T0285809

All-India
and
Down Under

All-India and Down Under

Peace, Partition and the
Game of Cricket
Richard Knott

First published by Pitch Publishing, 2023

Pitch Publishing
9 Donnington Park,
85 Birdham Road,
Chichester,
West Sussex,
PO20 7AJ
www.pitchpublishing.co.uk
info@pitchpublishing.co.uk

ISBN 978 1 80150 388 4

Typesetting and origination by Pitch Publishing
Printed and bound in Great Britain by TJ Books, Padstow

Contents

'Even when the guns had ceased fire, I could not come back to cricket for a season or two.'
Edmund Blunden, Cricket Country

'So innate is the cricketing skill of the Indians that the day will come when they will defeat both England and Australia.'
The Cricketer, 1946

'Listen, I didn't come through six years of war to be treated like a schoolboy.'
Joe Hardstaff Junior, Nottinghamshire and England

'Hammond and Bradman had completely divergent views on the meaning of cricketing goodwill.'
Clif Cary, 'Cricket Controversy'

'Can I take my cricket bat to Pakistan?'
Moniza Alvi, At the Time of Partition

Introduction

IT IS 29 July 1944 and the Middlesex batsman, Jack Robertson, playing for the Army against the RAF at Lord's, is about to take strike against Bob Wyatt, a former England captain. The score is 57/1. As Wyatt approaches the wicket, there is the drone of a doodlebug flying bomb and each player flings himself to the ground, the game momentarily forgotten, survival paramount. Thankfully, the bomb lands a few hundred yards away in Regent's Park. Robertson, after the over has been resumed, promptly hits Wyatt for a flamboyant six high into the Grand Stand.

Among those who sheepishly stood back up as the doodlebug passed over, brushing grass stains from his whites, was another England captain, Walter Hammond, whose presence looms large in this book, and of whom the poet Edmund Blunden wrote:

'Not to have seen him leaves us unaware
What cricket swiftness, judgement, foresight truly are'

Hammond captained his country in both the cricket tours which form the core of this book: the All-India series of 1946 and England's premature return to the Ashes contest in 1946/47. He was just one of many cricketers whose working life was interrupted by six years of war.

The close connection between war and cricket has been made by many, both writers as well as cricketers themselves:

the playwright Harold Pinter, for example, described the game as 'a wonderfully civilised act of warfare', while, when the English went to Australia to play the first Ashes series after the war, they were obliged to 'relearn the art of waging war against the Aussies', to borrow Stephen Fay and David Kynaston's telling phrase. The Sussex and England bowler Maurice Tate, a longstanding hero of another key figure in this book, John Arlott, had been through the real thing, serving in France with the Royal Artillery in the 1914–18 war, and he too recognised the connection. Moreover, for cricketers playing the game in 1939, the Great War seemed very close and often cast a shadow over their lives: Walter Hammond's father, for example, was killed in action on 5 May 1918, just six months before the Armistice was signed.

The transition between war and peace and what it meant in this greatest of sports was the genesis of this book. Given the juxtaposition of the last All-India cricket team arriving in England and the imminent Partition of that country into India and Pakistan, the links between cricket and politics are necessarily part of the context and story of the tours of 1946 and 1947. Cricket is deeply entrenched in the cultures of India, Pakistan, Australia and England. For one writer, 'the game is an Indian game accidentally discovered by the English', while the Victorians regarded cricket as an example of English cultural supremacy. No doubt, Australians would look at such sentiments with a wary eye. At all events, the links are close between the nations and cricket has helped cement them. Indeed, when cricket threatens to erupt in some way – be it over 'Bodyline' or apartheid in South Africa decades later – politicians inevitably become involved.

The writer Marina Wheeler, in her excellent memoir of Indian Partition, *The Lost Homestead,* at one point describes her visit to the Lahore Gymkhana ground – now called the Bagh-e-Jinnah after Pakistan's first prime minister. She describes the sheesham trees, the British-built Victorian pavilion and the impressive cricket museum. There she realises 'how cricket helped bond the new nation together and continues to be an integral part of its story'. Cricket and politics are 'intimately linked', Wheeler says, noting that the man who took Pakistan to its World Cup win in 1992, Imran Khan, became his country's prime minister. As if to reinforce the point, the city's principal cricket ground is named after the former Libyan leader, Colonel Gaddafi. For the Indian cricketers of 1946, politics would loom large in their lives and to a far greater extent than to their English or Australian counterparts. For the latter those post-war years were preoccupied simply with trying to return to the game they loved.

Note

Throughout the book I have chosen to use the cricketing and geographical terms that applied at that moment in time, while recognising the legitimate sensitivities around this choice. Hence Mumbai is 'Bombay', Pune is 'Poona', Sri Lanka is 'Ceylon' and so on. Batsmen remain as 'batsmen' not 'batters' too, as they were in 1946.

PART 1

THE ALL-INDIA TOUR OF 1946

April to September

The All-India Tour of 1946

The Itinerary

May 4, 6, 7	Worcestershire	Worcester
May 8–10	Oxford University	Oxford
May 11, 13, 14	Surrey	Kennington Oval
May 15–17	Cambridge University	Cambridge
May 18, 20, 21	Leicestershire	Leicester
May 22–23	Scotland	Edinburgh
May 25, 27, 28	MCC	Lord's
May 29	Indian Gymkhana	Osterley
June 1, 3, 4	Hampshire	Southampton
June 8, 10, 11	Glamorgan	Cardiff
June 12–14	Combined Services	Portsmouth
June 15, 17, 18	Nottinghamshire	Nottingham
June 22, 24, 25	**ENGLAND**	**Lord's**
June 26–28	Northants	Northampton
June 29, July 1, 2	Lancashire	Liverpool
July 3–5	Yorkshire	Bradford
July 6, 8, 9	Lancashire	Manchester
July 10–12	Derbyshire	Chesterfield
July 13, 15, 16	Yorkshire	Sheffield
July 17, 18	Durham	Sunderland
July 20, 22, 23	**ENGLAND**	**Manchester**
July 25	Club Cricket Conference	Guildford
July 27, 29, 30	Sussex	Hove
July 31, August 1, 2	Somerset	Taunton
August 3, 5, 6	Glamorgan	Swansea
August 7–9	Warwickshire	Birmingham
August 10, 12, 13	Gloucestershire	Cheltenham
August 17, 19, 20	**ENGLAND**	**The Oval**
August 24, 26, 27	Essex	Southend
August 28–30	Kent	Canterbury
August 31, September 2	Middlesex	Lord's
September 4–6	South of England	Hastings
September 7, 9, 10	H.D.G. Leveson-Gower's XI	Scarborough

1

Mr Gupta and Mr Arlott
April–May 1946

MR GUPTA'S blue trilby provided a flash of colour in the sober gentility of Westminster's Berners Hotel. London, in that first post-war year, was more used to khaki, bitter winter and grey skies than it was to the glittering prospect of cricket's return. Gupta was a small, harassed-looking man, only too aware of what could go wrong in the weeks ahead and of the fickle nature of an English April. The weather in England made him shiver, encouraged him to think kindly of Calcutta's unfailing heat, forgetting its clammy intensity. April 1946 in London was cold and wet; the telephone system was cranky; food was in short supply; the mood was dour, the country emphatically austere – and Gupta's cricketers were missing, scattered somewhere between India and Britain. And their kit was also at sea, which left him, the manager of the last All-India cricket team to tour England, with nothing to oversee and nobody to manage.

In the back of Mr Gupta's mind lurked the bad blood of his appointment – he was, after all, a hockey man rather than a cricketer. Then there had been the unseemly trouble over the appointment of the captain: should it be Vijay Merchant or the Nawab of Pataudi? With his urbane manner, well-heeled Bombay background, and cricketing pedigree, Merchant was the more obvious choice. But he had been turned down in a

10–8 vote in favour of Pataudi – even more well-heeled, but whose cricket was decidedly rusty. Added to that was the strange fact that the Nawab had played for England some 13 years previously. His ringside seat at the diplomatic crisis brought about by the 1932/33 Bodyline tour of Australia perhaps fed the political ambitions which, by 1946, were well-established. At all events, Pataudi's appointment as India's captain was a controversial one. As well as the cricketing tourists, he ruled his own small kingdom of 53 square miles in the north of India, close to Delhi, a responsibility acquired courtesy of history and the East India Company. Educated at Balliol College, Oxford, where he had been a triple Blue (cricket, hockey and billiards), he had an uncomfortable introduction to Test cricket – an Indian playing for England – and had been obliged to serve under the resolute, unforgiving captaincy of Douglas Jardine in Australia. The 22-year-old Pataudi had met up with the MCC party in Colombo, the rest of the players having sailed weeks before from Tilbury. He would go on to play in the first two Tests, scoring 102 at Sydney in early December 1932, followed by disappointing scores of 15 and 5 at Melbourne over the New Year. He was not selected for the remaining Test matches of that tour.

By 1946, Pataudi was 36 and had played little cricket for the previous eight years, his time spent instead on running his kingdom. In terms of cricket in India, he was inexperienced. Indeed, in his career overall, he had played far more cricket at Lord's than he had in India where he had only played in six first-class games: three in 1932 (in Patiala, Lahore and Delhi); once in Poona in 1944; and twice more in 1946 (in Patiala again and Bombay). Between 1938 and 1944 he had played no first-class cricket all. He did, however, already have first-hand experience of cricketing politics, having closely observed the combative confusion of England's 'Bodyline' tour.

Also in the hotel foyer was a man from the BBC, a radio producer (of poetry) whose cricketing credentials were largely confined to a star-struck passion for the game. John Arlott was 32, a man with a rich radio voice, a distinctive Hampshire burr. In that April of 1946 he was about to embark on a summer doggedly following the Indian tour, equipped with a 40-year-old typewriter, a clutch of pencils and a pristine notebook, and dressed in comfortable tweed. He would make it his job to get as close to the Indians as possible, an observant friend, with the players' interests at heart.

'All-India' – the description glosses over powerful undercurrents, political sensitivities arising from the country's religious differences and Britain's bankrupt, moth-eaten empire. India's landmass was vast, stretching from Balochistan in the west to the border with Burma in the east and from Kashmir to the Madras states in the south, and while the term 'All-India' suggested cohesion and unity, in reality it described an agglomeration of varied states over which British influence held some kind of sway, a creaking, sometimes malign, sphere of influence. With the war over, but the government in London grappling with a collapsing economy and urgently seeking to extricate itself from its imperial past, the lifespan of 'All-India' was limited. All-India was on the verge of Partition, the old order dying, to be replaced by India and Pakistan.

If imperial politics induced headaches, so too did the administration of cricket. Pre-war All-Indian cricket tours had been marked by tensions about the captaincy (along the shameful lines of 'would he be at home with a knife and fork?') and about the potential religious divisions within the squad (in 1932, seven Hindus, four Muslims, four Parsis and two Sikhs). Moreover, the 1936 tour had been marred by the early return home of the all-rounder Lala Amarnath for 'insubordination' (an unseemly thirst for women, it was said – although he claimed that he much preferred playing cricket).

But in 1946, at the beginning of the tour at least, the outstanding problem was the fact that the players arrived in the UK in instalments. It seemed to symbolise their inherent differences of faith. Some flew in by flying boat – Karachi to Poole – while Pataudi, Lala Amarnath and the pace bowler Shute Banerjee arrived via New Delhi, Karachi and Cairo, their BOAC flight finally landing at Bournemouth airport. They were photographed on the aerodrome tarmac in the rain, flaunting wide smiles and fedoras, arm-in-arm, swaddled in heavy winter overcoats donned somewhere between Karachi and England's south coast. They did not look like cricketers, but to be fair, the weather was more suited to rugby. Indian optimists likened Banerjee to England's Maurice Tate but, standing outside the aircraft, he looked frankly portly, resembling a prosperous restaurateur rather than a ferocious fast bowler, while Pataudi, behind the diplomat's smile, looked haunted and careworn. He would need, one commentator suggested, to 'retain reasonably good health'.

As the rain fell and summer refused to show its face, Mr Gupta and the Nawab of Pataudi contemplated the daunting prospect of playing 33 matches over four months. It would not be easy. Only six of the squad had played Test cricket before; the batting was better than the bowling, on paper at least; Banerjee's lost years in the war had seen his fitness slowly decline – he had played only at weekends and had been caught up in war-work. The tour schedule was quixotic, shaped by someone with little grasp of geography, or a nasty sadistic streak; early nets were a farrago of mud and rain; the light after the brilliance of Calcutta, Bombay and Delhi, was funereal; the food was British stodge made worse by rationing and showing little understanding of the dietary needs of Indian vegetarians. Meanwhile, post-war restrictions on clothing produced problems over the acquisition of cricket boots and white flannels. Rationing also affected the supply of cricket balls and the re-blading of bats.

Arlott's management of time and logistics was infinitely easier: pack a suitcase with pencils and a change of clothes and get to Worcester in good time for the first game of the tour. His complex system of laundry-by-post pleased his sense of order. So, on 4 May 1946, he left his terraced house in Crouch End, north London, in good spirits and arrived in Worcester before the Indian cricketers. Their journey to the Midlands was poor preparation for a game of cricket, their coach driver contriving to get lost en route. In that motorway-free age, the web of dark country roads was evidently baffling and the charabanc's precious cargo of sleep-deprived touring cricketers turned and twisted as it headed (mostly) westwards. It was three in the morning before the coach finally turned into the hotel's darkened car park. Mr Gupta's patience had been severely tested, while the players were numbed by travel and all too aware that they were due to walk out on to the New Road grass in less than eight hours' time.

The eager Arlott was awake early on the morning of the match, looking out of his window at threatening clouds sweeping in from the north-east, but comforted by the fact that he would soon be watching his first cricket match for more than six years. Outside there was a cold wind and the light was gloomy at best. For the Indians it would be a three-sweater day and Pataudi's first big test surely would be winning the toss, thereby ensuring that only two men – the batsmen – need be out of the pavilion's warmth at any one time. He called correctly – but then chose to bowl after all, presumably to get it over with – and the Indians filed out uneasily into the English spring weather to face the music. Around the ground, a record crowd of some 8,000 spectators sat, wearing trilbies and raincoats, a ring of damp grey encircling the rich green of the pitch and surrounds. The wicket itself, though, was lifeless and the ponderous Banerjee proved to be no better than military medium, despite a gallant, rolling approach to the stumps. He looked like a man struggling against the tide, his boots weighted with lead.

What did Pataudi learn from those three chilly days of spring in Worcester? He already knew that English weather was fickle, its cold a test for fielders' fingers, the light lacking warmth and clarity. The batting might lean over-heavily on the diminutive Merchant, while Vinoo Mankad's slow left arm was both inventive and aggressive – he had been his side's outstanding performer – and Banerjee's carefree batting was everything his bowling no longer was. Overall, Pataudi would not have been too downhearted by the 16-run defeat inflicted by Worcestershire, although perhaps worried by the weather forecast which did not augur well for the days ahead. The forecast proved accurate, the rain completely ruling out the first day's play in the next game, against Oxford University at The Parks. It confined the players to the pavilion, its windows blurred by the storm, while outside the circle of tall trees dripped and swayed in the wind, and pools of water spread across the outfield. It proved a long day for the Indians, without the compensation that Arlott found in scouring Oxford's bookshops.

While the prospects for cricket were shrouded in the gloomy downpour – would it rule out any hope of play on the second day? – the tourists' evening was pre-booked and unaffected by the bad weather. Instead of a quiet night in, it was off to a celebratory dinner at Oxford's Angel restaurant. Organised by Amalendu Bose, a student at Christ Church, it promised to be an evening of conversation far beyond the borders of cricket, since Bose was a passionate convert to the cause of Indian independence. He had taught at the University of Dhaka during the war and had been greatly influenced by the horrors of the famine in Bengal. The university was a hotbed of political activity with a strong pro-independence following. The Bengal famine was in part a consequence of Britain's wartime policies and was responsible for the deaths of several million people.

No doubt Bose had attracted the attention of Britain's intelligence agencies, while the Majlis Society – under whose banner the dinner at the Angel was being held – was regarded by MI5 as having communist connections. Imagine, then, a lamp-lit backroom and an eclectic mix of fiery radicals, high-born Indian cricketers, 'ordinary' squad members more interested in the provenance of the food and the next day's weather than radical politics, and harassed waiters, plates held high over the sheen of players' black Brylcreemed hair, soup of dubious origin spilling on to laundered tablecloths. Three courses: a dreary hors d'oeuvre; anonymous soup and a mildly spicy chicken served with vegetables that had been boiled to a watery death. Trifle to follow, a bland concoction of gloopy custard with a fleeting drop of liquor. Finally, speeches – these were not confined by rationing, unlike the unappetising fare – votes of thanks, and then a hurried stroll through persistent drizzle to the hotel and a night of listening to a room-mate's snores. They left behind a menu dutifully signed by each of them: Mushtaq Ali sprawling across the top; Vijay Merchant's resembling a caterpillar, initials and surname shunted together; Nayudu's smudged; and Vinoo Mankad, spread across the bottom, carrying the rest of the team, names penned in a kaleidoscope of styles from spidery to assertive.

They woke to a very different England with an early-morning sun shining in a cloudless sky. There was a full day's play which John Arlott watched from a bomb crater in the company of three poets: Dylan Thomas, Louis MacNeice and Cecil Day-Lewis, each of whom had worked with Arlott at the BBC. Poetry, cricket and peacetime in close harmony. The game was drawn, its highlight the batting of the New Zealand Test cricketer, Martin Donnelly (177 runs for once out). For India, Abdul Hafeez batted against doctors' orders with his fingers strapped together after a fielding injury, scoring 30 not out, batting down the order.

Later that afternoon, the Indians headed for London where on the following day they were due to play Surrey at The Oval. It was 11 May 1946, the day the County Championship fully resumed after a gap of nearly seven years, although Middlesex had begun the season three days earlier with a comfortable victory over Leicestershire at Lord's, despite a whole day being lost to rain. As well as India playing at The Oval, there was also a busy programme of county matches at Cardiff, Gloucester, Southampton, Lord's, Trent Bridge and Taunton. In a hint of what lay ahead in that summer of 1946, Middlesex's star batsman Denis Compton scored 147 not out; the Gloucestershire and England captain, Wally Hammond, made 134 before a strained back prevented him batting again in the match; and Yorkshire's Bill Bowes, for whom the war had been particularly traumatic, failed to score a run or take a wicket against Glamorgan. Despite that, the 1939 county champions won comfortably inside two days, with Len Hutton making 90 in a low-scoring match. It seemed to be business as usual for Yorkshire, despite having to wait seven long years to begin their title defence.

2

'Will I Ever Play Again?'

September 1939

YORKSHIRE'S HEDLEY Verity's artful slow left arm had brought the curtain down on the cricket season of 1939. The final act took place at Hove on the Sussex coast, just 48 hours before war was declared. Here was a man who had taken the incomparable Don Bradman's wicket in the Yorkshireman's fourth Test match (at Adelaide in 1933) and who went on to dismiss the great Australian seven more times before his career was over. At Hove, on the first September day in 1939, it took Verity the same number of deliveries to secure a Yorkshire victory: seven Sussex men dismissed for just nine runs. His slow, almost ponderous approach to the wicket and the uncomplicated, oiled arc of his bowling arm were in stark contrast to the spit, bounce and turn he extracted from the pitch. It was a virtuoso performance and it confirmed Yorkshire as county champions.

The two sides had met a little over a month before at Scarborough, a game in which the Yorkshire pace bowler, Bill Bowes, had taken 7-54 in the Sussex first innings. When Yorkshire batted, Len Hutton made 177 in a total of 386. Four wickets for Verity in the Sussex second innings gave Yorkshire a comfortable victory by ten wickets. In the return game, Sussex fared marginally better, with a first-innings score of 387, although centuries from Hutton and Norman

Yardley gave Yorkshire a slender first-innings lead. Verity's remarkable spell, however, saw Sussex all out in their second innings for a paltry 33 and Yorkshire's margin of victory this time was nine wickets. The game was only completed because Yorkshire's captain, Brian Sellers, aware that it was J.H. Parks' benefit match, insisted that it should be played through to a finish. The celebrations were muted – the German invasion of Poland began on the same day – and the players were preoccupied with how the team might get back home, given the problems with the railways and the regulation that obliged the Yorkshiremen not to use cars south of Birmingham. The expectation of war had resulted in widespread confusion. The crisis meant they made the long journey north by hired coach, each player's thoughts more on what lay ahead than in contemplation of a memorable victory. Verity was one of those who wondered if he would ever play cricket again and, indeed, for four of the players involved over these three days, it proved to be their last game.

That evening, as the coach and its subdued cricketers travelled home, the prime minister, Neville Chamberlain, was on his feet, addressing the House of Commons in his dry, strained voice, and struggling to seem in control of faraway events on the other side of Europe. Plummy *sang froid* was not enough to calm the nation's nerves and the evidence of disquiet, even panic, was all too visible to Verity, Len Hutton, Bill Bowes and the rest as the coach approached London: the Great West Road was choked with cars streaming out of the capital. It proved a slow journey north, progress hindered by a practice blackout and it came to a temporary halt at Leicester where they stopped for the night and ate a subdued dinner of oysters and champagne. They resumed the journey at dawn, finally stepping down from the bus, weary and unsettled, into the City Square in Leeds, then shaking hands all round before going their separate ways. It was a ritual enacted across the country. Warwickshire's Tom Dollery and Eric Hollies, for example, parted company at Birmingham station at the end of August and would not see each other again until April 1946.

The signs of imminent catastrophe had been clear for a good while: when Yorkshire were playing against Kent at Dover in late August telegrams kept being delivered at the ground calling up reservists. In truth, anticipation of war had been a fact of life for many months across the nation and cricketers were no different in wondering how and when the world would change forever. As far back as October 1938, members of the MCC party setting out on a tour of South Africa were preoccupied with the uncertain state of the world. The party had sailed for Cape Town on 21 October that year on board the *Athlone Castle*. Just three weeks before, Hitler had met Chamberlain at Munich and already the latter's boast of 'peace in our time' was sounding distinctly hollow. The voyage south to Cape Town took a fortnight, long enough for time to hang heavy and provoke unwelcome thoughts of German air raids, troubling the cricketers, all too conscious of their families left behind in England. There was an ominous feeling aboard, not helped by Norman Yardley's fall on deck – he cracked a rib against the ship's rail in a fierce Biscay swell and needed three stitches in a cut under his right eye – provoking rumours in the press of an ill-tempered brawl. The ship docked at Cape Town on the first day of November, in the early morning, with Table Mountain wreathed in cloud.

It would be almost five months before they returned to England and, by then, 'peace in our time' had been replaced by 'war, perhaps within days'. The increasingly volatile political situation resulted in a decision to call time on the 'Timeless Test' being played in Durban. The plan had been to play on until a definite result had been achieved, but events conspired against that intention: political uncertainties of course, but also the pitch was dead – a 'shirt front' was how the England leg-spinner Doug Wright described it. The bowlers were utterly spent and runs came at a funereal rate. The days passed and victory or defeat seemed as far away as ever. Nearly 2,000 runs were scored in the match which stretched from 3 to 14 March 1939. Paul Gibb, Hammond and Bill Edrich all scored hundreds (Edrich's was a double) in England's abandoned second innings. Earlier the Essex quick bowler Ken Farnes bowled 68 eight-ball overs, while Hedley Verity got through nearly 96 in the match. Rain fell and the heavy roller made a placid pitch even more lifeless and leaden. How far from home it felt! The players' exile seemed to be symbolised by the flying boat thundering low over the ground, its hold heavy with mailbags destined for England. After nearly a week's play the *Athlone Castle* left for Cape Town, bound ultimately for home, sounding its siren three times as it nosed out of the harbour, leaving the players behind. Time was finally called on the tenth day, the last rites of the drawn game played out to the accompaniment of ominous stabs of lightning and eventually a conclusive downpour, with England 654/5, chasing 696 to win. Instead of scoring 42 more runs, or losing five wickets, the MCC party was obliged to take a two-day train journey to Cape Town to rendezvous with the *Athlone Castle*. The ship duly sailed out of Table Bay, bound for England, on Friday, 17 March 1939. Two days before, German tanks had crossed the Czechoslovak border.

Spring in England that year brought snow for the start of the cricket season and, soon after, the silvery, bloated shapes of barrage balloons could be seen twisting and turning over London. For Yorkshire's players the season began on 3 May (at Oxford against the university) before moving on to Lord's (to play MCC) and then Kent and Gloucestershire in God's Own Country (Leeds and Bradford). And so the long trek that would end at Hove in late summer had begun.

That summer West Indies toured England, playing three Tests: there were two drawn games and a win for the hosts at Lord's in June. The final Test, at The Oval, ended on 22 August. The following day the agreement between Russia and Germany – the Molotov–Ribbentrop

Pact – was signed. Unsurprisingly, there were doubts about fulfilling the next fixtures – Sussex at Hove on 26 August and Kent (at Canterbury) on 30 August – and, in the event, the tourists departed in a hurry, leaving from the port of Glasgow on Saturday, 26 August. It proved a troubled voyage, disturbed by reports of prowling German submarines which necessitated frequent avoidance manoeuvres. As war drew closer, so the manifestations of its impact multiplied: on the 29th The Oval was requisitioned by the army; then the round of matches beginning on 30 August was affected, all but two being concluded within two days. Lancashire's game with Surrey at Old Trafford, for example, was abandoned as a draw on the Friday morning, with Lancashire needing 352 to win. Instead of a day seeking a 12th win of the season at Lancashire's expense, the Surrey players took the train south, eventually arriving in the chaos of Euston station. The platforms were crowded with evacuees. The players threaded their way through the confusion: cricketers and their coffins, stuffed with hurriedly packed kit, were heading home; those with gas masks and suitcases were intent on escaping the capital, hoping to find a bomb-free, rural peace.

3

'And That, Gentlemen, is Stumps'

1939–45

OVER THOSE last few days of late August, and at Hove on the first day of September 1939, on cricket grounds across the country – at Worcester, Taunton, Lord's, Leicester, Manchester – men in white coats removed the bails and pulled the stumps from the ground for the last time before the war began. What thoughts went through the various umpires' minds as they watched the players troop off the field not knowing when – or if – they would ever return? Players and umpires normally lived in a world of certainty, its boundaries the fixture list and railway timetables. Doubt and uncertainty were confined to the weather, the state of the pitch and whether a catch had carried. But the outbreak of war had led to a profound fear of what might lie ahead. Early autumn always brought with it worries about the future, whether contracts would be extended and, for the professional cricketers, how they would earn a living through the winter, but things now were infinitely more uncertain and there was no end in sight.

The uncertainty was not just confined to Britain. Its empire too was necessarily caught up in the conflict, the war affecting the cricketing countries, Australia, West Indies, New Zealand and India. In an act that encapsulated how Britain regarded India, the viceroy, Lord Linlithgow, acting on his own initiative, and without consulting any Indian politicians, had declared that India too was at war with Germany – and did so within hours of its beginning. As for English cricketers, obscure county professionals as well as established Test-match players, each of them was now at the mercy of wartime vagaries. The game's authorities were equally uncertain about how cricket itself might survive: would it be possible for some form of the game to continue during hostilities? In 1914, when the First World War had begun, Lord's had ruled that the game was suspended for the duration. This time, however, there was a realisation that sport had an important role to play in helping to sustain morale, both of the population as a whole and those in uniform. Given the nature of the German propaganda machine, it was thought vital that the 'free hit' of the home of cricket being closed down, should not be offered to the enemy. But where did the crisis leave the county cricketer on 3 September 1939? For some, the likelihood was that their career was over: Eddie Paynter, for example, of Lancashire and England, was in the twilight of his career and it didn't take him long to realise that the time had come to hang up his boots, at least in county and Test cricket. The County Committee awarded him a cheque for £1,000 when he decided to leave to play league cricket in 1946, by which time he was 44. Yorkshire's Herbert Sutcliffe, J. H. Parks of Sussex, Jack O'Connor (Essex), Ted Brookes (Surrey) and Alan Watt (Kent) were among those who never played for their counties again.

Early in the war, MCC's advisory committee decided to rule out any kind of regional competition, while judging that to continue the game in some form or other was the right thing to do. The glorious weather in the summer of 1940 seemed to reward such a decision. It hardly rained and only one game of the 26 played that year was affected by the weather. It was decided that games would be played over one day and the County Championship would be suspended. In general there was a rapid exodus of cricketers into uniform;

cricket grounds were requisitioned; heavy rollers were scrapped for their valuable metal; and the neglect of grounds – repairs and painting indefinitely postponed – began as autumn turned to winter.

In June 1940 an inaugural game involving a British Empire XI was played at Lord's. League cricket continued in Yorkshire and Lancashire and the Bradford League attracted a number of high-profile players, including Len Hutton (with Pudsey St Lawrence), Eddie Paynter (Keighley), and the West Indian fast bowler, Learie Constantine (Windhill). A London Counties team of professionals toured locally, while club cricket kept going partly through the efforts of those too old for military service (but fit enough to run between the wickets or round the boundary edge), as well as youngsters yet to be conscripted, or too young to volunteer. Problems for the game were considerable, however, ranging from where to place the treasures and artefacts normally held at Lord's (they were removed and buried in a secret location); the ongoing shortage of cricket equipment of all kinds; the frequent late arrivals at matches by players hindered by the night-time work of the Luftwaffe, or by travel chaos – something which resulted at times in unprepared lower-order batsmen being promoted to fill gaps created by the absent or delayed. The use of Double British Summer Time also caused some problems and confusion. Cricket grounds were acquired by the military, or to house prisoners of war, while some – Southampton, Edgbaston and Old Trafford for example – were bombed while others needed to ensure that they were not susceptible to enemy aircraft landing on the grass, or targeted by parachutists exploiting broad, flat open spaces. Later in the war, a further problem arose: an increase in the number of cricketers being posted overseas.

For the county professional past his best years, perhaps feeling the effects of too many seasons pounding the turf with an overlong run-up, knees and shoulders complaining, and first team place no longer guaranteed, these were disturbing times. Inevitably the most pressing question was whether his career was over, although there was some minor comfort to be gained from the fact that autumn – the close season – had arrived. In the early months of the war there was much anxiety but little in the way of open warfare. But just when the 1940 cricket season would have begun, in early May, the German blitzkrieg cut its way through France towards the Channel.

In the event, wartime cricket was very popular, no doubt because it helped people keep some kind of hold on better times. At Lord's cricket continued through the war years: in the summer of 1943, for example, a quarter of a million people watched the game there. Cricket matches were even played while the British Army retreated towards Dunkirk – and the desperate escape by boat from the French coast – was going on. While men in whites paced out run-ups, or took guard, less than a hundred miles away across the Channel others in khaki were dying in blood-stained seas. It wasn't easy to keep games on during that first summer – there was the fear of invasion, aerial dog fights over Kent and Sussex, a chaotic transport system and designated 'defence areas' on the coast. For some cricketing servicemen, the demands of the war and cricket were closely interwoven. The diminutive and pugnacious Bill Edrich of Middlesex, England and 107 Squadron, flew an operation one morning over the North Sea attacking enemy shipping in which several aircraft were lost; in the same afternoon he turned out to play cricket at Massingham Hall in Norfolk.

It wasn't just domestic cricket that was affected. MCC's winter tour of India was cancelled. The plan had been to play three Tests – in Bombay, Calcutta and Madras – but as the summer of 1939 passed it became increasingly clear that the tour would probably have to be called off. At the end of July, it was announced that there had been talks with the Indian Cricket Board about whether it would be wise to delay the tour until the winter of 1941. A week later, however, on 2 August, the news came that the tour would indeed go ahead, the squad leaving from Tilbury on Friday, 22 September on board the P&O liner RMS *Strathmore*. It was a decision in the best tradition of stubborn, blinkered British empire-building. The touring party would dock in Bombay on 8 October and then take the train north at ten o'clock that night. In the event, it was not until 4 September, the day after the war began, that the tour was finally cancelled. For the players originally selected the cancellation would have been anticipated some time before, but it was a great disappointment nonetheless.

The selectors – who included Yorkshire captain Brian Sellers – had named the squad some time before and the men named revealed a lot about the state of the world politically and, perhaps, a hint as to the relative importance attached to the tour by MCC. No Hutton, Hammond, Compton, Verity or Bowes; not one Yorkshireman; some quirky selections of cricketers who had played little first XI cricket in 1939; others with averages scarcely designed to disturb the opposition. For example, Worcestershire's Roger Human was a schoolmaster who had played just four times that summer, all in the school holidays. In six completed innings he had scored only 63 runs and in his career until that point he had played 59 times without scoring a century. Such outlandish selections spoke of a lordly condescension by the English cricketing establishment towards the 'plucky' Indians, an attitude which would continue for decades. The man selected as captain, Flight Lieutenant Jack Holmes (Sussex), was a popular figure with experience of India; but as a cricketer, he was second rate. Of the others, Sussex's James Langridge – the man who would take the last wicket of 1939 – soon withdrew. Roger Human, denied his Indian tour, and having left his teaching career for service with the Oxford and Buckinghamshire Light Infantry, died in November 1942 – poignantly, in India.

The man nominated to manage the tour, Lt. Col. Claude Rubie, also died during the war, suffering a fatal heart attack in November 1939. As for the players whose chances of an England cap were denied, there was the prospect of military service instead: two Sussex men, Hugh Bartlett and Billy Griffith, would later be involved in glider operations during the invasion of France in 1944 – after the war Griffith captained his county, with (Major) Bartlett as his vice-captain. Peter Smith joined the Essex Regiment and, in May 1943, was posted to the Middle East to take up a staff officer role at Combined Operations HQ in Alexandria. Jack Holmes became a Wing Commander in the RAF; James Langridge and Harold Gimblett were in the Fire Service. Instead of tiger hunts, official receptions and banquets, elephant rides, leopard shoots and cricket, there was the all-consuming world war.

Moreover, the longer the war went on, the less likelihood there was of earning a second chance at Test cricket and, in the event, only four of those selected to go to India in 1939 went on to play international cricket after 1945 (Tom Dollery, S.C. (Billy) Griffith, James Langridge and Peter Smith), and they accumulated only 13 caps among them. James Langridge, who had played seven pre-war Tests, played just one after it was over – against India at The Oval in August 1946, when he did not bat. For one member of that squad, there was some consolation after the war. Lancashire's Brocklebank – Sir John Montague Brocklebank – was captured on the Greek island of Cos in 1943 and became another cricketing prisoner of war (these included Wilf Wooller of Glamorgan, Bill Bowes of Yorkshire and the future England captain, Freddie Brown, then of Surrey and later, Northamptonshire). Brocklebank bowled both leg spin and medium pace – and was chairman of the Cunard Line – and would find himself in India, the small matter of eight years later, turning out to play for Bengal against Holkar in the Ranji Trophy at Eden Gardens, Calcutta, over the New Year period (31 December 1947 to 3 January 1948). By then 'All-India' had become India and Pakistan.

4

The End of Summer

September 1939

HEDLEY VERITY and Bill Bowes, once back in Yorkshire with the war about to begin, talked long into the night about what might happen in the days ahead and what the best thing to do might be. Once hostilities started, the future became even more disturbingly shrouded in uncertainty. In common with millions of other people, England's cricketers found their lives disrupted, particularly so since they were in an occupation with no obvious future. Each player was faced with the hard decision about how best they might contribute to the war effort. Should they sit tight and wait to be conscripted, for example, or rush to the nearest recruitment office? To complicate matters for Bowes, his wife was imminently expecting a baby. After much talk, it seemed that the wisest course of action was to sign up for service with the ARP (Air Raid Precautions) and so, instead of an autumnal last fling for the White Rose at Scarborough – the game against MCC had been cancelled anyway – it was off to the ARP Centre for a spell of night duty. Just days after the birth of the Boweses' daughter, both Bill and Hedley Verity signed up at a recruitment centre in Bradford and soon after they were posted to a searchlight unit in Selby, ten miles south of York.

Herbert Sutcliffe had been the first of Yorkshire's cricketers to be called up. This was in August and, as a result,

34

he was not available for the game at Hove that clinched the Championship. Instead, he was already serving with the Royal Army Ordnance Corps (RAOC) where he would rise to the rank of major. The times were abnormal, deeply unsettling, and even where attempts were made to cling to normality, the war found a way to intrude. For example, when Len Hutton (Yorkshire and England) got married at Wykeham near Scarborough in mid-September 1939, the guests arrived carrying both confetti and gas masks.

The day-to-day conduct of the war was, in some ways, as socially divided as the game of cricket; a former player's place in the scheme of things was often determined by his status, amateur or professional, officer or otherwise. Cricket had long been a game where the gap between the privileged and the working man was wide, despite the fact that in both club and county cricket, sides included both the titled at one extreme and the labouring man at the other. Having said that, it was the case that men who earned a living by playing the game as 'professional' cricketers were usually bowlers – consigned to summers of sweat and hard graft – while captains were invariably batsmen, harlequin-capped and public school-vowelled. Once in the armed services, the same principle applied: the amateurs for the most part became officers and the professionals were other ranks, obliged to do as they were told. Moreover, the professionals who were turned down by the army – like Kent's Arthur Fagg, who suffered from rheumatic fever – had suddenly lost their peacetime source of income.

As each former cricketer embarked on his journey to the war – those hours spent on painfully slow cross-country trains, standing in smoke-filled corridors beside a forlorn kit bag – what memories of cricket would sustain or haunt him? And how would life change in the months and years ahead? Each cricketing summer was a punishing schedule – the same trains criss-crossing England, but for a different purpose – since the counties played as many as 30 games a season, perhaps 90 days of cricket in all. In the weeks immediately before hostilities began, the Yorkshire players were required to travel from Cardiff to Leeds, then on to Leicester, Bradford, Scarborough, Sheffield, Dover and Bournemouth, before turning up to face Sussex at Hove. As for Sussex, their itinerary in the same period took in Bristol, Birmingham, Chelmsford, Nottingham, Hove, Worcester, Hastings and Eastbourne.

In the early months of both world wars, there was a widely expressed view that 'it would be all over by Christmas', but the thinking cricketer would have harboured doubts about such trusting optimism. Inevitably, thoughts drifted towards the future: when – if – there was to be a resumption of the game after the war was over, which of its time-honoured rituals would survive? What was in store for the out-of-the-way venues – Tewkesbury, Stroud, Lydney and Gloucester Wagon Works for Gloucestershire, for example? Or Huddersfield and Hull for Yorkshire, or Gillingham (Kent), Kettering (Northants), Ilkeston (Derbyshire), Dudley (Worcestershire) or Bath (Somerset)? How would county cricket's principal grounds recover from being taken over by the military? Bristol's grounds and buildings, for example, were requisitioned by the War Department, initially for use by the army, then the Royal Navy and finally the Americans, while Old Trafford was used as a transit camp for troops and a storage facility for the Ministry of Supply. Would the time-honoured rites of festival cricket survive, the brass bands, deckchairs, black-frocked waitresses with silver trays and china cups serving tea on the pitch? And what of the numbing treadmill of batting and bowling day after day (46 innings in a season for Herbert Sutcliffe, for example, and Verity's near one thousand overs in 1938)? Or the Victorian hangover of cricketers being deemed either professional ('Call me *Mister* Jardine!'), or amateur (a status which made it possible to captain England)? Some of these would not be missed, but the essential beauty of the game, what of that?

THE END OF SUMMER

Then there was the biggest question of all: how much of each cricketer's life would be consumed by the war effort? Imagine: you are a 23-year-old quick bowler just on the point of securing a county place – and suddenly it all stops. Worse, you have yet to find out that you will be nearly 30 before you get the chance to bowl again for your county, your best years spent in the Libyan desert, or Burma, or in a prisoner-of-war camp.

5

'Can't Wait to Have You Back'

Spring 1946

THE WAR ended in the middle of summer: the Germans signing the surrender in May 1945 and the Japanese three months later. It was inevitable therefore that a resumption of 'proper' cricket would have to wait until 1946. After all, by August 1945 there was already a hint of autumn in the air. Some first-class cricket was played that year, however, including five games that were billed as unofficial three-day 'Victory' Tests: an England XI (with Flight Sergeant C. Washbrook and Squadron Leader W. J. Edrich included, for example) played 'Australia', in fact, a strong Australian Services team (whose ranks included Pilot Officer K. R. Miller and Warrant Officer A. L. Hassett). The first game, at Lord's, began on 19 May, less than a fortnight after VE Day and was won by Australia by the comfortable margin of six wickets against an England XI that included five men who would tour down under in 1946/47. Further 'Tests' were played at a bomb-damaged Bramall Lane in Sheffield, at Old Trafford, and twice at Lord's. Wally Hammond scored a hundred at Bramall Lane where Lancashire's Dick Pollard took five second-innings wickets; Len Hutton (104) and Cyril Washbrook (112) both made hundreds at Lord's. The series ended at Old Trafford where another England win ensured the series was drawn, Pollard taking 25 wickets in all.

Keith Miller was Australia's star man, a cavalier cricketer if ever there was one – he was reputed to have remarked, after stepping out from the wreckage of a wartime air crash, that the moment had been 'nearly stumps' for him. In that peacetime summer of 1945 he made scores of 105 and 118 (against England at Lord's), and 111 (for the Australian Services against Yorkshire). Cricket's return was slow and tentative, its uncertain first steps taken as the war drifted towards its end. Sometimes the two seemed uncomfortably out of step with one another: for example, when long queues waited outside Lord's in bright sunshine on the very same day that the atomic bomb was dropped on Nagasaki.

* * *

With the first post-war season not beginning until 1946, it meant that 17 county clubs had eight months to prepare. In Gloucestershire the Cricket Committee wrote to the county's captain, Wally Hammond, excited about his anticipated return to the club and its first game – they couldn't 'wait to have [him] back in 1946', leading the team out at Gloucester on 11 May against Lancashire. Hammond had played as a professional from the start of his career in 1920: it had proved an inauspicious start, beaten inside two days by Lancashire at Cheltenham in August that year, with the 17-year-old Hammond scoring 0 and 7 not out. In 1937 he had given up his professional status, becoming an amateur and thereby allowing him to assume the captaincy of his country. (Len Hutton, in 1952, would become England's first professional cricket captain.) Hammond had ended the 1939 season as county captain and in imperious form. He had scored seven hundreds that season, averaged nearly 64 and taken 35 catches. The sharp reduction in the amount of bowling he did, however – just 72 overs when he had bowled over 2,000 in 1938 – was an indication perhaps that time was beginning to catch up with him. Before the war only Don Bradman rivalled – or surpassed – his standing in the game. That rivalry cast a shadow over the majestic Hammond which never truly faded during the 1930s and would darken immeasurably in the post-war Ashes tour of 1946/47. For Gloucestershire supporters, though, paradise was watching Hammond at the crease, perhaps with Charlie Barnett, the scoreboard ticking over faster than the clock, the sun high in a cloudless sky and the Bristol wicket at its most docile. 'See him while you can' was the message.

John Arlott warmed to Walter Hammond in that first post-war season, the 35-year-old novice commentator grateful for the 42-year-old England captain's shy generosity, the occasional dinners and the shared insights into the game of cricket. He was also, in Arlott's view, a great cricketer, in the same elite category as W.G. Grace and Jack Hobbs. Hammond seemed somehow to be only ever truly alive on the field of play; once he had stepped over the boundary rope, an innings or a day's play over, the aura faded, the trademark confidence and athleticism, the power of his batting, left out on the square. Away from cricket he was shy, with a preference for his own company. These were characteristics which did not impact on his batting or bowling – or indeed his fielding which was outstanding too – but they did not sit comfortably with captaincy.

Hammond was much travelled, courtesy of both cricket and the war. His career would see him make four tours of Australia and South Africa, for example, and two to the West Indies. He never toured in India. Over the period 1925 to 1939, he was away from home playing cricket for some 30 months altogether, missing the English winter each time, typically from October or November and returning in the early spring. Each time meant a lengthy journey by ship, out and back. In the war years he was constantly travelling too, often abroad, safer than many servicemen, but still wearied by the journeying, the sense of always being on the move.

Hammond had joined the Royal Air Force in October 1939 and was soon commissioned as an officer. He had been posted to an Initial Training Wing in Sussex before moving to Torquay in Devon where he acted as an officer charged with inculcating military discipline into young recruits. Too old, in his own words, to fly a Spitfire, he was part desk-bound airman and part cricketing ambassador, often in Africa. The fibrositis in his back got steadily worse – a cruel blow to a man admired for his athleticism – and that finally brought an end to his war service when he was discharged from the RAF at the end of 1944. As well as physical decline, Hammond faced mental challenges too. His first marriage was effectively over and the new love of his life, Sybil Ness-Harvey, a South African beauty queen, would become the second Mrs Hammond after the war. Despite the passing of the years, signs of physical decline and his shifting domestic arrangements, he remained a great cricketer, a player whose presence could make a day's play gloriously special.

Gloucestershire had finished third in the County Championship of 1939, with a relatively young team: the XI who played West Indies at Cheltenham in August that year had an average age of 27. Seven years later, when the county played Lancashire at Gloucester, the average, unsurprisingly, was 34. Four of the side were born in the county and two more hailed from other West Country counties. Hammond's reply to the warm words from the committee was both bullish and disingenuous: 'Feeling pretty good. See you for pre-season. We want to win the Championship.' They trained hard that spring and it showed: one opponent observed that Gloucestershire now played as if they were Yorkshire.

Hammond's batting was integral to the side's potential success – and it was as if he had never been away. It seemed he had lost nothing of his unequalled bravura at the wicket. It was a kind of majesty he conveyed: those powerful, imperious drives through the covers; the flawless timing and quickness of eye; that ability to pacify a difficult wicket. In his first five Championship matches before the first Test, he scored 134 (against Lancashire); 59 not out (Warwickshire); 143

41

(Yorkshire); 104 (Somerset); and 80 and 63 (Kent). Going into the Lord's Test he was averaging just over 116. With form like that what could possibly disrupt Gloucestershire's title challenge? Well, there was Wally's troublesome and persistent back problem for one thing. He was too unwell to bat in the second innings against Lancashire after his first innings hundred and he missed three of the next seven games. Indeed, he only completed 16 innings for the county all season, averaging 108. Next highest in the season's Gloucestershire averages was Barnett at 35 – achieved in 41 innings.

Then there was the question of his captaincy and the atmosphere and culture of the Gloucestershire dressing room. Despite the Labour election victory in 1945, the country was deeply divided in terms of class, and cricket reflected that. When Sam Cook, the newly recruited slow left-armer, turned up for the first time at Bristol's County Ground, he was overawed by Hammond's grand, regal presence. 'I'm Cook from Tetbury,' the spin bowler mumbled, head bowed, while the great man looked him up and down, cigarette smoke spiralling up from his leathery fingers. Wally was, quite simply, a batting god, but as a leader of men he was cold, hard, to reach, taciturn and moody, despite a deep understanding of the game. His contemporaries were awed by his batsmanship, but troubled by the kind of man he was. His predecessor and successor as skipper, Basil Allen, thought him 'an absolute shit' and was quite happy to tell the world. For some reason, Hammond had it in for the batsman George Emmett, who would ask his team-mates what the captain had against him. Emmett is a member of the 'one-Test wonder' group of cricketers (selected to replace Hutton at Old Trafford against the 1948 Australians, he was undone by Ray Lindwall's shattering pace and never played for his country again). Good enough to play for England he might be, but he would still get the sharp end of Hammond's tongue if he played a bad shot. When one of the team asked why Emmett had been dropped down to bat at number 6, Hammond's response was snappy and irritable: 'Because he *is* a number 6!' The captain, it seems, was not good for Emmett's cricket: he played under Hammond's leadership for two seasons – 1939 and 1946 – and his batting average in both was a fraction under 25. In 1947, after Hammond had gone, it was almost 35. He scored one century in 1938; none in the Hammond seasons, but six after the captain had been replaced.

Another Gloucestershire and England batsman – and a friend of Emmett's – Jack Crapp observed that there was only one occasion when his captain offered him a word of helpful advice. His batting statistics are as revealing as Emmett's: under Hammond, he averaged 35 in both 1939 and 1946. In 1947, it was 41.5 and the following season 48. It seems Crapp was inhibited, rather than inspired, by his captain. It was as if the latter's manner and astonishing batting performances (he topped the national averages in 1946) worked against the team. Others, however, recognised Hammond's genius: Tom Goddard, an outstanding spinner for the county, acknowledged the greatness of W.G. Grace, but added, 'If he was a better [cricketer] than Wally, then, with all respect, my cripes!'

The Gloucestershire players knew each other well; after all, the composition of the 1946 XI was scarcely different from that of 1939, just the small matter of all being seven years older. The routines and jokes would have been resumed; the fielding positions much the same; and the behaviours, foibles and mannerisms little changed – Charlie Barnett's preference for being addressed as 'Charles'; George Lambert's quick wits; Tom Goddard's loud, impassioned appeals; and the class divide that split the team in two, those with aristocratic leanings typified perhaps by Barnett and Basil Allen (Clifton College and Caius, Cambridge). They both rode to hounds; were both Masters of the Hunt, Barnett with the Beaufort Hunt and Berkeley Vale, and Allen with the Mendip Hunt. Known as the 'Guv'nor' in the dressing room, Barnett had been commissioned in the RAF during the war and photographs of him in uniform reveal, in his eyes and the set of his jaw, a man sure of his worth. He looked a dasher and his batting was nothing if not flamboyantly powerful: he would startle his team-mates by the ease with which he drove 'on the up' on the slow, sandy Bristol wicket. There was, though, a more pensive man behind the suave façade. Sharing a cabin with Hedley Verity in the SS *Orion* bound for Australia with MCC in 1936, he also shared the Yorkshireman's copy of *Seven Pillars of Wisdom*. He was a *Wisden* Cricketer of the Year in 1937, along with Vijay Merchant. Sam Cook represented the other half of the social divide with his bucolic ways, stolid humour and wry smile. His was an unflappable nature, typified by his between-the-overs chat with his batting partner in the midst of a desperate last-wicket stand against Yorkshire: 'How are your onions, Andy?'

Without the war, Gloucestershire might well have had a Championship-winning season, perhaps in 1942 or 1943, with a majority of their players then at their peak. They had the country's best batsman; an outstanding spinner in Goddard; a triumvirate of Test-quality batting in Barnett, Emmett and Crapp; and two useful quick bowlers (Colin Scott and George Lambert, who was believed by some to be as quick as anyone in England, at least for his first five or six overs). By 1946 decline had set in, epitomised by Scott's loss of pace and fire. Nonetheless, it seems that their shared love of the game sustained them well past an age when retirement might have been expected. Goddard played until he was 52, driven by his determination to reach 3,000 career wickets (he fell short in the end by 21, having caught pneumonia); Emmett continued to the age of 47; Wilson to 45. On average the team continued playing until the age of 43. It was a praiseworthy collective determination to make up for lost time.

6

The Oval
May 1946

THE SURREY medium-pace bowler Alec Bedser was
21 when the war started, having made his debut (against
Oxford University) at The Oval in June 1939. He played just
two matches that season – and didn't take a wicket – and
within a year he was caught up in the chaos of the retreat
at Dunkirk. His next game for Surrey would be nearly
seven years later, in May 1946, against the tourists from
All-India. Alec and his twin brother Eric both played for
Surrey and had received their call-up papers as early as June
1939 before eventually joining the RAF Police. Theirs was
an eventful war: in 1940, for example, they had witnessed
German aircraft flying low over the airfield at Merville in
northern France. The fear of strafing had provoked chaos,
with men fleeing in all directions, their haste spurred by
gunfire sweeping the runway and airfield buildings. As they
retreated, the French lanes were increasingly choked with
large numbers of British troops heading for the coast and
anticipating capture, or worse. Eventually the two Bedsers
were recognised by a Surrey member as he was single-
mindedly driving towards the English Channel, the enemy
in close pursuit. 'Can't leave you behind!' he said as the
future England cricketer and his twin brother climbed on
board for the desperate drive west.

In 1943, the Bedsers had been posted, sailing from Greenock for Algiers: seven days on board a Dutch ship, then by cattle-truck to Tunis. Thereafter, they joined the War Crimes Investigation Branch in Italy before being demobbed in March 1946, just in time for the new cricket season. For more than two years, while in North Africa during the war, Alec didn't touch a cricket bat or ball; instead, a world of sand, heat, and the treadmill of military duty.

Both Bedsers were stolid, brawny yeoman cricketers and Alec would in time prove to be a stalwart for his country. Over his career he would play 51 times for England, taking 236 wickets (at an average of 24.89). On Saturday, 11 May 1946, pounding in to bowl at a succession of Indian batsmen, he was of an age – 27 – when, without the war, he would have been established as an experienced professional cricketer. He was three years younger than John Arlott, who was at The Oval watching – there for pleasure, not work. Both men were learning a new trade and the apprentice broadcaster greatly admired Bedser's heavy-weighted bowling, recognising that his hunger, aggression and energy came in part from waiting so long for his real career to begin.

Arlott was no great fan of The Oval, thinking it ugly and he invariably felt uneasy whenever he was there. The ground had suffered during the war, its broken-down state a symbol of the depredation inflicted on London and other major cities. At the start of the war The Oval had been requisitioned for military use and inevitably its green expanse of grass was pitted with bomb scars, while the surrounding fabric of stands and pavilion underlined the fragility of the city's bricks and mortar under the onslaught. Seven high explosive bombs and two incendiaries fell nearby, causing major damage and fires. The ground itself went through a variety of wartime guises: a prisoner-of-war camp for German parachutists (who never materialised); an anti-aircraft gun emplacement; a drifting shoal of barrage balloons; a searchlight site and, finally, an assault training course, what was left of the grass serving as a substitute for the sandy beaches of Normandy. The Oval was a sorry sight when peace came and the return of cricket there seemed at least two years away.

The groundsman, Bert Lock, whose house in Exeter had suffered a direct hit from a German bomb in May 1942, thought otherwise, however. Herbert Christmas Lock – to give him his full name – played 35 games for Surrey between 1926 and 1932, taking 81 wickets, and later played for Devon in Minor Counties cricket. He was finally released from the RAF on 5 October 1945 and began the restoration of the Kennington ground just three days later. The work required was considerable: rats had eaten the nets; the grass was long; there was a profusion of poles concreted into the ground; four military huts stood as a bleak reminder of what had passed over recent years; there were unsightly pits, weeds and brambles; and the outfield resembled a barbed-wire-strewn battlefield. Lock showed great persistence and determination, however, and with the aid of an army of young lads and pensioners labouring through the autumn, the outfield was cleared; the near-meadow of grass scythed and sickled – and grazed by goats – while 45,000 turves were brought in from the Hoo marshes in Kent to lay the foundations for the return of cricket in 1946.

There were other problems too: in 1939 strict emergency controls had been placed on the manufacture of sports equipment and so bats and nets were in short supply for the duration of the war and beyond. The priority for the production of bats, balls and footballs was for men in the services with kit being supplied to every theatre of war. Machines which before the war had been producing cricket-shoe spikes, for example, had shifted to the production of assorted military hardware during the war years (Nettlefolds of Birmingham assuring the cricketing public once it was all over that 'we haven't forgotten how to make them'); grass cutting was hindered by a shortage of hand and motor mowers (Alexander Shanks & Son of Arbroath, for example, were manufacturing again, but an advertisement in the 1946 *Wisden* noted that there were limited supplies, although the company would be pleased 'to put your name on the waiting list'); even Ellimans Athletic Rub was in short supply, advertisements exhorting potential users 'to be careful how you use it'.

* * *

On Saturday, 11 May 1946, two diminutive Indians – Merchant and Hazare – walked out to open the tourists' first innings. The Surrey bowlers given the responsibility of the opening overs were quintessentially English, both Surrey-born, but at the opposite ends of their careers. Alf Gover was 38 and in the twilight of his career; Alec Bedser was very much the junior partner. Gover had been in the army during the war and had badly injured his right knee while still in the UK before making matters worse on board a ship bound for South Africa. He had two operations in a Cape Town hospital; two more in England and three months' physiotherapy before being finally discharged from the army, with a right leg which would not fully straighten. He was told he would not play cricket again and joined the Entertainment National Service Association (ENSA) to talk cricket to the troops. Gover was the son of a chartered surveyor while his opening partner, Bedser, was a bricklayer's son, both men with backgrounds sharply different from the Indian opening batsmen – gentleman cricketers, with reputations boosted by sheer weight of runs scored during India's Pentangular tournament during the war.

* * *

Hazare's stay at the crease on that morning proved short-lived – both he and Rusi Modi, batting at number 3, failed to score – but Merchant (53) and Gul Mohammad (89) batted well. Gover pulled up with an injury after just seven overs. A damaged tendon in his heel prevented him from bowling again in the match and he made only seven runs with the bat (in two innings). Nonetheless, at a few minutes after four o'clock, India were struggling at 205/9, before an extraordinary last-wicket stand between C.T. Sarwate and Shute Banerjee of 249 runs shifted the balance of the game. It remains the second-highest tenth-wicket stand in first-class cricket. Alec Bedser took five wickets, the first such triumph on The Oval's new Kentish turves. Surrey, facing an Indian total of 454, struggled, scoring only 135 in the first innings and, despite a better showing second time around (338), India won the game comfortably by nine wickets.

John Arlott, who was yet to achieve his later ample, claret-fed girth, instinctively warmed to India's Banerjee, his tendency to frivolity in the field and his contented slide into corpulence. The Indian paceman was in the twilight of his career: he had been 24 when he toured in 1936, and, ten years later, he had lost some of his pace and occasionally suggested undue weariness in the field. He had yet to play a Test match. But Arlott took pleasure in his evident enjoyment of the game – unsurprisingly since the broadcaster was an inveterate admirer of cricketers as a breed. It was typical of him that, in the early 1950s, he was a founder member of 'The Master's Club' in honour of the great Surrey and England batsman Jack Hobbs. Gover was another founder member. It was a sharp reminder of how much time had been lost by the war: over those years Gover had progressed from a bowler in his prime to the lower slopes of an honourable career. He went on to take 119 wickets in 1946 (at an average of 23.92), but the following year he retired. His experience was matched by other Surrey cricketers, each one acutely aware of what the war had taken from them. That side in 1946 had an average age of 36, and yet a good number were inexperienced in county cricket, their golden years spent in uniform. Those difficulties were made worse by an administrative gaffe: the man appointed to be the county's captain was out of his depth. The story was that the club had mistakenly invited N.H.

Bennett to lead the side, rather than the better-qualified 'Leo' Bennett. N.H. Bennett played 31 matches in 1946, averaging a mediocre 16; he struggled with the demands of captaincy, and never played first-class cricket again.

* * *

During May, Arlott had arranged for the tourists to visit the BBC in order for them to send messages home: fronted by the team manager, a perky-looking Pankaj Gupta, the squad was photographed in a studio, its confines necessitating a cheery huddle of smiling cricketers, prim and proper in suits and ties. Following the tourists' progress around the country in that summer of 1946, still bewitched by the thrill of watching cricket day after day, Arlott was diligent in observing and noting down the essential characteristics, the foibles and qualities of each player: how Banerjee ran in as if battling against the forces of nature; the spin bowler Shinde's frailty – how he felt the cold – and the gangliness of his frame, so out of step with the conventional view of a cricketer; Vijay Merchant's feline manner, his white muffler; Amarnath's jauntiness; Hazare's aversion to walking in the rain, his shyness ...

Presiding over the tourists was the captain, the Nawab of Pataudi, whose appointment had been controversial and whose health was already proving a cause for concern: he had played in the first two games, but he was too unwell to appear at The Oval. The bitter cold of mid-May triggered a bout of malaria, threatening his fitness for the first Test at Lord's which was only a matter of six weeks away. The tourists were growing used to the criss-crossing of the country, looking out of rain-swept carriage windows at the sodden fields of England and wondering who would make the cut for the much anticipated game at Lord's in June. Cricket in England seemed too often blighted by heavy rain and thunderstorms and the weather remained damply quixotic for week after week as they became accustomed to the vagaries of the railway system, the sequence of journeys from Cambridge to Leicester, then Edinburgh, London, Osterley, Southampton, Cardiff, Portsmouth and Nottingham.

Winning at The Oval had been a great boost to the Indians' morale and confidence, however, and they travelled to Cambridge for a match against the university in good spirits. It proved an ill-matched contest, unsurprisingly since the tourists had the advantage of having played cricket continuously throughout the war, while the opposition was a motley collection of war-weary students. Arlott watched uneasily, consoled to some extent by the students' cheery good nature and their hospitality, but unsettled by the opposition's somewhat contemptuous attitude. It was, it seems, men against boys, with the latter being beaten by an innings and 19 runs (hundreds for Modi and Pataudi; wickets for Hazare, Shinde and Sarwate). The Cambridge attack was disappointingly bland, while the university's batting never fathomed the Indian spin attack. Despite the one-sided nature of the game, Arlott enjoyed his cricket in Cambridge, the peacetime sleepiness of the city and its second-hand bookshops whose attractions were sometimes enough to warrant a delayed appearance at Fenner's. Flushed with the effort of digesting as good a breakfast as rationing allowed; then a quiet half-hour casting an attentive eye over shelves of poetry; followed by a slightly guilty, half-walk, half-run to the ground; eventually he would arrive to the treasured sound of bat on ball, the ripples of applause or a raucous appeal.

7

Pataudi, Hammond and Bradman
Down Under, 1932/33

THE CRICKETING careers of the three captains of the
two Test series in 1946 and 1946/47, Hammond, Pataudi
and Don Bradman, were closely connected for many years:
Hammond and Bradman's rivalry went back to 1928, while,
with the selection four years later of the Nawab of Pataudi
for the 1932/33 tour down under, the trio's connection was
complete. Each man would have a very different memory
of that incendiary Test series. When the photograph of the
1932/33 English touring party was taken, there was no hint
of the bad blood that Bodyline would cause, the rattling of
diplomatic cages, the exchanges of angry cables from one side
of the world to the other. There are 19 men in the photograph,
17 playing members of the squad and two suited, proprietorial
players from a previous generation standing respectively on the
left and right fringes of the group. The players are standing
in three ranks: the back row raised up on an unseen bench;
the front row of five on uncomfortable-looking wooden seats;
the middle row flanked by the officials – Messrs Pelham
Warner and Richard Palairet – but dominated by the tall
figure of Yorkshire's Bill Bowes, his glasses and blond quiff
giving no hint of his fast-bowling credentials. The squad
looks formidable, purposeful, serious-minded. There are few
smiles (the most engaging from Maurice Tate of Sussex, for

whom the tour would be largely uneventful). The blazers and white shirts are smart; so too the white flannels, while three players are sporting what look suspiciously like silk cravats – the Nawab of Pataudi (Balliol, Oxford); Freddie Brown (St John's College, Cambridge) and, unsurprisingly, the captain Douglas Jardine (New College, Oxford), all three of them present or future Test match captains.

In the Ashes series played in 1930, Don Bradman had batted like a god, making nearly a thousand runs, averaging just short of 140 over the five Test matches and making a top score of 334 at Headingley. Hammond, by contrast, made 306 runs at an average of just 34. Bradman's remarkable batting raised the chilling spectre of a decade at least of Australian dominance. For the English, it was like playing against a team with 15 men in the side, more than half of them batsmen full of runs. It was a dominance which, reasonably enough, resulted in secret English plans to make things more equal, to make Bradman somehow mortal. What turned the discussions and planning into something more inflammatory was the nature of the men most closely involved.

The England captain, Douglas Jardine, was flinty, relentless and stubborn. He it was who seized on what he considered Bradman's only weakness: a perceived uncertainty when faced with high-class fast bowling aimed at his body – or his throat. Jardine was convinced that 'the little bastard' was 'yellow' and had plotted the means to cut him down to size. Over dinner, in a swish London restaurant, moving silvered salt and pepper pots like chessmen across the white tablecloth to stand in for menacing fielders, and surrounding a lonely 'Bradman' with a circle of tableware breathing down his neck, the English captain described in icy detail what would be required. With him, no doubt remarking how different the restaurant milieu was from their Nottinghamshire roots – both of them were from mining stock – were the two principal English fast bowlers, Bill Voce and Harold Larwood. Of the two, it would be Larwood who proved the more successful, or unprincipled, even demonic, if you were looking with Australian eyes. What is certain is that, after that 1932/33 tour, his life would never be the same again. It was all designed to put the mighty Don on the back foot or, better still, on his backside.

The Bodyline tour had started well enough, with Pataudi scoring a hundred in his first Test, but the planned onslaught on the Australian captain – the disingenuous 'leg theory' – was not to his taste, much to Jardine's profound irritation. 'Pat' baulked at fielding close in, part of the predatory arc, prompting his captain to hiss, 'I see his Highness is a conscientious objector,' a term freighted with images of white feathers being handed to those who refused to fight in the Great War. Soon after, Pataudi broke a finger, then fell ill and was dropped. He would play only one more Test for England – at Trent Bridge in 1934 – and, until returning to the country as the newly appointed captain of India, his career seemed to be in terminal decline, or indeed over. He had been named a *Wisden* Cricketer of the Year in 1932, but his overall batting average for England was a disappointing 28.8. Arlott admired the subtlety of his batting, his humour and intelligence, and his captaincy. He also liked the fact that Pataudi had the grace to pretend to recall Arlott fielding as an emergency 12th man for Hampshire at Worcester before the war.

As for Jardine, unlike Pataudi, he never had the chance after Bodyline to restore his reputation. With his harlequin cap and stern manner, he was always unlikely to endear himself to the Australian public. Told that they didn't like him, his response was succinct and characteristic: 'It's fucking mutual.' Indian-born (in Bombay), his swansong as a cricketer was leading an MCC tour to India in 1933/34; after that it was all over, all cricketing achievement and prowess submerged in recrimination, a scapegoat with little hope of redemption. By 1939 his connection with the game was as a cricket writer for the *Daily Telegraph*, announcing in a report on a game between Surrey and Yorkshire that he was 'off to camp with the Territorials'. Soon he would be in France with the British Expeditionary Force and, in the summer of 1940, surviving the mayhem that was the retreat at Dunkirk. Later he would be posted to India, where he spent the rest of the war: in Quetta, then Simla as a major in the Central Provisions Directorate. On a few occasions he exchanged his officer's uniform for cricket whites, turning out for the Punjab Governor's XI in Lahore in November 1942 alongside Lala Amarnath and the Nawab of Pataudi, all three men scoring runs: a double century for Amarnath, 109 from Pataudi and 67 not out from Jardine in his penultimate game. Opening the batting for Jardine's team was one of the architects of Indian Partition, George Abell, and a young cricketer who would tour England in 1946 and become one of the key figures in the shaping of Pakistan cricket, Abdul Hafeez Kardar.

8

Captain, My Captain
May 1946

THE NAWAB of Pataudi had been given the captaincy of the All-India tourists by the narrowest of margins (10 votes to 8) over Vijay Merchant. Both men had leadership credentials, were urbane and well-born, although Merchant was now regarded as the better batsman. Perhaps he would have been the logical choice to captain his country, given Pataudi's ill health, an issue which had manifested itself as far back as 1933 when he had been playing for Worcestershire. Moreover, Merchant had been in superb form through the war years, while Pataudi was decidedly rusty, more statesman than cricketer. Both factors, taken together, raised the likelihood of dissent and mutterings against the skipper, particularly if things went wrong. Moreover, a tour by All-India necessarily had the potential for internal feuding, given the religious differences within the squad.

Pataudi's recent captaincy experience was limited to statecraft, cricket largely forgotten while he was addressing the various demands of his small country, a desk and state papers replacing bat and pads. His life over the preceding six or so years could not have been more different from the England captain, Gloucestershire's Wally Hammond. Hammond had enjoyed playing cricket during the war years in sun-blessed locations where the Germans were far away

– the Gezira Club in Cairo, in Kenya, and in a two-day game for the South African RAF against the Transvaal in Johannesburg starting on Boxing Day 1941. He took five wickets and scored 130 with four sixes.

In 1946 the England captain had worries on his mind, but they had less to do with cricket, or the progress of the war, than with his failing marriage, a love affair and a bad back. Pataudi's thoughts, by contrast, were filled with the anxieties of the touring skipper: the omission of good players from the original squad; the English weather (the sky never anything but grey, it seemed, and rain either falling, or just about to start); the constant travelling; the placid pitches; and the English food, since rationing was very much in force and the visitors were not exempt. Moreover, the strict vegetarians were troubled by what to eat and Pataudi felt it necessary to warn his players against visiting any of England's Indian restaurants (he was profoundly suspicious of the cooking oil). Merchant, for example, lost a stone in weight on the tour, although his more svelte self scored heavily, while he combated the cold conditions by wearing three sweaters and a muffler.

After the comfortable win in Cambridge, the Indian party travelled to play Leicestershire in a game marred by rain and violent thunderstorms. India batted first with the run-hungry Merchant scoring an unbeaten hundred. Leicestershire's reply was feeble and slow, so much so that Amarnath's 15.3 overs went for just 14 runs while he took four wickets. The rain-ruined draw completed, the team travelled north to Edinburgh to face Scotland beginning on the following day. The result was an innings win for the tourists, with Hazare scoring a hundred and Sarwate's perplexing spin earning him 12 wickets over the two innings, including a hat-trick in the second. Scotland was also memorable for the food, the best of the tour it was generally agreed: curry, rice and fruit.

And so to Lord's for the first time on the tour. In an unconsidered display of religious harmony, a Hindu

(Merchant) and a Muslim (Mushtaq Ali) opened the batting.

'All-India' of course meant just that, the selection of players irrespective of their religion or caste. Inevitably, though, some parts of the country were more in evidence than others: Bombay, historically the hub and spiritual home of Indian cricket, was heavily represented – Merchant; Hindlekar, the wicketkeeper, who worked on the Indian railways; and R.S. Modi, a Parsi and a student at Bombay University, and whose thin, frail physique seemed too tender for a damp English summer. Mankad – who had played against Lord Tennyson's tourists in 1937/38 as a 16-year-old – was 'attached professionally' to an Ahmedabad businessman, while several of the team (Amarnath, Mushtaq, Hazare, Gul, Sarwate) were in the employ of various Indian states, often with military rank. Banerjee (who wasn't selected at Lord's) was an officer in the Tata Steel Company's transport department.

Pataudi was injured after a fall on the pavilion steps at Lord's, missing the MCC game as a result. Unperturbed, India batted in stately fashion, the stand-in skipper Merchant anchoring the innings at the top of the order and exemplifying his side's steady resolution. Their total of 438 looked secure even before the rain interfered, turning an easy wicket into something much more spiteful. At one point John Arlott found himself in the Indian dressing room playing a makeshift game of cricket as the weather closed in, flummoxed by Nimbalkar's googlies bowled on the pavilion's coconut matting floor. By four in the afternoon on the final day, play had resumed, a grim session of defence which in the end came to nothing. India had beaten MCC by an innings. It had been dour cricket in Arlott's view, with India resolute in seeking the win. It would not have escaped the tourists, however, that the defeated MCC side contained no one regarded as certain to make the England XI for the opening Test match.

* * *

John Arlott had been a policeman in Southampton for more than a decade, a time which included the war years. By VE Day he was an acting sergeant in the town's force, but with a glimpse of what his future might hold, thanks to his distinctive voice and his taste for poetry, judged a whimsical interest for an ordinary copper. As a result he was heard on the BBC Home Service's *Tribute to the King* broadcast at 8.30 that evening. Thereafter, to his satisfaction, he began to pick up some broadcasting work and his rustic burr would become instantly recognisable across the cricket-loving world, including in India.

A little over a year from that VE Day broadcast, he was back in Southampton, revelling in being there for the cricket – and being paid for it too. Inevitably, the game between the tourists and his native Hampshire had a special resonance: his affection for the county's cricketing stalwarts – Philip Mead and the rest; fond memories of the cricket ground he knew best, now battered by the years of neglect and warfare; the companionship of old friends; the sense of loss he felt when confronted by the widespread bomb damage. The summer's persistent rain somehow fitted the mood, but, nevertheless, between the storms, there was enough play for the Indians to win a low-scoring match, despite Charlie Knott's 7-36 in the first innings. The tourists batted consistently to win the game, losing just four wickets in reaching the required total, with Modi and Hafeez top-scoring, but with everyone who batted contributing solidly.

Fresh from getting much the better of a draw against Glamorgan in Cardiff, a game marked by the running into form of Lala Amarnath (104 not out), the Indians flew to Portsmouth to play a Combined Services XI, a strong side with two future England Test players – John Dewes and Donald Carr – in the team. Leo Harrison of Hampshire, who would become John Arlott's greatest friend in the game, was behind the stumps. Instead of taking yet another train, five hours travelling by rail, it meant a mere 40 minutes in the air. They were pioneers, the first sporting team, in its entirety, to fly to complete a sporting fixture. Pataudi sat in the Dakota, alternately looking at the early-evening sun, green English fields below, and at Vijay Merchant sitting just across the aisle. He found himself revisiting the raw politics of his appointment as skipper, a decision taken amid bruising argument and political machinations. For many, Merchant was the obvious choice – hadn't Pataudi declined to play for India twice during the 1930s? Wasn't he uncomfortably short of game-time? Wasn't Merchant a run machine, steely and uncompromising? When the Indian Board met to discuss the issue at the Connemara Hotel in Madras – a meeting that was later dubbed the 'Mad Hatter's Tea Party' – Merchant's name was pencilled in as captain. Over the course of a long, charged meeting, it emerged that the appointment was anything but a foregone conclusion. Discussion was fractious and the decision to opt for Pataudi was far from unanimous. Now, as the Dakota struggled with turbulence – appropriately – Pataudi stared at Merchant's profile, his thin face and the understated moustache, that look of, what, disdain? Or was it pride? Anyway, he seemed always to favour that look when facing a camera, or an opening bowler. Pataudi's unease wasn't helped by his own uncertain batting form and his dubious fitness. So far on the tour, Merchant hadn't missed a match and was averaging 56, while the skipper had made just 167 runs in four innings, of which 121 were against the raw young men of Cambridge University.

With a shake of the head, Pataudi began to reflect on what he had been planning to do on the flight: the selection of his preferred eleven to face England in the first Test, now less than a fortnight away. The batting? Maybe four or five safe picks: Merchant (him again!), Modi, Sarwate and Hazare. Only Banerjee of the bowlers was a worry, with just eight wickets at 44, scattered over seven games. Not ready for Test cricket. There was some consolation in the creakiness of the English bowling attack, which seemed to lack pace and venom. Their batting was a different matter, making the Indian captain shift uneasily in his seat as the Dakota began its descent towards the south coast. He ran through some of the likely names, remembering how, nearly 14 years before, he and Hammond had batted together at three and four against Australia at Sydney and Melbourne. Now, both were older, wiser and, in Pataudi's case at least, struggling to relive past glories. Hammond's own struggle was against his painful and persistent fibrositis. As well as its imperious captain, England's batting had a lordly look to it – Denis Compton, Cyril Washbrook and Len Hutton. Hammond, however, would have looked at his batting line-up and worried about current form: Compton and Washbrook both out for nought in their last outings; Hutton had made two scores in the 20s; Hardstaff out for 16 while Jack Ikin had made only 25 and 5 – figures shaky enough to give India hope.

9

The First Test

June 1946

AFTER A month's cricket, the tourists could feel pleased with their progress towards the opening Test match to be played in the third week of June. They had played nine first-class games, winning six and only losing one (that inauspicious opening match at Worcester). John Arlott dutifully trailed after them, keeping close, except when he was obliged to take the slow train to Portsmouth while the cricketers made that first collective foray into air travel. He was happy enough, comforted by the reassurance of the dining car, a glass or two of something uplifting and warming, and a good book. That was the kind of comfort much needed in that wet summer. Rain was never far away and it was perhaps predictable that the final game before the Lord's Test, against Nottinghamshire, was abandoned, the first day entirely washed out and showers bringing the game to an early close. The Notts captain George Heane chivalrously allowed the Indians first use of an easy-paced wicket and Pataudi's men took full advantage, enjoying some batting practice, Merchant making a graceful 86 and the captain completing a chanceless century. After an Indian declaration, there was only enough time for 15 overs before the rain returned. Arlott was partly consoled by the proximity of the Trent Bridge Inn.

* * *

India's team for the Lord's Test was little changed from the eleven that had beaten MCC there the previous month: Mushtaq Ali and Sarwate were replaced by Hafeez and Nayudu. England, by contrast, selected a very different side from MCC's, its strength acknowledging that India would provide a real threat, not least because England had clear weaknesses, partly the result of the absence of any competitive cricket through the war years. India's Pentangular competition, on the other hand, had continued. England's players were all involved in the war – four of them in the RAF and seven in the army. Two – Compton and Joe Hardstaff – had even served in India. Overall some ten county cricketers played in India during the war, including Battery Sergeant-Major Hardstaff and Company Sergeant-Major Compton. The men picked for this Test to represent England were an older side, man for man, than India, with an average age of 33 (compared to 29.6); Alec Bedser was the youngest Englishman, at 27, while India had four players who were 25 or under. Hammond was 43, and certainly looked it; his principal fast bowler, Bill Bowes, was 37 and still recovering from his years as a prisoner of war.

The Test began on 22 June: English high summer. It was the first Test England had played since the war ended, after 13 months of preparation and expectation. The last pre-war Test had concluded on 22 August 1939, England drawing with West Indies. The 13 months since hostilities had ceased was a significantly earlier return to Test cricket than in the aftermath of the Great War when it had been more than two years before England faced Australia in Sydney towards the end of December 1920 – and were duly crushed by 377 runs.

Long queues formed outside the St John's Wood ground from early morning, a densely packed line, reminiscent of the press of eager young men outside Army Recruitment offices, seven years – and 32 years – before. Flat caps, overcoats (the miserable summer of 1946, remember), even a muffler or two among the largely male throng standing in the shadow of the red-brick wall that hid the ground from view. The attendance that day totalled 29,000. Pataudi won the toss and chose to bat, trusting that, after the weeks of rain, the pitch would be slow and benign. He was right, it was indeed easy-paced, although there would prove to be some help for the bowlers. Hammond lobbed the new ball to Bowes and, at last, normal service was resumed.

Bowes had last played for England in July 1939 when he had demolished West Indies, taking six wickets. Posted to North Africa as a gunnery officer, he had been taken prisoner at Tobruk in June 1942, one of 20,000 men captured at the city's aerodrome, and then marched to the rear in a shambling trail of dazed and dispirited soldiers, systematically fleeced of their watches, rings and cigarette cases by the Italian guards. Bowes had been at his peak in 1939, although he didn't conform to the stereotype of a fiery, rugged Yorkshire fast bowler. He was 6ft 4in, gangly and bespectacled. Batsmen would see the sun reflecting from his glasses as he loped in to bowl. Early in his career, while on the ground staff at Lord's, he had bowled with pince-nez hanging from his ear on a chain. His stance and specs gave him the air of an earnest academic. Approaching the wicket, he looked as if he was running to catch a bus with a pile of books under his arm.

Bowes' Test career had begun in 1932 and he had played in the notorious Bodyline series (just one match then and a single wicket – although it *was* Bradman, and for a first-ball duck). In those days he had been a high-class fast-medium bowler, lacking Larwood's raw pace, but able to move the ball both ways, while his high action produced uncomfortable lift and bounce. The war, however, diminished him. Time would have done so anyway, but the three years he spent behind Italian, then German, barbed wire, accelerated the process. From Tobruk, Bowes had been taken to Benghazi, then flown to Lecce in the heel of Italy before being transported to a transit camp at Bari, about a hundred miles to the north along the coast of the Adriatic. He was there for some seven weeks, bored and hungry, *bêtes noires* of the POW. Food was provided in a tedious, repetitive cycle: counterfeit coffee at six in the morning, soup and fruit at lunch, then a second bowl of soup at 6pm. Bowes grew thinner and weaker. Eventually he was taken to a permanent camp at Chieti, further up the coast. Unknown to him, his close friend and Yorkshire team-mate Hedley Verity was on the other side of Italy in the summer of 1943. After the Italian surrender, Bowes was transported, along with other prisoners, including the future England captain, Freddie Brown, to a squalid camp in Germany, where they were obliged to wait for the war to grind to a conclusion. On 12 April 1945, the Americans liberated the camp and a few days later Bowes was climbing down from an aircraft on to a runway in Buckinghamshire. He weighed nearly 29kg (4½ stone) less than he had in 1939.

Now, 14 months later, the Yorkshire fast bowler was running in from the Pavilion End to bowl to Vijay Merchant … *'And Merchant leans forward and flicks it away gracefully to leg and they run two …'* At the end of the over, Bowes was seen walking down to third man, with tears rolling down his face, overcome by the emotion of the moment, back at Lord's after his long wartime incarceration. Once Bowes ended his career in 1947, John Arlott would stay with him when he went to Yorkshire and they drank together at the Menston Arms in Wharfedale. All that lay ahead, however. Now the commentator was intrigued to watch Bowes bowl again – that laconic style, the evident loss of pace, his unblemished subtlety, but the old hostility quite gone.

Hammond turned to Bedser to open from the Nursery End. It was the Surrey bowler's first Test match in what was virtually his first season – he had only played twice for the county in June 1939, against the two university sides, Oxford and Cambridge. That had been a distinctly low-key beginning: 18 overs bowled; 59 runs conceded; and without taking a wicket. Over the war years he had changed from a raw 21-year-old to a man in his prime. Arlott admired his coltish strength and eager willingness in his opening overs, describing him in his notes as 'young', as if the war years somehow didn't count. That he had avoided Bill Bowes' fate had been a close-run thing, thanks to his escape from Dunkirk in 1940. In 1946, before the Lord's Test, he had played only ten first-class games, but had taken 46 wickets at an average of 16.7. Against Lancashire at Old Trafford a fortnight before the Test, he had taken 11 wickets in the match (for 89), while in the Test trial in the preceding week, he had got the wickets of both Len Hutton and Wally Hammond. Joe Hardstaff of Nottinghamshire, one of the team's oldest players, presented him with his England cap, telling him to take it home for his mother. Three months after his demobilisation, Bedser, in his size 15 boots, enticed the bothersome Merchant to nibble at a ball which Paul Gibb behind the stumps duly caught.

India were soon in deep trouble, sinking at one point to 87/6, before Modi, with 57 not out, and a pugnacious 43 from Abdul Hafeez, swinging his bat freely, steadied the ship. It was a rare interval of Indian resistance: Bedser's swerve and cut bowled at a brisk medium pace was irresistible and the Indian innings closed at just 200, considerably below par. England's reply began inauspiciously, with Hutton, Washbrook, Compton (for a first-ball duck) and Hammond all out, leaving England at 70/4, all four wickets falling to Lala Amarnath. The English recovery was significantly less flimsy than India's had been: Hardstaff, batting bareheaded with an Edwardian grace, and Gibb putting on 182 for the fifth wicket. Hardstaff ended the innings undefeated on 205. Arlott judged Gibb's invaluable contribution as perhaps the least impressive match-saving innings ever played – he never seemed secure or in control – but the upshot was a first-innings lead of 228.

India batted rather better in the second innings, reaching 275, with Mankad and Amarnath both making fifties, but on the final day the innings petered out, leaving England to score the 48 required for victory without either of the two opening batsmen being dismissed. It proved to be Bedser's match: he took 11 wickets, bowling 62 overs and, in the process, exposing by his strength and energy what time and the Germans had taken from Bowes. The Yorkshireman took just one wicket (Hafeez) in the match and bowled only four overs in the second innings.

The arrival on the ground of King George VI to be introduced to the players somehow hinted at the fading days of empire; it certainly delayed the inevitable England victory, though not for long. By 1.30 in the afternoon of the third and final day the game was won and lost. The tourists had acquitted themselves well enough, although the captain had failed twice with the bat, leaving the responsibility for saving face to a core of senior players – Mankad, Amarnath and, of course, Merchant. There was little time for a post-mortem since the next match, at Northampton, was due to start the following morning. As for Bill Bowes, he headed north, preoccupied with the harsh reality of life's rapid passing.

Bowes was not the only England cricketer to feel disappointed with aspects of the Lord's Test. Hammond's captaincy had caused some unease: it was acknowledged that he was a keen student of the game with a wealth of experience, but his manner was not always seen as helpful. He was not an effusive man at the best of times, unlikely to put an encouraging arm around a young cricketer's shoulders or find the right words to settle a bowler's nerves or fire a player's passion. Bedser thought him unduly cold and was perturbed by the perfunctory welcome to the England dressing room he had received as a debutant; Hammond's reluctance to talk through the pros and cons of fielding positions; and his unwillingness to emerge from his very private world. For his part, Bowes thought Hammond lacked subtlety and guile as a captain and was too much of a lone wolf. The captain himself would have left Lord's content with the overall performance but feeling the pain in his back and the passing years. In the back of his mind, too, would have been the forthcoming tour of Australia and whether his body would stand up to one last Australian hurrah.

10

The Seven Year Gap
1939–46

YORKSHIRE'S BRAMALL Lane ground in Sheffield had
been badly damaged in a bombing raid in December 1940.
The county's cities had been regular targets for the enemy
bombers: Hull, for example, paying a price for its dockyards,
while Leeds and York were also subject to raids. If the state
of the cricket grounds in the county was a cause for concern
in early 1946, so too was the age and fitness of the Yorkshire
playing staff. The cricket committee's collective view was
that the necessary work on the grounds was perhaps less of
a concern than the threadbare look of the team. Take the
age of the players: the eleven who had put Lancashire to the
sword in August 1939 had an average age of just under 30,
with only three players below that figure. Len Hutton was
the youngest at 23. If the county had fielded the same team
for the fixture in 1946 – something that wartime casualties
made impossible – some of them would have been frankly
over the hill. An infusion of new blood was needed and
a high priority was finding replacements for some of the
bowlers. That included a young, fit, slow left-armer and a
new pace bowler.

A month before the war broke out, Yorkshire had
played Lancashire at Headingley, Leeds: the Roses match,
intense 'proper' cricket. Bill Bowes opened the bowling, not

enamoured of the slow wicket or the sullen gloom and chill of the morning. It was traditional Roses cricket with Lancashire grafting their way to 54/1 at lunch. A cold wind had not stopped blowing across the ground throughout the two hours' play. The cricket writer Neville Cardus, who was watching, fretted at Lancashire's slow progress, but consoled himself with the amusement afforded by Bowes' fielding. The pace bowler was an idiosyncratic figure in the field. He looked the part, watchful and alert, until he was obliged to chase the ball, whereupon he set off in a high-kneed gallop, before philosophically recognising that others did it better and leaving the ball for someone better placed. He would have a quiet game overall – just the one wicket – since the damage was done by Yorkshire's spin bowlers, Hedley Verity taking six wickets in the game and Ellis Robinson 13, including 8-35 in the Lancashire second innings. A century from Len Hutton – 'the marvellous boy' in the poet Edmund Blunden's telling phrase – cemented the victory. Hutton hit 105 not out in a total of 147/5 as the rain threatened. For those with a poetic turn of mind, the heavy, black clouds sweeping over Headingley suggested more than the threat of an imminent storm. There was a heavy hint of the dark times that lay ahead. Seven years later, Lancashire's Cyril Washbrook and Yorkshire's Hutton would open the batting for England down under. Now, on 8 August 1939, Washbrook reached for – but missed – a difficult last chance off Hutton's bat, and the White Rose had won.

A month later, both sets of players were more preoccupied with the war and its consequences than the past summer's cricket. Of the Yorkshire side that faced the Red Rose at Leeds, Maurice Leyland and Brian Sellers would soon be serving in the Royal Artillery, the latter assuming responsibility for the defence of the English coastline between Kent and Sussex. Leyland's military service would take him to North Africa, Italy and Greece. Turner and Robinson went into the RAF. Hedley Verity and Norman Yardley were in the 1st Battalion of the Green Howards, serving in Northern Ireland, India, Iran, Egypt and Sicily. Len Hutton and Turner were also in the army. Hutton volunteered early in the conflict, becoming a sergeant-instructor in the Physical Training Corps, his cricket limited to appearing for Pudsey St Lawrence in the Bradford League. Although not in the war's direct firing line, in March 1941 he sustained a serious, career-threatening injury …

… Sergeant Hutton is in the city of York. It is springtime, but, being the north, the daffodils are still dormant on the grassy banks below the city wall. The war is not going well – the German offensive in North Africa is showing no sign of petering out, for example, while the weather is equally unpromising. It is the final day of a commando training course and Len Hutton is in the gym. The afternoon session sees him demonstrating, his singlet and kit as crisp and neat as his cricket whites. He has performed this particular manoeuvre many times, alone or watched intently by apprehensive troops. It is the 'fly-spring' where he must run hard, do a handstand at pace – and then flip over, flying momentarily. It is very different from an elegant push into the covers and an ambled single. As he reaches full speed, his plimsolls slapping the gymnasium floor, the mat slips and sends England's treasured opening batsman flying. He lands awkwardly, his left arm caught at an unnatural angle. There is a stunned silence and, for a moment or two, no one moves.

Sergeant Len Hutton's forearm was fractured and his ulna dislocated at the wrist. A sister at York's Military Hospital gave him a large brandy for the pain – a kindness which he would long remember. He was transferred to a hospital in Wakefield under the care of an orthopaedic surgeon, Reginald Broomhead. For anyone, this would be a serious injury, but for a cricketer it might well mean that he would never play again. Certainly the prognosis was not good: the surgeon took a bone graft from Hutton's right leg to his broken left arm; followed it soon after with a second operation; then took another bone graft, this time from his left leg. Instead of a life of press-ups and parallel bars, still less playing cricket, he was obliged to rest and submit to extensive post-operative care. The long-term outcome was that England's opening batsman now had a left arm two inches shorter than his right.

Discharged from the army on medical grounds, Hutton consoled himself with reading (James Boswell's *Life of Samuel Johnson* was a particular favourite) and contemplating how best to accommodate his newfound disability when he was at the crease. Lacking full movement in his left wrist would mean a permanent change in his batting technique with an altered grip on the bat handle. With that major adjustment he might be able to resume his career – his livelihood, since Hutton was a professional. However, he would never regain full movement in his wrist and was obliged to avoid playing the hook or pull shots. That was a limitation which Australia's bowlers would note and exploit mercilessly in the post-war Tests. Thereafter Hutton would forever be troubled by a swollen wrist and sore shins – the consequence of the bone grafts taken from both legs. The hard grounds overseas were particularly wearing for him. He knew too that any crushing blow to his left forearm would mean the end of cricket for him. As far as the Indians were concerned, however, in the 1946 series against England, they lacked quick bowlers who could make a batsman duck, dive or flinch. The real challenge would come some months later, on England's tour of Australia. There Hutton would face the high pace and aggression of Lindwall and Miller, later describing the experience as being as if he were back in the wartime Blitz.

* * *

Unlike Verity, Bowes had not been accepted into the Green Howards – the plan had been for both men to join up and get commissioned as officers together. Bowes' fast bowler's knees had put paid to that idea. Instead, the two close friends went their separate ways, Verity to find that the Green Howards proved to be little more than a Yorkshire County Cricket Club reunion – with them he joined forces with Hutton, Maurice Leyland, Arthur Wood and Herbert Sutcliffe. It gave them a cricket XI that would test any county side's quality, Yorkshire apart perhaps. Verity was a thinking man and had seen the war coming; he also read a lot about military matters, enjoying the connection between tactics on the battlefield and a slow bowler's guile; the thinking ahead, the disguise, the feint, the artful trap. Being a professional, Verity had never been regarded as captaincy material by his employers. The army saw things differently, and Hedley Verity became Captain H. Verity.

There were aspects of the military life which did not come naturally to him. Verity trying to strip a Bren gun, for example, was an embarrassment. One might have expected that someone who could make a cricket ball talk might show a degree of manual dexterity, that fiddling with a weapon's intricacies would come easily; on the contrary, he was all spinning fingers and clumsy thumbs. After training in Yorkshire he was posted to Northern Ireland. This was in the summer of 1941 and, for a while, the war was a succession of easy-going cricket matches, playing for the battalion against Irish opposition, in Strabane, Armagh and other towns in the province. It was a fine summer, days of long spells bowling in the sun, savouring subtle variations of flight – red ball, blue sky – and the outwitting of rustic gung-ho batsmen, intent on bludgeoning unsubtlety. It couldn't last. In 1942, he was stationed for a while at Walton Heath in Surrey; then suddenly came a posting overseas. There was time for a brief goodbye in London with his wife, Kathleen – he remembered hugging her, turning to wave and his boots echoing in the frost as he walked away. Then, a grim train journey north, to Liverpool, a marathon of packed corridors, chain-smoking tommies, the smell of damp uniforms and fear, before arriving at the city docks.

The troopship made the wartime railways seem luxurious by comparison. This was one tour that Verity would have been wise to avoid. His thoughts would have turned to his previous long stretches at sea – Australia and New Zealand in 1932/33; India, South Africa and Jamaica – weeks of enforced idleness, as MCC's select cricketers dined, perhaps, at the captain's table; slept on deck to escape stifling cabins; swam and enjoyed the games deck (where Wally Hammond, if he was touring, invariably prevailed); smoked, sitting on the sun-deck; wrote stilted letters home and danced in the evenings as the sun set into the ocean. On the 1936/37 trip to Australia, Verity spent many hours reading. The ship on that occasion was RMS *Orion*, which later was one of the 'Winston Specials' ferrying troops in convoy to South Africa, India and the Middle East. As Verity soon discovered, troopships offered a very different cruising experience: overcrowding, discomfort, military discipline and the fear of prowling German submarines.

Once he was in India, things did not improve. Verity suffered from dysentery; made a slow and partial recovery, but felt his strength being sapped by the regimen of drugs he was obliged to take. He was now 37 and with his fitness increasingly undermined. The postings that came thick and fast did nothing to improve matters: the hills of Persia, then Iraq, Syria and Egypt, before a move to the east bank of the Suez Canal. There preparations were well advanced for the invasion of Sicily.

* * *

Three years later, the Yorkshire committee anxiously perused players' names: who would want to return to the game they had been obliged to leave suddenly in 1939? Who would be fit enough? What sort of playing budget could the county afford? How many players needed to be recruited? Who would replace those no longer available? Above all, could the county win the Championship again, seven years after that ominous September day at Hove?

Committee men across England might have worried about how their county would cope with the restarting of cricket after such a long time. But such anxiety was nothing compared to that felt by players resuming a mothballed career. Somerset's Bill Andrews spoke for many when he revealed how 'strangely nervous' he was at the resumption, comparing it with how he felt at the beginning of his career. Denis Compton, back from service in India, was apprehensive too, wondering if he could still play the game to the level he had shown before the war. Some, like Chick Cray of Essex, were still overseas and in uniform: he would not get home until the winter of 1946/47, a shock after Rangoon, and his first post-war game wasn't until early May 1947. Len Hutton, nursing that serious wartime injury, was acutely aware of the challenge he faced in recapturing his pre-war form. This was a man who had scored 364 against Australia at The Oval in August 1938. Now though would a fast, lifting ball directed at his weaker arm be a test too far? For each man strapping on pads or marking out a run-up in that first game of genuinely competitive cricket since September 1939, emotions would have run high: excitement, pleasure, nervous tension – and, at some level, a fear of failure.

11

Far East and Up North

Summer, 1946

JOHN ARLOTT was stunned at the thought of his Hampshire burr rolling right across India, courtesy of the BBC. His cricket commentaries were increasingly popular there, to the extent that the BBC's man in New Delhi felt obliged to cable London and report how successful they were and how important it was for them to continue whatever the cost. For a man whose idea of travel had once been bicycle rides around the Hampshire byways, the world had suddenly opened up. Hitherto he had never been north of the Trent. The cricketing enclaves of Yorkshire and Lancashire were a foreign country to him – so much more so was India. He imagined legions of cricket fans, leaning in to catch every word of his broadcast from Lord's, their ears pressed to radios across the subcontinent, village by village. My goodness, the ex-bobby from Basingstoke speaking direct to Bombay, Bhopal and Bangalore!

As well as his eloquence and feel for the game of cricket, Arlott took very seriously the need to understand and empathise with the men whose arrival from a foreign land had persuaded the BBC to commission him to follow the All-India tour. The long rail journeys from one venue to the next gave him time to get closer to the players, ask earnest questions and offer sympathy and his wry humour. Hours on trains also allowed him to window-gaze, to acclimatise to the unexpectedly different faces of the north and Midlands of England and to research the cricketing world of the exotic tourists. With him he carried a copy of *Presenting Indian Cricket*, a slimmed-down post-war volume, and was touched by its introductory letter from the Nawab of Pataudi (dateline, the Ibrahim Palace, 20 March 1946). To underpin his broadcast commentaries he needed to know about the nature of India's Pentangular competition, in which the teams were determined not by city, or region, but by religious belief. Cricket continued to be played throughout the war in India and, in some ways, it prospered there, notably in the quality of its batsmen. But the country's fragile peace was all too evident in the unwillingness of the Hindus to take part in the Pentangular in 1937 and again in 1942. In the former year, it stemmed from Hindu dismay about the inadequate provision of seats for its followers in the Brabourne Stadium, Bombay – the very name of which hinted at India's other seemingly intractable problem, since the ground was named, not to commemorate a legendary Indian cricketer, but for a former British governor of the city, Lord Brabourne.

It was in Bombay, in early August 1942, that Mahatma Gandhi launched the 'Quit India' movement, speaking at a rally on one of the city's sandy beaches. He was subsequently arrested. By this third year of the war, an active campaign against 'communalism' in Indian cricket interfered with the game. Inescapably, India had become a powder keg. For all that, there were those who could see beyond the bitter religious rivalry. The Hindu, Vijay Merchant, and the Muslim, Mushtaq Ali, opened the batting for All-India and were friends. During the Pentangular final between Hindus and Muslims in 1944, the game was held up after Merchant, captain of the Hindus, asked if poor footholds on the bowling crease could be filled in. The Muslim captain, Mushtaq, consulted his team who were keen to refuse Merchant's request – but Mushtaq overruled them, arguing that the game should be played in a sporting spirit: losing it would not be a disaster, not leading to slavery or a death sentence, as he put it. The footholds were duly filled in and, for a moment, bitterness was set to one side. The Muslims, set to make 298 to win, reached the target with only one wicket remaining, the opening bat, K.C. Ibrahim, batting undefeated through the innings. Seven of that Hindu XI would tour with All-India in 1946 as well as three of the Muslim side. After the game Merchant went to the Muslim dressing room, embraced Mushtaq and congratulated his team on the win. It had been deserved, he said, and, if they had lost, the sport would have suffered.

* * *

After the Lord's Test, the Indians headed north, with Arlott dutifully following suit. This was the moment when he was obliged to face his preconceptions about the north of England. The comfort of the south's bucolic charm, as he saw it – its church spires, downland, cornfields and thatched cottages – had been left behind and he anticipated a sprawl of grim smoke-stacks, pit villages and slag heaps. If Arlott was uncertain about heading north, how much more wary were the tourists, although some had experience of playing league cricket in Yorkshire and Lancashire. Their itinerary too was an unforgiving one, a four-week trek to and fro across the Pennines, with just one day without any cricket (and that spent travelling back from Sunderland for the Manchester Test).

It was evident that the Indians' preparations were focused on the second Test, with much thought expended on the squad fitness and the form of key players. Arlott was intrigued by the fact that the players' kit bags somehow seemed bigger, their laundry arrangements more complex, and their packing more idiosyncratic, as if for extra comfort while on the road. Merchant, for example, packed extra writing paper; Pataudi ensured that he had his address book; and, strangely,

Hindlekar (affectionately nicknamed 'Handlebars'), was actively investigating the possibility of buying a sewing machine. Was Pataudi planning an overnight stay at the Midlands home of a fellow Balliol man? (He would choose not to play in the next match at Northampton.) Did Merchant intend to write an account of the tour, or was he perhaps drafting a business plan for the family firm of Thackersey of Bombay? Was Hindlekar contemplating a gift to take home, or his life after cricket?

In terms of deciding selection for the second Test (just over three weeks away), the game at Northampton offered little information of any value. The performance at Lord's had already confirmed some certainties: Merchant, Modi, Amarnath and Hazare. The captain, by dint of his role rather than his fitness or form, would also play at Manchester. But the bowling remained an issue, with no one, it seems, able to emulate what Alec Bedser had done for England at Lord's. At Northampton, Merchant scored heavily, making 110 out of a total of 328 in the first innings, following that up with 72 not out in a second innings of 171/1. Both Amarnath and Modi again made runs, while Mankad and the spinner Shinde took eight wickets between them. Mankad's control of length and his variety were exceptional. It was stately cricket, however, with the county meandering along at two and a half runs an over, while India were content with unhurried, elegant batting practice on the final day. It was, in Arlott's eyes, a 'harmless' draw of the sort which required a pint, a post-stumps pipe and nostalgic conversation about 'ten to make and a match to win' to rekindle one's spirit. If nothing else, Merchant and Amarnath's unflurried soporific batting somehow confirmed that peacetime had truly settled over England.

With the match over, it was a hurried departure for Liverpool: bats and pads, batting gloves and the rest of the kit gathered up, a last check of the visitors' dressing room, and then yet another train journey. On arrival in the north-west, the players spilled into the hotel foyer, tired from travel, cricket and, perhaps, of each other. The hotel's greeting, however, was effusive, the beds comfortable and the hospitality warm, all of which left the visitors with a highly favourable view of the northern city. The weather, though, proved as capricious as elsewhere, punctuating the first day with showers. Welcome to Aigburth in the rain.

Lancashire, like its northern neighbour to the east, had lost a number of players because of the passage of years: Eddie Paynter's career was effectively over (he was now 44 and since his debut for the county in 1926 he had scored more than 20,000 runs at an average of 42); 'Buddy' Oldfield – another of England's one-Test cricketers (his sole appearance was against West Indies at The Oval in August 1939 when he had scored 80 and 19) – had left the county, although he would have a protracted swansong with Northamptonshire from 1948. Bill Farrimond, a wicketkeeper with four Test caps, had retired, aged nearly 43 when cricket resumed in 1946. Jack Iddon had played five Test matches in 1934 and 1935, four of them on a tour of the West Indies. He survived the war, but not a car crash on the drive home from a business meeting at the Rolls-Royce works in Crewe on 17 April, less than a month before Lancashire played their first post-war county match, at Gloucester.

The sun shone on the Sunday – no help since there could be no play on the Sabbath – and by Monday when play resumed, the pitch had turned hard and pacey. Lancashire were hustled out for a feeble 140 by the bowling of Amarnath and Banerjee (4-32), the latter at last finding some form, and a surface he liked, for the first time on the tour. Until then he had taken only nine wickets in eight games at an average of close to 50. Suddenly, given a firm pitch, he was a genuine handful, so much so that when he bowled the all-rounder Eddie Phillipson, one of the stumps was shattered.

Pataudi watched Merchant and Hafeez go out to begin India's reply, reasonably confident that the Test XI's batting selection was secure enough, apart from finally settling on who should open with Merchant. An hour or so of limp batting was therefore disturbing, with four of the first five batsmen (Hafeez, Amarnath, Hazare and the vice-captain Merchant, failing for once), contributing a total of just six runs between them. Pataudi, with 35, top-scored in a total of 126, 14 runs short of the county's total. The Lancashire quick bowler, Dick Pollard, took 7-49 in 19 impressive overs. When Lancashire batted again, the Indian bowlers limited them to 185, leaving India 200 to win, a target reached comfortably thanks to a fine stand between Pataudi (80 not out) and Merchant (93 not out). Abdul Hafeez failed again, dismissed for 10, but only three Indian batsmen were required to secure a comfortable win.

Leaving Liverpool behind, the tourists were in good spirits for the upcoming match against Yorkshire at Bradford. Both Arlott and the Indians were struck by the county's stark differences from the world they were used to – the grey-stoned villages and bleak hills beyond the coach windows as the team travelled by bus from Leeds to Bradford each day; the inelegant stolidity of the ground itself; and the flat-capped directness of Yorkshire 'folk' which Arlott thought was fittingly represented by the weighty meatiness of the county's pies, chewed grimly while the first shower of rain fell. That squall scuppered Pataudi's game-plan: he had won the toss, eyed a promising pitch, then watched as the rain exposed its devil.

Things did not go well. Forty-three-year-old Arthur Booth, replacing Hedley Verity, made the ball spit and bounce: India subsided to a feeble 138 (top score 29, achieved by both Hazare and Nayudu). Then Hutton outscored them on his own, encouraging Arlott to pen a short riff in his notebook on the nature of cricketing 'greatness'. This son of Pudsey, in the Hampshire man's eyes, was without a blemish in his batting and so – emphatically, indisputably 'great'. Thereafter the sun came out and the wicket eased; Yorkshire declared and then, as if orchestrated by their captain, Brian Sellers, the rain fell again, just enough to spice things up. India's second innings was even more humbling than its first – all out 124 (Nayudu 28) – and the resulting innings defeat was the worst possible preparation for the Test now just over two weeks away. The debacle was encapsulated by a tale of two wicketkeepers: Yorkshire's Arthur Wood, a late replacement, caught five and stumped two, while conceding just a single bye; by contrast, India's stumper, 'Handlebars' Hindlekar, was forced to leave the field after an attack of lumbago.

* * *

On 29 June, the first day of the game against Lancashire at Aigburth, when Shute Banerjee's dispiriting run of poor form was dispelled, the British government's three-man mission returned from India empty-handed and despondent. The viceroy, Viscount Archibald Wavell, duly cabled the cabinet informing them that, with the collapse of talks, the prospect of serious public disturbances was now higher than ever. The task facing the mission – the Three Magi as they were termed – that of negotiating the British withdrawing from India without losing face, was fraught with difficulties and the price of failure was the strong probability of civil unrest, then Partition on religious lines, splitting British India into two: India and Pakistan. Back in April, at much the same time as the Indian tourists were arriving in England's cold, wet spring, the British prime minister, Clement Attlee, had secretly authorised the Partition of India as an option. Attlee had attended Haileybury School as a boy, an institution with long-standing and deep connections with India to the extent that its boarding pupils stayed in houses named for Indian states. In the ensuing weeks, the mood in India worsened, in part because of an election in which only 10% of the Indian population were eligible to vote. Relations between Hindus and Muslims deteriorated. There were riots in Bombay, the United Provinces and Bengal and predictions of civil war. The British found themselves side-lined, on the very edge of the bitter divide, the tension between the two communities so great that one Englishman reported that two fighting gangs had stood back from each other to allow his wife to cross the road. Safely on the other side, neutral and forgotten, she sensed the rival mobs resume their bloodletting.

And yet the cricketers of India stood side by side, the Hindu Vijay Merchant opening the batting against Yorkshire with the Muslim Abdul Hafeez. Just how did that work? Both men were politically aware and, moreover, not averse to speaking their minds. In the squad photograph of the 1946 tourists, Merchant looks every bit of his 34 years. Blazered, like the rest of the team, he looks neat and assured with deep-set eyes and a toothbrush moustache over a haughty top lip. His hands are crossed loosely on his lap, hinting at an inner calm. The bulky shoulders of the team-mates on either side – Pataudi and Mushtaq Ali – are invading his space, but he seems untroubled by it, somehow content with the comradely contact. They are team-mates, after all. For all that, he had form politically: as far back as 1932 he had shown his support for the Civil Disobedience Movement in India by staying away from the trials for the forthcoming tour of England. The movement's leader, Gandhi, had been arrested and jailed. Merchant had gone on the 1936 tour, however, content that political prisoners had been released. His batting on that tour was good enough to earn him a place as one of *Wisden*'s Cricketers of the Year in its 1937 edition. The Merchant family held Gandhi in high regard, so much so that when MCC toured India in 1933, Vijay's sister, Laxmi, asked Gandhi for his autograph. The great man duly signed, adding his name and signature and thereby casting himself as the 17th member of the 16-man touring party.

Abdul Hafeez, at 21, was much younger than his opening partner. He had only made his first-class debut in 1944, scoring 94 for Northern India. In the team photograph he is directly behind Merchant, a shy smile on his thin face, hair swept back with a touch of flamboyance, his blazer hanging loosely on him. He looks strong-willed, determined, with a hint of the enigmatic quality that Arlott had noted. The commentator, failing to see the way India would split apart in little more than a year's time, predicted that he would do well for India for many years to come. But by 1952, Abdul Hafeez Kardar, as he had become, was captain of Pakistan. Like Merchant, he was politically engaged, but as a Muslim he was a keen supporter of the Muslim League leader, Muhammad Ali Jinnah. Once his cricket career was over, he would enter politics, serving for a time as the government's minister for food and later as Pakistan's ambassador to Switzerland. Conversation between Merchant and Hafeez as they walked out to bat no doubt concentrated on the clarity or otherwise of the light, whether rain was likely, or who should take first strike. Matters of religion and nationhood were probably best avoided.

There were still three games against the counties to play – plus a token two-day match with Durham at Sunderland – before the second Test. Rain prevented all but four hours of play against Durham, where a draw was inevitable. The games against Lancashire at Manchester and Yorkshire in Sheffield were also drawn, both fixtures notable for heavy run-scoring: Merchant making 242 against Lancashire, and Hazare 244 not out against Yorkshire. The batting looked solid enough and there were encouraging signs from the bowlers too with Sohoni bowling with some pace and occasional lift at Manchester, taking five wickets in the Lancashire first innings. The batting of the Lancashire and England pair, Washbrook and Ikin, who both scored hundreds, hinted though at the overall fragility of the Indian attack. Pataudi's score of 113 against Derbyshire was a major factor in winning that game by 118 runs, success coming in the final over of the game.

For Pataudi, there was much to ponder, not least keeping a sense of unity among the All-India squad at a time when the country back home was in turmoil, although he knew that touring sides typically develop a togetherness that rises above winning or losing. There was, though, the weather to face up to – the need for resilience against the gloom provoked by the wet English summer. Finally, Pataudi was exercised by the composition of the team to confront England in Manchester. For example, there was still the question of who should open with Merchant. Abdul Hafeez's scores of 21 and 8 at Bradford were unconvincing. Should Mushtaq Ali be slotted back in? The captain found himself watching him closely – a tall man, with Bollywood good looks, sufficiently handsome for the Australian all-rounder Keith Miller to compare him to the actor Errol Flynn. He had high cheekbones, sleek skin and eyes that drew you in and spoke of a steely confidence. He wore his cap at a slightly rakish angle and sometimes indulged in wearing a white kerchief round his neck which, with his half-turned-up shirt collar, gave him a piratical look. John Arlott admired his wide shoulders and the conscious elegance of his walk. He was 'dashing' and that manifested itself in his batting which could be unduly extravagant, throwing his bat at balls best ignored. How would that cavalier spirit cope with Alec Bedser and whoever was selected as England's other opening bowler? He seemed to like quick bowling and he evidently warmed to playing at Old Trafford – he had scored a hundred there ten years before (batting with Merchant, Pataudi remembered).

The rest of the batting picked itself: Amarnath, Hazare, Modi, Mankad. Hafeez bolstering the middle order and tail; bowlers Sohoni and Sarwate to add to the all-rounders; Hindlekar behind the stumps, nursing his bad back. What could possibly go wrong? And so, on the morning of Saturday 20 July, Pataudi and Hammond walked out to the middle to toss the coin, both conscious of the rain and what it might do to the wicket. It was many years since the two of them had scored hundreds together for England against Australia in Sydney. Now they were both approaching middle age, their best years behind them.

The coin settled on the damp grass. Hammond smiled twice: once when the awkward choice fell to Pataudi; then again when the Indian captain defied logic and asked England to bat first.

12

Manchester

July 1946

PATAUDI'S QUIXOTIC decision had England's early
batsmen padding up when they might have anticipated a day
in the field. As it was, the English bowlers could relax with the
prospect of a quiet day in prospect. Hutton and Washbrook
would be in the firing line first thing and after them the
sumptuous middle of the England batting: Hammond at
number 4 and, first wicket down, Denis Compton. Compton
had played his first Test aged 19 in August 1937, a drawn
match against New Zealand at The Oval. He made 65, the
prospect of scoring a hundred on debut ruined by a run-out, a
lapse that he put right in his next Test – 102 against Australia
at Trent Bridge in June 1938. There were seven more caps
before war intervened during which time he accumulated
468 runs at an average of 58.5, his form recognised by *Wisden*
choosing him as one of its Cricketers of the Year in 1939.

   Like the tourists, Compton had travelled to the UK
from India in the spring of 1946 – he had served in the
army there during the war – and he knew a number of the
Indian team. In early 1945 he had played for Holkar in the
Ranji Tournament alongside Sarwate, Mushtaq Ali, Nayudu
and Nimbalkar. The volatile nature of Indian politics was
inescapable, its dangers brought home to him when he was
playing at Eden Gardens, Calcutta for East Zone against the

Australian Services in November 1945. Five of Compton's team-mates in the Indian side subsequently toured England the following year, while Lindsay Hassett and Keith Miller were in the Services XI. Compton had scored 94 when a riot broke out on the boundary edge, the game's peace suddenly broken by banner-waving, angry protesters. After being run out without scoring in the first innings, the timing of this interruption was unfortunate. Moreover, matters rapidly got worse. One of the leaders advanced on to the field, moving with intent towards an increasingly uneasy Compton, who tightened his grip on his bat, now transformed into a potential defensive weapon. Batsman and firebrand faced each other. 'Mr Compton,' the latter said, 'you are a very good player, but the game must stop.' The resumption of play was clearly impossible in the short term, although eventually the Middlesex man was able to complete his hundred, his progress and the earlier confrontation watched with a smile by the Australian all-rounder, Keith Miller, who was fielding at slip.

Compton had only been demobbed a couple of months before the new season started, but he had been able to play cricket through the war years – as many as 19 games for example in 1942 when he was still in England. Once he was posted to India, however, his opportunities to play were considerably reduced to the extent that he only played a handful of first-class games in the years 1943 to 1946, the last of them for the Europeans against the Hindus in mid-January 1946 in Bombay.

Six months later and Compton travelled to Manchester with some disquiet about his form. He had failed to score in the Lord's Test (one of Lala Amarnath's five victims), while a double hundred against Cambridge University had been distinctly scratchy and uncertain. His batting early in the new season had been sound enough, averaging around the mid-40s, but the 202 scored at Fenner's against the university had made his figures unduly flattering. In 14 innings since Lord's he had scored ten or less on nine occasions. To make matters worse, the weather in the north-west looked unpromising and, in Compton's eyes, the captaincy of the England XI was equally depressing: he recognised Hammond's great talent as a batsman, but found him an isolated, uncommunicative figure as captain. The weather forecast was for heavy cloud drifting overhead for the three days of the game and that meant regular interruptions for rain and desultory games of cards in the pavilion. As for the match itself, Compton anticipated over-cautious captaincy, ill-thought-out plans and a plodding Micawberism – keep plugging away, something will turn up. In the event, though, it was India's captaincy that attracted scepticism, even surprise. What on earth was Pataudi doing, winning the toss and then asking England to bat first?

Both teams had made changes, England recalling Bill Voce (the pace bowler who had been Larwood's new-ball partner in the Bodyline series), to replace Bill Bowes. Voce, at 36, was only a year younger than the Yorkshireman. A third seamer was included: Lancashire's Dick Pollard, playing on his home ground, but no novice himself at 34. E.W. (Jim) Swanton, the *Daily Telegraph*'s cricket correspondent, was not the only traditionalist who regretted the absence of both an orthodox slow left-arm bowler and an off-spinner in the England selection. As for India, Gul Mohammad, Shinde and Nayudu were replaced by Mushtaq, Sohoni and Sarwate, the latter two making their Test debuts.

The Monday of the match would be Sarwate's 26th birthday; he was one of the game's few young men. Watching more rain sweep in from the west, John Arlott found himself thinking back to The Oval in May when Sarwate and Banerjee had both scored defiant hundreds against Surrey. Sarwate looked very young and his manner somehow conveyed self-doubt, as if he felt unsure of his right to be in the Test arena. The team photograph has him sitting boyishly on the grass, his head alongside the knees of the

older and more established players. Nonetheless, his was a
logical selection – he would strengthen the batting and his
mix of leg and off breaks might suit Old Trafford. He had
taken 41 wickets on the tour thus far, although only 19 were
against first-class opposition. Chandu Sarwate was evidently
a man for whom fingers mattered, either wrapped tightly
around a cricket ball, or in his job as a fingerprint specialist
in Holkar state.

Ranga Sohoni was a more left-field selection. An all-
rounder, he had had a miserable tour up to that point, taking
a mere eight wickets (at just over 51 runs each) and scoring
123 runs at a measly average of 12.3. His one respectable
score, however, had been at Manchester two weeks before
when he had made 44, albeit in a big Indian total. Handsome,
with a determined set to his jaw, hair swept back from a
noble forehead and eyes with a haughty look at odds with his
mediocre form, Sohoni's engaging manner may have helped
his selection. Arlott certainly warmed to him: his evident
pleasure in the game, his easy smile, his lack of malice.
Looking him over racehorse-style, the commentator took in
his upright guardsman's stance, his breadth of shoulders and
his general fitness.

Pataudi's seemingly capricious decision to bowl first left
Sohoni stretching and staring philosophically out of the
pavilion window, trying to still his nerves. Suddenly, on a
damp day in the north of England, his moment had come. He
would be bowling his first ball in Test cricket, a great moment
for him, but Manchester's damp air and outfield was a long
way from the hard, true wickets of Bombay. Had Pataudi
judged the wicket, the weather and his bowlers correctly?
England had not lost a Test in Manchester since the end of
the Great War, an impressive fact, although ten full days of
cricket had been lost to rain over those 14 matches. What was
certain was that at Old Trafford captains usually chose to bat
first. Only twice had that basic principle been broken: in 1931,
in a rain-affected match with New Zealand which ended in

a draw; and in 1939, when West Indies had asked England to bat first. On that occasion, the home side had struggled to a measly 164 all out, although that was still enough for a first-innings lead. Again the game was drawn. So Pataudi was ignoring the lessons of history – unless he remembered the embarrassment of India's visit to Manchester ten years before when they had been skittled out after winning the toss and then conceded a first-innings lead of 368. His decision in July 1946 went against accepted theory: win the toss; bat first and control the game. The side batting first at Old Trafford typically scored around 340 on average.

Play did not begin until after lunch. The ground was crowded, another sea of flat caps and raincoats, while the grass arena was patched with sawdust, neat stooks of it at the beginning of the bowlers' run-ups and yellow-white islands of dust where Indian boots had pressed it down over the vivid green. On the boundary edge, the crowd sat on damp grass contemplating the progress of the clouds and how the debutant Sohoni would cope with the pressure and a wet wicket. He proved innocuous – indeed he would complete the game without taking a wicket – and it was left to the old hands, Amarnath and Mankad, to try and redeem the captain's ill-judged decision. Amarnath had been struggling with a knee injury (another reason to bat first?), and he had treated the problem with a bizarre remedy involving grapefruit halves, salt, mustard oil and turmeric. Warmed, the grapefruit pieces were then applied to Amarnath's knees. It worked. The Indian all-rounder went on to bowl 81 overs in the match – 70 more than Sohoni.

It was 2.15 in the afternoon before Len Hutton and Cyril Washbrook walked out to open the England innings, with the Yorkshireman feeling – appropriately – under the weather with a chill. His back was also bothering him (what is it with cricketers' backs?) and, in consequence, his batting was cautious and preoccupied. The shortened day ended with Pataudi's gamble in shreds. England progressed to a comfortable 236/4 – well on the way to a par score – with each of the top four scoring fifties. But perhaps the weather might still have a say. The Indian captain would have looked out of the hotel window on the Sunday morning, seen the rain falling over Manchester's blackened chimney pots, dark puddles filling and spreading, and wondered if the game could be saved after all. Throughout the day the Indians watched the weather, calculating the likely outcome from the interplay of rain, the uncovered wicket, a drying wind and the passing hours.

On Monday morning it began well enough, with six England wickets falling in an hour, thanks to the guile and accuracy of Amarnath and Mankad. Later that season, at Taunton, Somerset's Harold Gimblett would ask the metronomic Amarnath whether he had ever bowled a half-volley; the bowler ruefully admitted that he had – just the once. In 1940. Now Amarnath dismissed Compton, Hammond, Jack Ikin, Hardstaff and Bedser – who would have looked hard at the wicket and its behaviour while contemplating his own efforts with the ball. England were all out for 294 (Hammond top-scoring with 69). Before India batted, the roller brought up enough water from below the surface to turn the pitch dark in colour and feather-bedded in pace. Mushtaq and Merchant batted serenely at the outset, reaching 124 before the first wicket fell – Pollard bowling Mushtaq Ali for 46. It seemed that perhaps Pataudi's decision to bowl first had been inspired. Then all ten wickets fell for 46, the rout compounded by the captain's perverse change to the batting order, promoting the mercurial Hafeez to bat at number 3. He lasted seven balls before being caught and bowled by Pollard for a single. The Lancashire pace bowler and Alec Bedser proceeded to run through the Indian batting, ten wickets falling in short order. Bill Voce took just one wicket (Hazare) in his 20 overs.

Day three proved eventful: India's first innings spirited away in a flash leaving them 124 behind; then England chasing quick runs but struggling against India's two best bowlers; before Denis Compton accelerated matters, with 71 not out, making a declaration possible. India were set an unlikely 278 to win, a task made more demanding when Merchant was out second ball. Bedser took seven wickets in quick time, four of them clean bowled, but the clock steadily marked out the turning of the hours. Only 13 minutes were left when Hindlekar joined Sohoni with nine wickets down. Sohoni's bowling had been limp and suggested that he might readily succumb with the bat. Not so – he defied the English for 55 balls and nearly an hour, scoring a match-saving 11 not out. It had been a damn close-run thing, but, in the circumstances, a draw was a kind of victory for the Indians.

Hands were shaken, stumps pulled, Hindlekar and Sohoni politely ushered off the field of play, shoulders patted, backs slapped, as the crowd swarmed around the players, then drifted away to Manchester's bus stops. The players gathered up the game's detritus – socks, gloves, green-stained whites – from the dressing-room floor. There were some tired legs and minds in both camps, and among the batsmen some anxiety, since this had been a low-scoring game, only Compton making good runs in both innings. Run-scoring had been hard work, both sides averaging only 2.3 runs per over throughout the match. It had been hard for some of the bowlers, too. Mankad had bowled 67 overs in the three days and Amarnath substantially more than that despite his wonky knees, while Bedser completed 51 overs and Pollard 52. Bedser had taken another 11 wickets in the match, despite the handicap of the team's insubstantial breakfasts – cricketers were not spared the rigours of rationing – and Bedser, who needed fuel, frankly struggled. A feeble, thin sausage, half a fried tomato, a lonely rasher of bacon and a slice of toast with a token pat of butter did not constitute sufficient substance for a fast bowler's constitution. The hungry Surrey man was to be seen during the three days prowling the streets of Manchester searching for fish and chips. No doubt still peckish, his weariness wasn't helped once the Test was over by having to catch the midnight train south, prompting a disquieting memory of wartime rail journeys at unseemly hours. The train pulled in at Euston at five in the morning. A few hours later he was back at The Oval for Surrey's game with Glamorgan. It was some consolation that Surrey batted first and Alec could put his large, tired feet up for a while.

13

Amarnath: Disgraced

Summer 1936

LALA AMARNATH was tired too, his knees sorely tested by his heavy workload over the Test's three days. It was 13 years since he had played in his first Test match (against England in Bombay). That had been India's first official Test. Photographed at the time (he was just 22), he looked like a schoolboy, toothy half-smile, cap proudly set, rakish over a dark-eyed stare, collar turned up on a shirt the top two buttons of which were undone, his thin arms emerging from wide sleeves. His batting gloves look as if they have been borrowed from the school's first XI kit bag – and there he was, batting at number 3 for his country. In a drawn game, he scored 118 in the second innings against Jardine's men (an England team that included Hedley Verity and Gloucestershire's Charlie Barnett).

Cricket must have seemed such a simple game to the young Punjabi then – ball, bat, stumps – but the events surrounding the 1936 All-India tour of England surely opened Amarnath's eyes to a more complex, darker world. It was an unpleasant, poisonous tour, the doubtful overture of which was the appointment of a high-born – but incompetent – captain, the Maharajkumar of Vizianagaram, a noble moniker usually reduced to 'Vizzy'. This was a man who travelled with 36 items of luggage, attended by two servants and who was invariably at pains to ingratiate himself with the viceroy. Cricket and politics were for him closely entwined. The decision to appoint him had been a political, rather than a cricketing one, and the wrong-headedness of it was soon revealed as the tour made its way around the cricket grounds of England, with India's batsmen struggling, and tactics frequently ill-judged. The weather as that tour began was cold and wet too: the 1936 and 1946 tourists both suffered in the English spring. Before the opening Test, Vizzy averaged a disappointing 16.85 with the bat. Early defeats damaged morale and Vizzy's bizarre captaincy: the irrational fielding placements and bowling changes; the whimsical alterations to the batting order; his patrician interest in the sartorial (an endless supply of white silk shirts) all made matters worse. Amarnath, by contrast, was in good form, taking wickets and scoring runs in a way which underlined Vizzy's struggles. By the middle of June, Amarnath had scored more than 600 runs at 32.3 and taken 32 wickets at 20 each. Vizzy's contribution did not stand comparison. There was an inevitable decline in the team's mood and dressing-room feuds between rival camps developed. At one point, Vizzy and the team manager remonstrated with the outspoken Amarnath on the grounds that they felt he was not sufficiently serious about his cricket. Hence, perhaps, the perceived fostering of internal division. 'Divide and rule'. There were those who said that the strategy had been learned from the perfidious British.

In the middle of June, during a game at Lord's against the Minor Counties, matters came to a head. Nursing a back injury, Amarnath was infuriated by the skipper instructing him to get padded up and ready to bat. Wickets steadily fell and Vizzy, despite his instruction to Amarnath, insisted on pushing the all-rounder further and further down the batting order. Eventually, after a long and inexplicable wait, Amarnath was sent out to bat at number 7 in the order when India were 328/5. By this point he was furious, profoundly irritated by yet another of the captain's aberrations, the anger he felt compounded by the fact that his back had become even stiffer and more sore from the long, uncertain wait. At close of play, he stormed into the dressing room, flung his kit into the corner and let rip with a burst of angry Punjabi. Things got worse later that evening. There was a meeting of Vizzy's supporters, some deeply perturbed by Amarnath's complaints ('I know what's going on!' he had shouted), others quite baffled by what the all-rounder's impassioned Punjabi actually meant.

Then the manager, Major Jack Brittain-Jones, and the Indian captain combined to insist that Amarnath should be sent home with immediate effect. There would be no appeal and no reprieve, the manager – an Englishman albeit born in Manila in the Philippines – insisting that Amarnath should vacate the team hotel at once and sail on the first available ship back to India. As a young man, in June 1922, Brittain-Jones had turned out for MCC against a Rhine Army XI in Cologne (he scored 86 in the first innings). In the following decade, in his mid-thirties, he had been on the fringes of cricket in India, playing for the Viceroy's XI, alongside the Nawab of Pataudi. He had been bowled by Hedley Verity playing against MCC, for a Viceroy's team which also included George Abell – a man, as we shall see, who would have a close involvement with Indian Partition. Brittain-Jones had also played for Vizzy against the Maharaja of Patiala's XI in Delhi in 1935. When he acted as manager for the 1936 tour he was only 36 and a member of the viceroy's staff.

Amarnath had crossed a powerful man and Vizzy was an adroit politician, albeit an inept cricketer, with the power of the British Raj behind him. A photographer was on hand to capture the cricketer's isolated figure boarding a liner at Southampton: wearing a loose-fitting suit with a neat tie and a snappy fedora, his face tight with resentment, the all-rounder is gripping the boarding rail, in disgrace, and obliged to leave his team-mates to face the English without a key player. This at a time when the next Test was only a matter of ten days or so away.

The Indians duly lost that game by nine wickets, bowled out twice for low scores, although they had earned a slender first-innings lead. Somerset's Harold Gimblett top-scored with 67 not out in England's untroubled second innings. Amarnath's runs and wickets would have been invaluable. Nine days after the game ended, Amarnath's ship docked in Bombay, the dockside crowded with supporters. The whole episode was a cause célèbre: at one point, it seemed that Amarnath would be called back for the second Test, only for that to be vetoed. Later, a commission of inquiry was held into the affair and the Chief Justice of Bombay, Sir John Beaumont, concluded that the captain was simply not up to the job. Vizzy's role as a leader of men was not helped by his lamentable form – 33 runs in the three Tests at an average of 8. The English establishment saw something in the unfortunate Indian captain, however: the Maharajkumar of Vizianagaram was knighted by King Edward VIII on 15 July 1936, the honour conferred with no sign on the horizon that such glittering prizes of empire would be so short-lived.

14

Amarnath: Triumph in Sussex

Late July 1946

THE INDIAN players of 1946 left Manchester in better spirits perhaps than their predecessors of ten years before when India had been obliged to use seven bowlers in an England total of 571/8 declared (Hammond making 167). The game had been drawn, but the second day had been painful, with the home side scoring 398 in the day, at that time a record in Tests. As for the Englishmen of 1946, a number had long rail journeys in order to play for their counties the following day: Washbrook and Ikin travelled to Maidstone to play Kent (and thankfully batted second); Joe Hardstaff turned out for Nottinghamshire against Warwickshire at Edgbaston, Birmingham (he was out for 0, one of Eric Hollies' ten victims); Doug Wright batted for Kent at Maidstone. The lucky ones had a chance to recover, either being rested or spared by the fixture list.

After Manchester, the tourists headed south: players, reporters and, of course, the man from the BBC, John Arlott, still pinching himself at his good fortune in being able to watch cricket for a living, without having to sacrifice his poetry responsibilities with the corporation. That summer, he was no longer obliged to take the underground into the London office on a regular basis; instead his travelling companions were All-India's cricketers on their progress around the country. That meant the ex-policeman acquiring the habits of hotel living, the hurried packing and managing the complex logistics of train travel from one cricketing oasis to the next ('I'll have to change trains at X to be there in time for Y'). Moreover, there was the need to stick closely to the Indian players and learn more about their personalities and foibles. It was that urge that convinced him, after an unsatisfactory week travelling third class, that he needed to join the players in the first-class compartment. He paid the difference out of his own pocket – the BBC would never countenance subsidising such seeming extravagance – but he reaped the reward of becoming an avuncular, trusted fixture among the Indian travellers.

Arlott decided to miss India's drawn one-day match against the Club Cricket Conference at Guildford on Thursday, 25 July, sensing that he needed to give some time to his other job: there was a string of poetry programme recordings that needed to be updated. That done, he was off to the Sussex coast. Unlike their predecessors ten years before, their morale was good – the second Test had been drawn after all; they had enjoyed two days of rest and, for the game at Hove which started on Saturday, 27 July, the sun emerged at last and turned Sussex into a little India. The tourists batted first on a wicket that reminded them of home, a zippy pitch in Bombay perhaps, rather than temperate Brighton. The Indian batsmen were in an expansive and unforgiving frame of mind, with four of them scoring hundreds, including Vijay Merchant who made 205. Indeed, only four Indian batsmen batted during the whole of that first day's play, while, in exceptional, broiling heat, the Sussex bowlers took just three wickets. At the close, India were able to declare with their score at 533/3. Apart from Merchant, there were hundreds from Mankad, Pataudi – and Lala Amarnath.

Seven years had passed since Sussex had lost the final game of the 1939 season against Yorkshire, but the team to face India on that July day in 1946 showed only three changes. Three Sussex men had been lost during the war. Robert Miller, who had kept wicket for the county for a dozen games in the first season after the Great War, had died in South Yemen in 1941; Kenneth Scott played six games for Sussex in 1937 but was killed during the invasion of Sicily in August 1943, hit by an enemy shell; and Captain Alexander Shaw of the 11th Sikh Regiment committed suicide in July 1945 in New Delhi. Before the war, Shaw had lived in India working as a tea-broker, an occupation which overshadowed his cricketing life. That was limited to just two first-class games, one for Sussex in 1927, keeping wicket against Cambridge University (his wicketkeeping victims and runs both totalled six); the other for Bengal against the Australians at Eden Gardens, Calcutta in December 1935 – a game in which he scored 0 and 1. Coincidentally, one of the 1946 Indian squad, Shute Banerjee, had opened both the batting and bowling for Bengal. Eleven years later, Banerjee, down to bat at number 8, sat in the sun in Hove with his feet up, contentedly watching the runs accumulate.

There is a photograph that captures that momentous day of Indian batsmanship, the scoreboard at Hove displaying the score as it was before Lala Amarnath was dismissed – 533/2. The scoreboard clock says 11.28, suggesting that the picture was a proud re-enactment of an historic occasion, perhaps on the morning after, and before play began. The scorebox is thick-set, chunky, more suited perhaps to some outpost of empire. The four centurions are dwarfed by it and look thin and pensive, three of them lined up shoulder to shoulder, while, to Pataudi's left, Merchant stands slightly apart. There is no sense of triumph, not much sign of a smile from any one of the four; indeed they have the look of men a long way from home, with many weeks of touring still ahead. Or, perhaps, such a dignified, stoic acceptance of success was simply in tune with the spirit of the age, the way international cricketers in those days acknowledged achievement – just another day in cricketers' lives.

Arlott savoured that day of cricket, feeling it was the moment when peace had finally arrived, though he recognised that Sussex's chastened fielders might have felt less benign about the sweaty day of chasing the ball around the ground. Moreover, the second day brought no respite from All-Indian dominance: Pataudi declared overnight (at 533/3) and then Shinde and Mankad methodically worked their way through the Sussex batting. The wicket had not been much affected by overnight rain, but the county side soon folded, falling short of the Indian first innings by 280 runs. Invited to follow on, the county made a better fist of things in the second innings, with George Cox scoring an unbeaten 234, but it was not enough to delay the inevitable, runs from Merchant and Modi taking India to a nine-wicket win. They left for Taunton in confident mood.

15

Undone in Taunton

Late July, early August 1946

THE INDIANS left sun-kissed Brighton on the penultimate day of July, heading for what proved to be a soggy Taunton to play Somerset, beginning the very next morning. There was a widespread view – certainly held south of Bristol and all the way down to the Dorset border – that by June 1946, Somerset were the most attractive cricketing side in the country. That and the sharp change in the weather might have signalled trouble for the tourists. There was cloud over the Quantock Hills on a day to gladden a seam bowler's heart. The ground was rustic, girdled by a river and blessed with a cockle stall outside, a gastronomic tempter for Arlott's increasingly sophisticated palate, despite the pleasures of the hotel's breakfast. The weather in the west was as different from Hove as Calcutta was from Auckland and there was every prospect of the new ball offering the bowlers considerable help – late swing and sharp pace, with the seaming ball hitting the wicketkeeper's gloves with a resounding, malevolent thwack.

Pataudi repeated his toss-winning trick, but where that had been a boon in Brighton, here it was a highly dubious benefit. Merchant went early; Mushtaq and the captain steadied the ship, but only briefly. Then things fell apart, dismantled by two middle-aged West Country stalwarts, the 38-year-old Bill Andrews, playing in his brother

Jack's borrowed size 12 boots, and 36-year-old Bertie Buse. Andrews would be sacked by the county in 1947 and the following year was playing for Stourbridge in the Birmingham League. He was considered by some as having been denied an England cap only by the war, although he blamed Wally Hammond's malicious veto. Buse continued playing for the county until 1953. On that summer's day in Taunton they were India's nemeses, both men taking five wickets. Arlott initially viewed the pair with some doubt, noting Andrews' shambling gait and the resemblance Buse had to a churchwarden delicately carrying an offertory plate, or an obsequious butler in some grand mansion. But they were good enough that morning to cut the Indians apart, dismissing them for a paltry 64 in 37 torrid overs. After Mushtaq and Pataudi were dismissed, the remaining eight batsmen made only 14 between them. Merchant, Hazare and Abdul Hafeez all failed to score.

Somerset's was an ageing eleven to the extent that the team which played the first post-war game had an average age of a fraction under 38, the oldest in the country (where the average was 34). Remarkably, in the country as a whole, there were 29 players over the age of 40 in the first games of 1946 and only three aged 23 or under. By contrast the Indian XI at Taunton averaged 27. But this proved to be a day for gnarled veterans and, by early afternoon, Somerset had begun batting and with real purpose, to the extent that by tea the West Countrymen were in complete control. Amarnath and Sohoni, who opened the Indian attack, failed to take a single wicket between them in 79 overs, conceding 206 runs. At 506/6, the Somerset captain, Bunty Longrigg, declared, setting India 442 to stave off an innings defeat. This they could not do, falling short by 11 runs, despite stubborn resistance by Merchant and Pataudi, and a stout last-wicket partnership between Sarwate and the wicketkeeper, Hindlekar. The team left Taunton troubled by the scale of this third defeat by a county side.

* * *

India's last-ditch defiance against Somerset had ended in whimsical fashion. The final-wicket stand of 52 runs, Arlott observed, resulted in impatient spectators (and commentators?) missing their trains out of Taunton station, a ten-minute walk from the ground. It ended with Dattaram Hindlekar being stumped by the 45-year-old Somerset keeper, Wally Luckes. It was a neat and tidy way to end proceedings, the two veteran keepers responsible for the game's final act. As well as their shared trade, they were both born in the same decade and both on the same day of the year, the first of January – 1901 in the case of Luckes and Hindlekar seven years later.

Arlott admired the Indian keeper, not least his ability to lighten the mood, to 'clown', but a photograph taken that summer in front of a marquee at one of the season's cricket festivals reveals a more philosophical, sombre side, his deep-set eyes harbouring some hidden pain. His was a sensitive face and, for a man with a reputation for laughter, he looks as if it wouldn't take much to make him cry. He looks boyish, hair neatly parted, but Arlott noted the grey streaks, thinking it made him seem 'wry'. First-choice wicketkeeper in both 1936 and 1946, Hindlekar's glovework was neat and unfussy, enthusiastic too – his team-mate Vijay Hazare thought him only surpassed by England's Godfrey Evans (whose time was yet to come). He was a dignified man, Hazare thought, appealing for lbw or catches behind the wicket, for example, with minimum drama, more in the way of a polite, gentle inquiry. Injury-prone, both his England tours were hampered by a chipped bone in his finger, blurred vision and, in 1946, a complaining back. Unlike many of his team-mates, and certainly his captain, he came from a poverty-stricken background. The son of a farmer, it was said that he couldn't afford wicketkeeping gloves and was obliged to borrow them. Perhaps it was a fear of penury that prompted his unguarded intimations of anxiety about the future which he revealed from time to time, usually in the quiet of an evening's reflection. Beyond cricket, his working life was spent in the port of Bombay on a minimal wage. His selection to tour England again in 1946 was unexpected, the result of his good form in the Bombay Pentangular final early in the year and, as things turned out, he would go on to play as many games that year (29) as he had ten years before. John Arlott would long remember Hindlekar's rakish cap when he was batting and the idiosyncratic cocking of his left boot, as well as his passion for narrow shoes, trilby hats and, most outlandish of all, English sewing machines. This last All-India tour was almost the last act of his cricketing career – he would play just five more games after his farewell performance at Scarborough in September 1946, bowing out for good the following year. Just over three years later, he died – on 30 March 1949, three months after his 40th birthday.

16

Goodbye to Country House Cricket

1939–46

SOMERSET'S WICKETKEEPER, Wally Luckes, outlived Hindlekar by more than 30 years and was as unassuming and placid as his Indian counterpart was outgoing and lively. Luckes first played for the county in 1924, became a fixture in the side by 1927 and was retained by the county through a three-year period of ill health, sufficiently severe to stop him playing at all in the summer of 1931. Such considerate employment practice was not typical of the way Somerset treated its professional cricketers. Bill Andrews, for example, was released by the club four times – as player and coach – over the years. Making his debut in May 1930, he missed the seasons of 1933 and 1934 and was obliged to play and coach in Scotland for those two years after the county had released him. His left-wing politics sat uneasily with the gentlemanly amateur culture that pervaded the club.

The club's finances always seemed to be precarious and its pre-war sides often included oddball characters and those who enjoyed at least one drink too many. The batting was often fragile, the fielding leaden-footed and its captains idiosyncratic. Amateurs and professionals were treated very differently and confined to different dressing rooms: a situation that militated against team spirit. This was a world where cricket scorecards distinguished between amateurs and professionals by having the formers' initials printed *before* their names and the concept of having a professional captain of England – or even of a county side – was regarded as unacceptable. In 1939 every county captain was an amateur, while all but one (Les Berry of Leicestershire) had that status when cricket resumed in 1946. 'An odd lot in there' was one professional's view of those behind the amateurs' door. Interestingly, after the war, cricketers were more restive, perhaps having seen more of the world, and sharing in the country's uncertainty about the way things were (hence the outcome of the 1945 general election and the ensuing Labour government). People in general – and some cricketers were no exception – were less inclined to be subservient.

At times, there was a flavour of 'country house cricket' in Somerset's approach to the game, typified by one of its captains, R.J.O. Meyer, who with aristocratic nonchalance, pulled the communication cord on the Manchester express in which the team was travelling. As the train ground to a halt, he asked the nonplussed guard to 'rustle something up' since several of his boys were peckish. Meyer, who was also headmaster at Millfield School, got his way and the hungry cricketers were fed. He would have expected no less. When the team played away and an overnight stay was required, the club could not afford hotels, so the players stayed in 'digs', sometimes with the players sharing not just rooms, but beds. For one game against Surrey at The Oval, four of the West Countrymen shared one room in a Paddington bed and breakfast.

* * *

During the war, Somerset lost six players in all, five serving in the army and one in the Royal Navy. The biggest loss was Peter McRae. He had played in the final game of the 1939 season before becoming the ship's doctor on the destroyer HMS *Mahratta*. He scored nearly a thousand runs for Somerset in 25 games, 13 of them in the 1939 season when he averaged nearly 31. At just 23, he was clearly a player with some potential: he had made his first century (107) against Hampshire at Taunton on the first Saturday in July 1939. His ship was torpedoed by a U-boat in the Barents Sea in late February 1944 and he was not one of the 16 survivors from the crew of 236. Before he drowned in the icy waters, he had willingly given up his place in a life raft.

Twenty-year-old Geoffrey Fletcher had made his debut in July 1939; a captain in the Rifle Brigade, he was killed in action in Tunisia in 1943. Major Ronald Gerrard, Royal Engineers, and a rugby union international for England, was killed in Tripoli earlier the same year. Sergeant Charles Mayo of the Royal Armoured Corps – and of Somerset for six games in 1928 – died in Egypt in April 1943, aged 40. William Baldock was shot after being taken prisoner by the Japanese in Malaya in December 1941. He had first played for the county in 1920; then twice more in 1921, but it would be almost 15 years before he appeared again, in May 1936, in a season in which he made seven appearances. He was destined never to play again. His highest score of 63 not out was scored at Taunton, coincidentally against the 1936 All-India tourists, their side including Merchant, Banerjee, Mushtaq Ali, Amarnath and Hindlekar.

Jack Lee, who was killed, aged 42, in an accident in Normandy two weeks after D-Day, was the only man able to approach something like a full cricketing career with the county, scoring nearly 8,000 runs and taking 495 wickets between 1927 and 1936. With the exception of Lee, all the other Somerset men lost to the war were former public schoolboys, educated at Taunton School, Marlborough, Christ's Hospital and Eton and therefore officers – and, for the most part, batsmen. Charles Mayo, however, spurned officer status for that of 'other ranks', in a way foreshadowing, perhaps, a more enlightened post-war world.

* * *

When Somerset defeated the Indians at Taunton in 1946, perhaps the key players for the county were the two opening bowlers – both old-school professionals – alongside two amateurs: Bunty Longrigg, who was a Bath lawyer and a Cambridge Blue, and Michael Walford, an Oxford Blue and a schoolmaster who played for the county during the summer holidays. The other main protagonist was the opening bat, Harold Gimblett, Somerset's pre-eminent batsman, a mercurial, troubled, enigmatic and hugely talented cricketer whose career laid bare the game's potential pitfalls as well as his employer's hard-nosed paternalism and bloody-minded parsimony. After scoring 310 in a game against Sussex at Eastbourne, a collection for Gimblett around the ground was suggested for the next home game. Refusing the idea, a Somerset official explained that he was paid to score 300 – that was his job.

Gimblett was selected for the 1939 tour of India (later cancelled), having played for England three times before the war. He would eventually play five unofficial Tests in India in 1950/51, but the experience was not a happy one – he lost two stone in weight and pined for home. His batting was explosive, compelling and formidably powerful; his mind, however, was fragile, unreliable and increasingly tormented with doubt and uncertainty. Gimblett was an inveterate talker on the pitch, full of nervy banter and badinage, but he had the knack of saying the wrong thing. Playing against Gloucestershire, for example, he could not resist asking the England captain, Wally Hammond, 'What do I have to do to get on this boat trip of yours then, Wally?' It is doubtful if Hammond's face did anything other than scowl. Born in a stone, creeper-draped farmhouse in the west of Somerset, on the far side of the Quantock Hills from Taunton, Gimblett was very much a country boy; the establishment freemasonry of Lord's unnerving him. Initially rejected by the county – too flashy by half, it was said – he was suddenly called up at short notice to stand in for someone who was unavailable. He missed the bus, hitched a lift to the game in Frome, batted at number 8, and scored a hundred. It was 18 May 1935.

By the time war broke out, Gimblett had become a fixture in the side. Somerset's final game before hostilities began was against Northamptonshire at Taunton, the home team crushing the Midlanders by an innings, with Harold scoring 67. It was the last day of August. With his season over, he and his wife planned to take themselves off to Scotland for a holiday. They got as far as Scarborough before the reality of what was happening in Europe became inescapable and a rapid return to the West Country seemed wise. His preference for war service had been the RAF, but to his surprise, a few weeks after his medical, he was posted to Taunton fire station. For the first two years of the war, opportunities for Gimblett to play cricket were minimal, but from July 1941 until hostilities ended in 1945, he played more regularly, turning out for a number of different teams, including the National Fire Service, the Civil Defence Services, a British Empire XI and, once, for an England XI. There were games at Lord's, Trent Bridge, Edgbaston and Bristol's County Ground among others. He played three games in 1941; six in 1942 (over a period of seven days in August); ten more in 1943; just one in 1944 and four in the final year of the war, the last, in Glastonbury, two days after the atom bomb was dropped on Nagasaki. He bowled infrequently – 29 overs all told over the five years, taking just seven wickets – but he batted regularly, scoring four hundreds, and making over a thousand runs at an average of nearly 41. His opponents included teams from the RAF, the Army, Southampton Police and the Dominions, while some of the individuals playing against him – Denis Compton, Alf Gover, Learie Constantine, Reg Wyatt and Keith Miller – illustrate the quality and competitiveness of the cricket. For example, in one game at Lord's, the first five in the batting order for the Civil Defence Services (against the Army) were J.H. Parks

(Sussex), John and James Langridge (Sussex), Laurie Fishlock (Surrey) and Gimblett.

In the first post-war season, Gimblett scored five hundreds, including a double (231) against Middlesex, and averaged nearly 47. He was, *Wisden* observed, 'merciless'. He was also visibly older, stockier, less flashy and, at 32, still with prospects of playing again for his country. He would be named a *Wisden* Cricketer of the Year as late as 1953. That would, however, prove to be his penultimate season. Against India in that one-sided thrashing at Taunton in 1946, he top-scored in Somerset's reply, hitting ten fours in an innings of 102, 38 more than the entire Indian team had managed on that cloudy morning in the West Country.

Gimblett, after the humbling of the Indian bowlers at Taunton, remained in the west of England for the derby match against Gloucestershire, led by Wally Hammond, at the County Ground, Bristol. As he walked in to bat on 3 August, the England captain had a distinctly prince-like quality about him, a coloured handkerchief fluttering from his back pocket, sharp eyes scanning the Ashley Down ground, fixing the field placements in his mind, getting used to the light. Before taking strike, he apologised to the opposition. He was obliged, he said – because of a substantial wager – to score a double hundred on that particular day. The sporting gamble was never in doubt: Hammond unreeled a majestic 214. His 52 not out in the second innings took him closer to 50,000 runs in first-class cricket. When it came to his turn to bat, after many hours in the field, Gimblett scored 133. On the Monday, the Bank Holiday, Bristol's Ashley Down ground held 17,500 watching these two stalwarts of the game reveal the essence of peacetime.

17

With Dylan in Swansea

August 1946

WHILE GIMBLETT and Hammond were making hay in
Bristol, across the border in south Wales, the Indians were
trying to erase the memory of the Taunton defeat in a game
against Glamorgan. As the train rolled into Swansea on the
first day, John Arlott had been preoccupied with the weather
and the imminent threat of rain. The view from the carriage
window of what the war had done to the Welsh town didn't
lighten his mood. Swansea's town centre had been heavily
bombed, leaving a wasteland of shattered bricks and scrawny
weeds. The prospect of cricket lifted Arlott's spirits, however,
as well as the energy of the large crowd and the whimsicality
of the hosts needing to recruit a 12th man from the crowd
(a Mr Morris from Pontardawe). The St Helen's ground was
uplifting, too, and different, separated from the sea by road,
railway and train station. It felt quite maritime, the trees
reshaped and stunted by the westerly winds blowing in over
Swansea Bay, while the pitch had a distinctly sandy quality.
Both these factors and the sea preoccupied the two skippers
before the toss – like Hove, Swansea's wicket changed
character with wind and tide. Glamorgan's captain, the
48-year-old John Clay, called correctly, looked at the clouds,
the wicket and, perhaps, the tide-tables, before eventually
opting to bat.

It was almost exactly ten years since the two teams had last faced each other at Swansea. On that August day in 1936 – it was 3 August since the first day had been washed out – India had won the toss, batted and soon came to regret the decision. Of that eleven, Merchant, Mushtaq Ali, Nayudu and Banerjee had all survived to return a decade later, while Glamorgan included three men who had been playing in that game in 1936. Of those missing from the Welsh side, the most significant was their former captain, Maurice Turnbull. He had played nine Tests for England between 1930 and 1936 (including one against India), but his cricketing life was replaced by service in the Welsh Guards. He was killed by a sniper's bullet through the head near Montchamp in Normandy on 5 August 1944. His absence inevitably weakened Glamorgan's batting and played on the team's mind, particularly on the Monday of the match against All-India, the second anniversary of his death.

Glamorgan were hustled out by late afternoon on the first day for a disappointing 238 and India, thanks to Merchant and Modi, were able to make good progress by close of play on the Saturday. It had been a satisfying day's play – a high point being when Clay hit Mankad for 24 in an over. Despite that, Mankad was much admired by Arlott, who thought he had become the best slow left-arm bowler in the world by the end of the 1946 tour. Deep-set eyes full of laughter, thickly creamed hair swept back, a face full of determined confidence, Mankad was a formidable cricketer, busy, inventive and insistent. He could bat too and scored 1,000 runs on the tour, as well as taking 129 wickets at an average of just under 21. At Swansea, Mankad took seven wickets in the match and bowled 58.1 overs. Sea air, a spirited Bank Holiday crowd and an exhibition of Mankad's full repertoire – it all contrived to make Arlott's Welsh expedition particularly pleasurable. India went on to win the game by five wickets, thanks to 93 from Mushtaq Ali and Mankad's bowling. That too pleased him, sharing in the team's success as the train headed for the English Midlands.

There was a further reason to remember Swansea. It was one of the occasions when Arlott's love of poetry and cricket coincided. The poet Dylan Thomas, ever nostalgic for Swansea, sat with him on the pavilion roof for part of the game. They were much the same age, good friends and Arlott used him regularly on his poetry broadcasts for the BBC, usually when the poet was in need of funds. Thomas's love of cricket was such that he would sneak out of school as a boy to watch a game at the St Helen's ground. Arlott 'worshipped' Thomas and, over the years, regularly donated £10 or so to the poet's empty wallet. Dylan Thomas made more than 100 poetry broadcasts for the BBC, 50 in 1946, most of them commissioned by Arlott. That year the poet earned some £700 through his radio work. When the Indians played at Oxford earlier on the tour, Arlott had stayed with Thomas in his Oxford house by the river.

The first day's play over, on the Sunday, Thomas showed him the sights of West Wales, its green hills and out-of-the-way hostelries. For his part, Thomas regarded Arlott as the best sports commentator there was, writing warmly to him on 11 June 1947 from Florence, while listening to his friend's familiar voice over the airwaves all the way from Trent Bridge, struck by its enthusiasm, warmth, authority and, not least, Arlott's ability to give the listener a visual picture of what he was watching. Arlott believed that Thomas read his verse like an angel, despite the dead cigarette in his hand as he leaned into the microphone. After Thomas died in 1953, John observed that the Welshman 'had a touch of divinity about him'. Memories of the poet curled up in the Swansea commentary box while the poetry of cricket was played out on the grass outside would never leave him.

18

The Outlook is Unpromising

August 1946

BUOYED UP by the win, the Indians left Swansea for Birmingham to play Warwickshire at Edgbaston, a ground that John Arlott didn't warm to. It was, he thought, Edwardian, draughty and not big enough for Test match cricket; worse, it was too large for an ordinary county game. During the war the ground had been bombed and a small scorebox near the pavilion had been demolished. Thankfully, the raid had spared the pavilion itself, an old-fashioned building from which Arlott took some small comfort. Warwickshire's playing staff had arguably suffered more than the ground and the county was obliged to make use of local club cricketers to make up the numbers: on average some six players per game were sourced from local clubs, while 24 of the club's players that summer were amateurs. As a result key players such as Tom Dollery and Eric Hollies were obliged to carry the side on many occasions: the leg-spinner Hollies, the man who took Bradman's wicket at The Oval in the Australian's final Test in 1948, took 175 Championship wickets that season (at 15) while Dollery's 1,861 runs (at 43) might well have earned him selection for the winter's Australian tour – but didn't. He was one of those cricketers who had been selected for the cancelled tour of India in 1939.

For Warwickshire's game against the Indian tourists, as so often that summer, there was rain about and the outlook was decidedly unpromising. The pitch on the morning of 7 August was rain-affected and the day's play was curtailed by the weather. The Nawab of Pataudi was still not fit – a worry since the third Test at The Oval was due to begin in ten days' time – and Vijay Merchant assumed the captaincy. At the game's preliminaries Merchant called correctly; took another quizzical look at the Edgbaston wicket and the clouds; remembered the dubious weather forecast; and decided to do the unexpected. It was probably a toss he would have much preferred to lose. Merchant turned to the Warwickshire captain, Peter Cranmer (Oxford University and an England rugby international) and politely asked the county to bat first. He signalled to his opening bowlers, Banerjee and Amarnath, that they should limber up. Did the fickle weather make Merchant ultra-cautious? Was he worried about any loss of confidence among the Indian batsmen, left exposed on yet another green English wicket?

Whatever the reasoning, it was a misjudgement: the pitch proved easy-paced and the Warwickshire openers began comfortably against the Indian opening attack, the luckless Banerjee unable to break free from his below-par form. The opening batsman, Richard Sale (another Oxford man), accumulated runs steadily, while the Indians spilled catches with frustrating regularity. The left-handed Sale batted for nearly five hours, survived a number of chances, and went on to score 157. He had played for Oxford University in both 1939 and 1946, and would earn a county cap twice, for Warwickshire in 1946 and Derbyshire five years later. He never surpassed his score against India that day. Not for the first time, it was Hazare and Mankad who took the wickets, the latter bowling a marathon 41 overs in Warwickshire's total of 375/9 declared.

On the second morning it was raining and the start of play was delayed until 4.30 in the afternoon. Merchant opened the batting with Mushtaq Ali – they would open in the forthcoming Test – and both made runs, the first wicket not falling until the score had reached 67. Thereafter things fell apart. The Indian batting was sedate at best and was discomfited by the presence on the field of a genuinely quick bowler – a rare breed that summer in England. Tom Pritchard was a New Zealander and despite the greasy ball, damp outfield and run-ups, he proved fast, accurate and hostile. Merchant was dropped and then Pritchard dismissed Hazare, Mankad and Gul Mohammad for a single run within a seven-ball spell. The phlegmatic Merchant watched his team-mates come and go, but stayed undefeated until the end, having scored 86 – this in a total of 197 eked out over 107 overs. Asked to follow on, India reached 21/1 before bad light intervened. The time lost to rain over the three days was enough to give India an undeserved draw. They left Birmingham for Cheltenham under heavy cloud, only partly meteorological.

Hoping for good weather, the tourists arrived in Cheltenham to face Gloucestershire on Saturday, 10 August. With just seven days before the final Test, India needed time at the crease, ideally a day and a half of measured batting practice, under a blue sky with Cleeve Hill in heat-haze to the east of the College ground. What they got instead was rain – a thunderstorm which battered the ground, blew down tents and marquees, and wrapped the hills in cloud. Cheltenham was not alone in seeing no cricket at all that day. There was no play in many places around the country, from Bradford to Weston-super-Mare. Only 50 runs were scored in the day at The Oval, while only the coastal fringes escaped the downpour – Clacton and Hastings, for example. Cheltenham was awash and no play was possible until after lunch on the second day, by which time a weather-savvy Arlott, after a treasured weekend at home, had arrived for broadcasting duty in the West Country.

India versus Gloucestershire meant a reprise of the duel between Hammond and Pataudi. Suspicion of a damp, green and unfriendly looking wicket was enough to persuade the Indian captain to ask the county to bat first, thereby echoing Merchant's misjudgement in Birmingham. Gloucestershire made steady progress, thanks to Charlie Barnett (20), his opening partner, Andy Wilson (45) and Hammond (30 not out), to the extent that the Gloucestershire captain felt able to declare soon after tea. Pataudi batted judiciously on a drying pitch against Tom Goddard's finger-spin – but the rest of the batting folded as if bewitched. Hazare made 11, while Abdul Hafeez and Gul, in the shaky Indian middle order, both failed to score. Somehow the two captains contrived a near-finish, the day and a half's play seeing all four innings, thanks to two generous declarations. Set 185 to win in three hours on the final afternoon, Pataudi came and went; Goddard's fingers gripped the seam; Amarnath hit out; Hazare hit form; wickets fell and the clock ticked; afternoon turned towards early evening and 12 runs were needed in the last six minutes. It ended as another draw, with Tom Goddard taking 11 wickets in the match; he was 45 and had a broken little finger on his bowling hand. Neither his age nor the injury could disguise his match-winning quality.

The recent form of the tourists, by contrast, was uncertain: two wins, two flaky draws and a thrashing by Somerset. The weather too remained ominous and the next (and final) Test was already upon them, beginning on 17 August at The Oval. It would be the final game of the series and the last Test to be played by eleven men representing the whole of India.

19

Dark Clouds Over The Oval

August 1946

AFTER CHELTENHAM'S stormy weather, the tourists returned to the capital. The two Test captains, Hammond and Pataudi, were both increasingly preoccupied with final preparations and selection permutations. Hammond would have been the more content of the two following the overall performance at Manchester. England's batting there had looked secure enough – each of the top six had had one decent score in the series. Admittedly, Lancashire's Jack Ikin, at seven, was a bit short of runs and the English tail didn't always wag. Certainly the bowling was good enough for the job, with Bedser the pick of the bowlers, having taken 22 wickets in the two previous Tests at just under 11 runs each, while Dick Pollard had taken seven wickets at Old Trafford. But the forthcoming tour of Australia was also a factor in the players selected for The Oval. There were disturbing, glaring weaknesses, not the least of which was the state of English fast bowling. Bill Bowes would not tour again – too old now and too weakened by his wartime tour of Italian and German POW camps. Bill Voce had vast experience, but his bowling was little better than military medium now. The next generation of English fast bowlers had never been identified, developed and blooded – except in the literal sense.

So there was scope for the England selectors to make changes: a new-ball partner for Bedser, for a start, and perhaps a replacement for Ikin in the middle order. As well as the missing English fast bowlers, there were issues with the team's spin options. The 1946 season would end with two men topping the bowling averages whose combined age was 91 (John Clay of Glamorgan and Yorkshire's Arthur Booth). How could they possibly stand up to the heat of Brisbane and Perth? The same issue affected medium-pace bowlers: the top-ranked fast-medium bowler, Austin Matthews of Glamorgan, was also into his early forties. Could the Ashes be won with a team of middle-aged men? After great deliberation, the England selectors made six changes, some as a result of injury. Both Voce and Doug Wright were deemed unfit and the job of partnering Bedser in the new-ball attack was given to Surrey's Alf Gover, another veteran at 38. Laurie Fishlock, also of Surrey, was brought in to bat at number 3. He was a year older than Gover and pushed up the team's average age to nearly 32.

Pataudi's selection options were more limited, inevitably in a squad of 16, where one player (Nimbalkar) had played only a single game since the Manchester Test. The opening pair of Merchant and Mushtaq Ali were both in good nick. Then Hazare, Modi, Pataudi himself and Amarnath were all obvious picks. Hafeez had completed only one decent innings (of 38) in the past month, so he was a risk, but who else was there? Amarnath and Mankad were certainties (both staunch batsmen and essential bowlers), though Mankad had only scored 40 runs in his last six visits to the crease. The wicketkeeper Hindlekar must play, given Nimbalkar's rustiness. None of the bowlers were obvious choices: Sohoni, Sarwate, Banerjee, Shinde and Nayudu had taken only 21 wickets among them in the most recent five games. There was no escaping the fact that the team was over-reliant on four or five key players. If the captain's eyes occasionally looked at the clouds over London and the daily weather forecasts, it was entirely understandable.

* * *

Welcome to the England dressing room before play begins: grizzled old pros (Hammond, Fishlock, Gover); and two playing Test cricket for the first time (the Kent wicketkeeper, Godfrey Evans and Peter Smith of Essex) – a mix then of cigarette-smoking sangfroid and nail-biting tension. Marooned in the pavilion, they watch the rain and each other, the long wait a test of fortitude, patience and nerves. The debutants – Evans and Smith – are fretting more than most. Denis Compton watches Hammond with mixed feelings, not enamoured of the captain's cautious approach and remembering how the England skipper had upbraided him for seeming to give his wicket away after scoring a hundred in his first Test against Australia at Trent Bridge in 1938. The players fiddle with kit, smoke, stare at each other and at the rain falling beyond the pavilion window.

Twelve months after hostilities ended, each man knew he was lucky to be there, even those whose selection was a formality. They were, after all, survivors. Five England Test cricketers were not so fortunate, having died during the conflict. Altogether, 46 county cricketers died in the war, with Middlesex and Kent hardest hit – seven players in both cases. Thirty-eight of the 46 were officers. The great majority of those who died were in the army, 28 in all, with some 16 killed in action; nine were in the RAF, six in either the Fleet Air Arm or the Royal Marines and one was in the navy. Two others were civilians. The causes of death were varied: some were shot down over enemy territory; others were killed in training accidents. Two died of wounds received; three were lost at sea. There were also two suicides and two instances of the Japanese shooting POWs. Five were killed in air raids, one as late as the summer of 1944 by a V1 flying bomb.

When cricket resumed in 1946, the players who had survived the war were all too aware of the absent faces in the dressing room and on the pitch. That was true of the game from the most rustic of club cricketers to members of the national side where it was England's bowling attack, both high pace and canny spin, that was significantly weakened. That was a big worry for England – and would become more so during the forthcoming winter in Australia. The war had removed two fine exponents of the art of bowling, one fast bowler and an incomparable left-arm spinner.

20

The Quick and the Dead

1941 and 1943

IF, AT the outbreak of war in September 1939, an optimistic dreamer had been contemplating the resumption of cricket at some distant point in the future and selecting the likely composition of an England XI, two names, both bowlers, would have been near certainties. The Indians of 1946 would have regarded both Hedley Verity of Yorkshire – even in his early 40s – and Ken Farnes (Essex) as major threats, while the Essex fast bowler would have given the MCC's touring side heading to Australia later in 1946 some much-needed firepower. Alec Bedser was clearly a formidable bowler, but of no more than medium pace; moreover, he was untried outside England and might well be hindered by the Australian climate and pitches. Certainly, looking through the counties' battery of fast bowlers, no one possessed the pace and aggression that Farnes had generated before the war. The list of alternatives was painfully thin, consisting of men who were too old to flourish in Test cricket down under (the 38-year-old Bill Copson of Derbyshire; Hampshire's 'Lofty' Herman, 39; Matthews of Glamorgan, 42); nor fast enough (there was a string of medium-pacers); men who had yet to be demobbed; were unwilling to travel (Alf Gover, who had been perversely selected for the final Test against India); or simply not good enough. The 6ft 5in Farnes, on the other hand, had taken 33 wickets in the month of August 1939 alone and, at 28, was then at his peak. That month he had taken his first hat-trick (against Nottinghamshire at Clacton – three good men too in Hearne, Gunn and Hardstaff), rattled batsmen with his speed and bounce, broken fingers and knocked off caps.

Farnes was chosen as one of *Wisden's* Cricketers of the Year in 1939, alongside Hugh Bartlett (Sussex), Bill Brown (Australia), Denis Compton and Arthur Wood (Yorkshire), and after his final game of the season, against Northamptonshire at Clacton-on-Sea, he went back to his job at Worksop College where he was a housemaster. Beyond the school gates the war closed in; inside, another autumn term began. Farnes busied himself with house matters, taught history and geography, and finalised the cricket book he was writing (*Tours and Tests*). The book was published by Lutterworth Press that year. He remained in school for the first half of 1940 while the grim realities of the German blitzkrieg and Dunkirk underlined the country's dire predicament. He was able to play some cricket that summer: at Lord's for Sir P.F. Warner's XI against a West Indies XI on 22 August (in the same team as Sergeants Denis Compton and Len Hutton, Freddie Brown, Billy Griffith and Gubby Allen among others), Farnes taking 1-31 in ten overs; and finally, at Cheltenham, for a British Empire XI (he took 3-59 and bowled Gloucestershire's George Emmett), but by then he had joined up for the RAF Volunteer Reserve.

Ken Farnes' rare cricketing ability made him a public figure – a suave, silk-cravated, cricket-blazered hero on a Wills's cigarette card; a tall, powerful, leggy giant on the cover of *Boy's Own Paper* (August 1939 issue). And, if you were lucky and a schoolboy, he was teaching you history, if only for a short while. Farnes was soon being trained as a pilot in Medicine Hat, Canada, after short spells in Torquay, West Worthing and Scotland. He earned his bomber pilot's wings

in Canada – he was too tall to fit comfortably in a Spitfire
– and, once back in England, he joined No.12 Operational
Training Unit (OTU) flying Wellington bombers.

On 20 October 1941, Farnes was the pilot of a four-man
crew on a night-flying exercise over Chipping Warden, an
RAF base some six miles from Banbury in Oxfordshire. It
was late – 11.10pm – and on that dark autumn night, he
was in terrible difficulties, struggling with the unfamiliar,
heavy controls of the lumbering Wellington and horrified at
the fast-approaching runway. It was too close, too short and
he knew that beyond the perimeter were the village houses,
blacked-out but certainly somewhere out there ahead of his
doomed aircraft. Moments later, the bomber hit the ground,
missing the houses, but crashing into a tennis court, then
bursting into flames. The crash and fire were witnessed by
Aeron Franklin, the girl Farnes was planning to marry and
who was waiting for his return to base. Farnes was killed
immediately, while his co-pilot died six hours later, both of
them suffering the same fate as many wartime trainee pilots
– in that week of 13–20 October, for example, there were
15 other such accidents, either in training or in so-called
'Nickel' operations (dropping leaflets over Germany), killing
36 men in all.

Ken Farnes' book *Tours and Tests* was published before
he died – and would later acquire considerable second-hand
value after many copies were destroyed in an air raid on the
warehouse where they were stored. In that book he expressed
his concern about the future of English cricket – as he saw it,
before the war intervened to make matters infinitely worse.
Batting and batsmanship caused him much less concern than
the state of bowling and bowlers. The latter were in short
supply, at least at the highest level, perhaps because talented
amateurs tended to be batsmen, while bowling was seen as
the appropriate role for horny-handed professionals. Farnes
himself was a rarity, an amateur who bowled fast. When
the game was eventually reborn, seven years later, he would

be greatly missed: quick, fiery, intimidating, but already a fading memory.

* * *

The autumn that Ken Farnes was killed, his England colleague Hedley Verity had yet to be posted overseas. A captain in the Green Howards, he had been in Northern Ireland earlier that year, a relatively peaceful posting, brightened with considerable opportunities to play cricket. He took wickets with great regularity on pitches that were perhaps more suited to fox-hunting. In June 1941 he turned out for the Army at Lord's against the RAF; the Army XI included Denis Compton, Jack Robertson and Billy Griffith, while the airmen fielded Cyril Washbrook, Les Ames and Charlie Barnett, an old friend from the Indian tour of 1933/34. It was Hedley's final appearance at Lord's and was distinctly low-key – he didn't bat or take a wicket.

Early in 1942, the 1st Battalion of the Green Howards was posted to India (to Ranchi, a town some 260 miles west of Calcutta and the birthplace of the great modern Indian cricketer, M.S. Dhoni). India provided a stark contrast to the world of the Marylebone Cricket Club, its red and yellow ties, rain stopping play and players fielding in three jumpers: there it was hot, sticky and tense with political uncertainty. Physically too, it was very demanding: Verity fell ill, eventually with dysentery, sufficiently badly for him to be considered suitable for repatriation. That idea was forgotten in the battalion's subsequent series of postings – Persia in the first instance; then in March 1943 to Kibrit Air Base in Egypt; and on to Syria. Verity was still weak from the disease he had picked up in India and, at 38, he was significantly older than those he was commanding. Moreover, the war was about to take a significant new direction. In July 1943, the Allies invaded Sicily and Captain Verity was soon caught up in fierce fighting, just at the time when he was close to being withdrawn from the front line to the relative safety of a staff job. The demands of the moment denied him this last chance to avoid the harsh reality of night attacks, artillery barrages and the desperate intensity of battle.

On 19 July, the Green Howards were caught up in a night attack, the darkness broken by the light from burning crops, trees and gunfire. The 15th Brigade came under heavy and sustained fire and B Company under Captain Verity found itself surrounded. He was hit in the chest by shrapnel, a wound sufficiently serious to rule out any prospect of escape. As the Company retreated, Verity was left behind, bleeding in the dust, but furiously exhorting his men to keep going, towards the German positions. Soon after, alone in no-man's-land, he was captured and taken to a field hospital where he was operated on.

Instead of a period of peaceful recovery, Verity was taken on a series of dispiriting journeys: across the Straits of Messina to mainland Italy; into a hospital in Reggio Calabria; then a two-day train journey to Naples; and finally, because the German hospital was full, to an Italian military hospital at Caserta. The travelling – boat, train, ambulance – weakened him further and another operation proved necessary, performed by Italian doctors. For a few days he seemed to be improving, but it did not last. There was a sudden catastrophic decline, accompanied by the loss of a great deal of blood, and on 31 July 1943 he died.

On 31 July 1939 Verity had been bowling at The Oval in a game that featured Len Hutton, Bill Bowes and Alf Gover. That day he scored just 5 and the following day he took four wickets, with no thought of how the world of cricketing green and white would be swept away so soon. Had he survived the war and played against the men from All-India in 1946, he would have been in his early forties, ground down perhaps by the war's demands, but still able to cause unease by his mastery of flight and turn. It was not to be, but at least his last month or so of cricket in 1939 was a final glorious, golden time: 61 wickets at an average just above 11.

On 19–22 August, less than a fortnight before the war began, Essex played Yorkshire at Bramall Lane, Sheffield, winning by an innings and four runs. The scorebook recorded that Ken Farnes took four wickets in the match, while, in Essex's only innings, Hedley Verity's slow left arm earned him 5-40 in 30 eight-ball overs. Among those five wickets was:

K. Farnes bowled Verity 0.

21

The Last All-India Test

August 1946

WITH ONE exception, the England XI at The Oval
were all former servicemen. Four were ex-RAF, including
Bill Edrich who had flown many operations over enemy
territory. He had been in the very eye of the storm, flying
Blenheim bombers, a tour that included daylight operations
over Germany, notably the attack on Cologne on 12 August
1941. It was for that he was awarded the Distinguished
Flying Cross. Acting Squadron Leader William John Edrich
appeared in the *London Gazette* in recognition of his gallantry
in attacking two power stations, an operation that involved
flying some 250 miles over enemy territory at an altitude
of 100 feet. He was one of those whose 'calm courage and
resolute determination' rendered the attack a success. These
were the very characteristics which rendered him invaluable
after he had swapped flying jacket and Mae West life jacket
for cricket whites. Of the others who had served in the Air
Force, Bedser had been in the RAF Police; Cyril Washbrook
had served as a physical training instructor and Wally
Hammond, before his discharge with a damaged back, had
been a privileged and shielded officer whose military kit bag
invariably included his bat and pads. Five men had served
in the army: Compton as a gunner in India; Evans in the
Royal Army Service Corps; Smith as an officer in the Essex

130

Regiment and Hutton and Gover as PT instructors, although the Surrey man would later become a major in the Pioneer Corps. James Langridge, like Somerset's Harold Gimblett, was in the National Fire Service. The exception was Laurie Fishlock who, as an engineer, made aircraft parts for the RAF. Inevitably, each man was much changed by the war and a different cricketer from the one who had played seven years before. Most had played a number of Tests before the war, with the majority making debuts in 1936/37. Hammond's debut was as long ago as 1927.

Waiting for play to begin, the England players were largely quiet, bar occasional complaints about the English summer, the new Labour government, and doubts about the prospects for the forthcoming tour of Australia. Reminiscence was limited to the last time players had shared a dressing room before the war; wartime exploits were set aside. Even if Hammond had been a loquacious, sociable extrovert, he might well have baulked at 'shooting a line' about his RAF service when Edrich was listening. Hammond's war was confined to run-of-the-mill flights to the Middle East and South Africa, his life a mixture of desk work (to do with the provision of sporting facilities for officers), quasi-ambassadorial activities, a love affair, and playing cricket, largely of an exhibition kind. He was based in Cairo for three years, a life of heat, dust, Shepheard's Hotel, the Gezira Club and, for a while, contemplation of what would happen if Rommel's tanks thundered into the city. Part of his responsibilities in Egypt included organising, promoting and playing cricket. As war experience, it did not stand comparison with that of the Middlesex all-rounder, down to bat at number 6 for his country.

The Indians in the away dressing room had very different wartime experiences, but the dictates of history – the life cycle of empire and the Raj – guaranteed that they too will have been marked by the war years, despite the game's continuation after 1939. There were a significant number of English county cricketers who had played the game in India at some time, both in peace and during the war, sometimes for the Army, or for the Europeans, in the Pentangular competition, or the Roshanara Club in Delhi, or the Viceroy's XI, or perhaps, for Bengal or Hyderabad. Some were killed in action – caught in the chaos of the retreat to Dunkirk, or in the North African desert, or Italy or Burma. One took his own life when his wife deserted him, just as the war ended. Thirteen of those cricketers who died in the war were Englishmen, but born in India, sons of parents whose working lives were in India, and who had consigned their offspring to boarding school life at Cheltenham College, Winchester, Haileybury or Harrow, before settling for a life in the army.

* * *

Lord's and The Oval: chalk and cheese – north and south London. In that first post-war year Kennington Oval was a gaunt place of gasometers, red-brick walls and windswept seats; on blistering summer days, there was minimal shade, and when it rained, shelter was hard to find. That was the way of things on the third Test's first day – Saturday, 17 August – when the sky was a mix of dark grey and black. It was more November than high summer, but nonetheless there were long queues standing patiently by the high walls of the ground from early morning. It was, in a way, a statement of post-war optimism.

It rained all that morning and it wasn't until five in the afternoon that play began. There was a feeling that the umpires had taken pity on the faithful huddled under umbrellas. Pataudi won the toss and elected to bat first, thereby breaking the pattern of the previous two games. Inserting the opposition had stood them in good stead previously: the Indians had won the toss seven times to that point out of 17, put the opposition in and subsequently had only lost once. The wicket was sodden and flat and the placid 90 minutes of play that ensued proved Pataudi's decision to be correct. Merchant and Mushtaq Ali survived until the close, despite Gover and Bedser's perseverance: stumps at 79 without loss.

The second day, Monday, felt like a proper Test match – a full day's play with both sides working to make progress: India 331; England, 95/3. Prime Minister Attlee was in the large crowd and the anticipation for the third day was considerable – the game poised. Predictably in that damp summer, however, the rain returned and no further play was possible. Merchant had scored another methodical, neat hundred before being run out (his opening partner, Mushtaq Ali, had suffered the same fate); Edrich took four wickets, and Hammond, 9 not out when play ended, had played for the last time for England on home soil. Indeed, there was only one more appearance for Gloucestershire and that was an ill-advised return in 1951 against Somerset at Bristol – he made a scratchy 7 runs (George Emmett whom he had too often belittled scored 110 and 102 not out going in first). At a wet Oval, Hammond was already thinking about Australia, with embarkation for down under only ten days away. The Indians, by contrast, were bound for Southend-on-Sea for a game with Essex, still with five more matches to play, their punishing itinerary taking in Canterbury, Lord's, Hastings and Scarborough before the five-month tour came to an end.

As for John Arlott, he left The Oval without a backward glance, its abiding memory for him one of grey rain clouds, soot-black buildings, and an arena empty, apart from city-stained sparrows and wet newspapers blowing in the wind.

22

The End of the Indian Summer
Late August 1946

BY NOW there was just a hint of autumn in the air and for the weary tourists the end was at last in sight. The three Test matches had come and gone, and this being England, with the first leaves beginning to turn, the weather showed signs of improvement to the extent that the sun emerged for the Indians' match against Essex at Southend at the end of August. The Indian tour would be over in only two more weeks and the seaside town was busy with East Enders enjoying the novelty of a holiday: bald heads pale under knotted handkerchiefs; long queues for eels and shellfish; the sun high and bright. John Arlott's walk through Southchurch Park was a pleasant pre-match interlude before the hostilities began.

Essex scored a respectable 303 on the first day, with the runs spread among the whole team. At one point there was the prospect of the county going beyond a position of respectability and dominating the day's play, reaching perhaps 350 or more. Sadu Shinde's googlies and leg breaks had done for both openers but Essex fell away from a promising 104/1 to a jittery 156/5. Vijay Merchant, captaining the side once again in Pataudi's absence, knew Shinde well – he had scored a triple hundred against him back in December 1943, when Shinde had bowled until his shoulders ached and his spinning finger burned (he completed 75 overs in all). Merchant's decision to bowl the young man against an Essex side progressing sweetly on a fine morning for batting was a brave one. He had to overcome an initial wariness about bringing Shinde into the attack, a feeling triggered by the bowler's diffident demeanour, a manner not put to one side when the field was set before coming in to bowl. Tall, gangly and frail-looking, he didn't have the look of a cricketer. Moreover, he had found the tour of England meteorologically challenging – too cold, wet and windswept. He had soon discovered how different the country was from home: it was one thing bowling in the heat and light of Poona on hard, fast wickets, but quite different when it came to the dampness of England, where the pitches were frequently rain-affected, slow and low. As for his fielding, he tended to make a skipper close his eyes and pray – or swear – frustrated by his spin bowler's leaden heavy-leggedness. He would fumble chances, as if his fingers were made of ice and the ball was toxic. At the start of a bowling spell, he was nervy and easily disconcerted: a talent certainly, but decidedly raw.

Sadu Shinde's selection for the All-India tour had been a surprise for some, but he had done well in the 1945/46 Quadrangular tournament. Aged only 23, he was still a student in Poona and his high forehead and thoughtful eyes gave him an academic look. Unusually, he had two varieties of googly and he certainly spun the ball prodigiously. In the first Test at Lord's, however, his bowling had been unexceptional (1-66 in 23 overs). Instead, it was his batting with Modi in the first innings, where he had shared a partnership for the last wicket of 43, that had caught the eye. His performances more generally, however, were not enough to earn him selection for the second and third Tests.

Shinde did not often get the chance to show what he could do with the bat: of the 20 matches he played on the 1946 tour, there were eight in which he did not bat at all. But on the final day at Southend he was to play a critical role.

India were set 367 to win with almost five hours in which to get them. In the event, the result came to depend on whether Hindlekar and Shinde could score 15 runs in the final 17 minutes. An elegant – if somewhat fortuitous – late cut by Shinde in the final over went for four runs, and India had won by one wicket with one minute left to play. The willowy, forlorn-looking student from Poona had confounded those team-mates in the pavilion who had been unable to watch, anticipating an anticlimactic failure.

The team left Southend in high spirits en route for Canterbury for the following day's game with Kent, where, being England, the rain returned, and with a vengeance. It fell for days, making a mockery of the idea of festival cricket. Instead there was a melancholy, end-of-term feeling to the St Lawrence ground, with the flags hanging heavily, bunting torn and twisted, and puddles spreading and merging across the field of play. There was only time for a single and incomplete innings in which Kent scored 248/3, with Arthur Fagg making 109. Ten years before, he had made 172 when Kent beat India by an innings. Now the tourists, pavilioned and dry, improvised a loud and intense miniature game inside, with the door acting as wicketkeeper. John Arlott, with work denied him, prowled the city, on the hunt for second-hand bookshops (and finding only one).

The Indian team returned to Lord's for the third time, on this occasion with autumn even more pronounced. The game against Middlesex began on the last day of August, the same day that the MCC touring party was due to sail for Australia. Once again, Hazare (193 not out), Modi (80) and Mankad (109 not out) scored heavily and All-India declared at 469/5, a prodigious total on a wet wicket. Middlesex, without the Australia-bound Compton and Edrich, duly folded twice, losing by an innings and 263 runs: they were poor in the first innings and worse second time around, all out for 82 in 36 overs. Shute Banerjee took four wickets for 21 runs, finding some form when it was far too late. The game was all over in two days. The third day – the seventh anniversary of the outbreak of the war – was not required.

That was the last of the games against the counties, but the tourists' cricketing obligations were not yet over. There were two more fixtures still to fulfil and the itinerary continued to be unkind: two seaside resorts – Hastings in the south for the penultimate game and then up to Scarborough in Yorkshire. The game in Sussex was against the South of England and victory was India's by ten runs, despite the rain falling harder by the minute at the end. There were more runs for Merchant (82 and 39) and eight wickets for Amarnath against a South team boasting Tom Goddard, Les Ames (Kent) and Jack Robertson of Middlesex. And so, the 300-mile haul to Scarborough and a festival game against H.D.G. Leveson-Gower's XI, a name that somehow conjures images of empire and an age fast drawing to a close. Worcestershire's Richard Howorth had dominated the game, scoring 114 and taking 4-38 and 5-34 when India batted. The tourists still required 12 runs with only two wickets left to fall in order to make the Leveson-Gower XI bat again; then after lunch on the final day, the heavens opened and so the game was abandoned. Instead of a dispiriting defeat for the Indians, the rain fittingly had the last word in this final game of the summer of 1946.

And so, on 10 September, it was all over, after 33 games, some 4,000 miles of travelling and five long months during which much in the world beyond cricket had changed. Ahead lay a return to the sub-continent, the anguished birth of both a territorially curtailed India, and the new land of Pakistan, split between its East and West and more than a thousand miles apart. For India's cricketers and the country's wider population it would be a grim time of chaos, political upheaval and appalling bloodshed. Each member of that last All-India squad would have wondered what the future held, for their cricket careers and their country.

23

Mr Arlott and Mr Gupta: a Retrospective

September 1946

IT WAS time to go back home, the season over and autumn scattering leaves on cricket grounds across the country. John Arlott shared a carriage with the Indian commentator Abdul Hamid Sheikh on the London train from Scarborough, both men companionably munching apples. 'I'm contemplating writing a book about the tour,' Arlott said, an observation which elicited little more than a murmured 'Yes?' from his companion, who promptly fell asleep. Deprived of an audience, Arlott looked out at the flat fields of the north-east through the smoke-dusted window and toyed with bookish ideas. He was also thinking ahead to the winter: back to BBC Centre for him and his care of the Corporation's poetry, rather than months trailing across Australia with the English tourists.

There was, though, the opportunity to reprise the summer's cricket through the writing of *Indian Summer*. Arlott's first cricket book, commissioned by Longmans, meant a punishing discipline of writing over the autumn and winter months. He saw the book as needing to strike a balance between insightful commentary on the game itself, painting a lyrical picture of an English cricketing summer, and revealing something of the warmth, generosity and skill of cricketers, both English and Indian.

John Arlott's take on the All-India tour of 1946 could afford to be tolerant of failure and disappointment; could digress on a player's foibles, his film-star looks or the idiosyncratic way he ran in to bowl. For those charged with management of the tour, principally Pankaj Gupta, but also the Nawab of Pataudi and his senior players, there were questions from the cricket authorities at home that needed to be answered. What could be learned for the next tours? What weaknesses should be addressed? Who might be held responsible for any shortcomings? What follows is *not* Mr Gupta's report; just a best guess as to what such a report might have said ...

A Report on the All-India tour of England, 1946

1. First, we shall deal with the initial selection of the Indian squad. A decision was made to take 16 players to England. With the benefit of hindsight, it would have been wiser to take one additional player. More troublingly, there were a number of players who should have been included and weren't (the medium-pacer, Fazal Mahmood for one) – and some who were in the party and might have been left at home without any loss to the strength of the side. The injury to Nimbalkar – a lengthy one – made matters worse and put great strain on the remaining players. Frankly, we could have used an extra quick bowler (an issue to which we shall return), as well as a genuine batsman capable of taking over wicketkeeping duties. Hindlekar's bad back and Nimbalkar's broken thumb, in combination, presented us with selection difficulties for the Test matches. A further issue was the overall quality of the squad – we shall return to this later in the report – and the consequence was that we were never able to pick a Test XI where everyone made a positive contribution. In each of the three Tests, some players were largely anonymous.

2. We batted better than we bowled, but in the Tests we only once topped 300 runs. Over the five innings we averaged just over 225 – simply not enough to win cricket matches. Only four players averaged over 30 and two of those only played in two Tests; it follows that some players selected for their batting underperformed. Vijay Merchant was outstanding, averaging 49 in the Tests and 74.5 overall. However, he was the exception: Abdul Hafeez averaged just 16; the captain only 11; Hazare, 16 and Amarnath 13.8. A sign of our fundamental weakness was the failure to settle on an established batting order. In the Tests, Merchant was the only player to bat in the same position on every occasion. By contrast, Mankad moved from opener to number 8 and the skipper batted at 3, 6 and

7. In conclusion, an analysis of our dismissals is salutary: Amarnath out bowled four times out of five; Pataudi the same. In all, 59% of our dismissals were clean bowled, with another six lbw. We seemed curiously vulnerable to the straight ball.

3. We turn now to our bowling. With the benefit of hindsight, we expected too much of Shute Banerjee. At 33, he no longer holds the same threat, except perhaps on hard, fast wickets (a rarity in this wet summer). A heavy man, he struggled for fitness and tired easily, while his fielding was sluggish. He was a cheerful and willing member of the squad, but he was rightly omitted from the Test side, never being a realistic option. The bulk of the bowling fell to Vinoo Mankad and Lala Amarnath. Between them they took 24 out of the 28 English wickets that fell during the series. The remaining four were shared by Hazare (2), Nayudu and Shinde. Even more disturbing was the fact that Hazare's two wickets cost nearly 90 runs each. All this meant that the team chosen to represent the country in the Tests invariably comprised two groups – the core (Merchant, Mushtaq, Hazare, Amarnath, Hindlekar and Modi), and those simply making up the numbers. It should also be said that there was a case for the captain leaving himself out of the side – he was never fully fit – and letting Merchant perform the role.

4. The standard of fielding was a further concern. Although sometimes excellent, it was never consistent. We could be over-anxious, slow or passive; too many catches were spilled, although the poor quality of the light and the dark background of English spectators in their drab and colourless raincoats didn't help.

5. We turn now to the players:
   • **V. Merchant**: An outstanding tour by a world-class batsman. Over 2,000 runs scored at an average of 74.5 (49 in the Tests). Determined, consistent and able to concentrate for long periods. A fine ambassador for his country.

- **V. Mankad**: Excellent. Perhaps the best of his kind in the world. 1,120 runs (average 28) and 129 wickets (at 20.8). Worked hard and never complained.

- **V. Hazare**: Disappointing overall, particularly in the Tests where he was an easy victim of the English pacemen. Bowled too short.

- **R. Modi**: Did well for a young man of 22, showing discipline and a good temperament. Tellingly, his batting average in the Tests and overall was very similar (37 altogether on the tour and 34 in the Tests). Quiet and earnest.

- **L. Amarnath**: A mixed bag overall although he took the most wickets in the Test matches (13). While Hazare reached the 1,000 runs/100 wickets target, Amarnath fell short.

- **S. Banerjee**: One outstanding batting performance; otherwise a poor tour.

- **Mushtaq Ali**: Inconsistent. Failed to score a single hundred. Had a tendency to waft the bat at balls he should have ignored.

- **C.T. Sarwate**: One Test: 2 runs, no wickets. Never threatened to make a Test place his own. Dozy in the field.

- **Abdul Hafeez**: Sharp fielder; fragile batsman. Top score of 43 and a Test average of only 16. Still young enough at 21 to have a future for his country.

- **S.W. Sohoni**: Two Tests and out only once – hence his solid average (43). His bowling wasn't strong enough for him to be deemed an all-rounder.

- **R.B. Nimbalkar**: Injury-plagued and made little impact.

- **D.D. Hindlekar**: Short of runs but showed courage and determination. Better when keeping to the medium-pacers. Troubled by back pain and obliged to play more than was wise by the injuries of Nimbalkar.

- **S.G. Shinde**: Played at Lord's but made little impression. Expensive with the ball and when attacked, tended to drop short.

- **C.S. Nayudu**: Another disappointment: two Tests, but a paltry return of runs at an average of 7 and just one wicket (a good one – Fishlock at The Oval). Little impact in the county games.

- **Gul Mohammad**: The tour seemed to pass him by: one forgettable Test where he was bamboozled twice by Doug Wright. Bowled just two overs.

- **Nawab of Pataudi**: A tour too far after a long period away from the game. Batted well enough in the county games, 981 runs at an average of 46.7, but fell away in the Tests (55 at 11). Often less than fully fit, or indeed in good health. Led the side soundly in the field but made some quirky decisions which worked against the side's chances. For example, Hazare was asked to open the batting against Surrey (and failed to score); was then pushed down the order before being used as a nightwatchman against Yorkshire – and going on to make 244 not out.

So, in summary, there are some key points of learning for future tours: a squad of 17 players would give greater security in the event of injury; the captain must be a player whose form is current and secure; and we need to develop quick bowlers if we are to challenge other major Test-playing sides. That last point has implications for the kind of wickets we prepare back home. These are often featherbeds, unduly favouring our batsmen, cosseting them and spiking the guns of would-be pace bowlers.

There are two other points to make. First, there needs to be greater scrutiny of the tour schedule before it is agreed – this tour was too demanding, involving far too much travelling. Second, it is perhaps the case that politics intruded in an unhelpful way during the summer. Players were inevitably all too well aware of the troubles back home. We return to an India very unsure about how events will impact on the game we all love. Can the game survive undamaged in these troubled times?

Submitted with respect,
P. Gupta

* * *

No one will ever know if this piece of fiction bears any relation at all to Pankaj Gupta's actual account. That the team manager was asked for such a document suggests that the Indian Board was looking to apportion some blame among the players for the overall lack of Test-match success. Gupta, however, was on good terms with most of the players and indeed the Indian Board and so he felt obliged to resort to mild skulduggery. He responded to the board's request by saying that he had indeed produced such a document, writing it on board ship as the party returned home. Ah, but ... much to Mr Gupta's regret, the wind had gusted across the ship's deck and blown every single page into the sea ...

PART 2

ENGLAND DOWN UNDER

September 1946–March 1947

The MCC Tour of Australia and New Zealand 1946/47

The Itinerary
Australia

October 2, 3	Northam and Country Districts	Northam, WA
October 7	Western Australia Colts	Fremantle
October 11, 12, 14	Western Australia	Perth
October 17–19	Western Australia Combined XI	Perth
October 22, 23	South Australia Country XI	Port Pirie
October 25, 26, 28, 29	South Australia	Adelaide
Oct 31, November 1, 2, 4	Victoria	Melbourne
November 8, 9, 11, 12, 13	Australian XI	Melbourne
November 15, 16, 18, 19	New South Wales	Sydney
November 22, 23, 25, 26,	Queensland	Brisbane
November 29, 30, Dec. 2–4	**AUSTRALIA**	**Brisbane**
December 7, 9	Queensland Country	Gympie
December 13, 14, 16–19	**AUSTRALIA**	**Sydney**
December 21, 23	Northern New South Wales	Newcastle
December 27	Southern New South Wales	Canberra
December 30	Victoria Country	Bendigo
January 1-4, 6,7	**AUSTRALIA**	**Melbourne**
January 10, 11, 13	Tasmania Combined XI	Hobart
January 15–17	Tasmania	Launceston
January 24, 25, 27, 28	South Australia	Adelaide
February 1,3, 4, 5, 6	**AUSTRALIA**	**Adelaide**
February 11, 12	Victoria Country	Ballarat
February 14, 15, 17, 18	Victoria	Melbourne
February 21, 22, 24, 25	New South Wales	Sydney
February 28, March 1, 3-5	**AUSTRALIA**	**Sydney**

New Zealand

March 10–12	Wellington	Wellington
March 15, 17, 18	Otago	Dunedin
March 21, 22, 24, 25	**NEW ZEALAND**	**Christchurch**
March 28, 29	Auckland	Auckland

24

Goodwill and Bad Blood

Autumn 1946

JUST AS the Indian tourists had left home at a critical moment in their country's history, so too did the English when they left for Australia five months later. For the Indians the issue was one of political fracture – would religious difference split the country irrevocably in two? Britain's preoccupation on the other hand was what the war had done to the nation, including its relationships with the empire. Seven years of war had both exhausted and impoverished the country. That poverty – reflected in the UK's crippling level of debt – had rendered the concept of 'Empire' both impractical and outdated, with the very word itself seeming increasingly archaic. Ironically, in a time of British economic crisis, 'Empire' was being replaced by 'Commonwealth', although 'wealth', common or otherwise, was in short supply.

The war had made the British poorer, while at the same time Indian demands for independence had flourished. Indian poverty was of a different order of course, and that had been made worse during the conflict – by aspects of British policy and the way Britain waged its war. Millions died of starvation in Bengal and the horrors of this contributed to India's growing political activism. The idea of Partition – the establishment of a Muslim state separate from the rest of India – was not the preferred option in

147

the spring of 1946, but as the summer progressed, and the Indian cricketers toured the bucolic cricket grounds of England, it became clear that 'All-India' was no longer viable. The country was in turmoil, with many Britons seeking to leave, and some members of the armed forces, desperate for demobilisation and home, on the point of mutiny. The Cabinet Mission sent from London to resolve the political crisis had failed and Viceroy Archibald Wavell had seen fit as a result to opt for an interim Indian government of six Hindus, five Muslims, a Sikh, a Parsi and a Christian. It was a selection that neatly mirrored the religious composition of the cricketing tourists.

On 10 August 1946, while the tourists were watching the rain beat down in Cheltenham – a town that retained a lingering hint of the Raj – Jawaharlal Nehru, the leader of the Congress Party and India's future prime minister – was letting it be known that he was in a position to form a government. That was enough to provoke the Muslim leader, Muhammad Ali Jinnah, into withdrawing his support. A 'day of action' followed which duly led to widespread rioting in Calcutta. Jinnah's view of the situation was clear: the country should be divided (on religious grounds, Hindu or Muslim), or failing that it should simply be destroyed. It was an impasse that sealed the fate of thousands who died as a result, as well as the countless victims of acts of brutality perpetrated by both sides. The chaos spread rapidly across India, through Bengal, Assam, the Punjab and the North-West Frontier. Meanwhile, in England, India's cricketers were preparing themselves for the third Test at The Oval. By the time they were close to returning home, immersed in playing festival cricket in Hastings in early September, the violence had reached Bombay, home to a significant number of the squad. In that bustling port city there was no sign at all of the tolerance and mutual respect manifest in the behaviour of India's opening batsmen – the Hindu, Vijay Merchant, and the Muslim, Mushtaq Ali.

* * *

As the Indian tour was drawing to a close, England's cricketers were aboard ship heading down under. The England party had been wined and dined at Lord's before leaving the country, the occasion marked by the presence of the prime minister, Clement Attlee, who made a short speech emphasising the tour's importance as a 'goodwill mission'. At the back of his mind would have been the gathering crisis in India: this was the week when Attlee decided that a date for withdrawal from the country must be set. There was no mention of that in his speech, unsurprisingly, but nor did he touch on Bodyline, although its unsavoury odour was clearly in the air. Instead he remarked on the nation's deeply felt gratitude for Australian support and sacrifice during the war. It was sound politics from Attlee and sincerely meant, but the England vice-captain, Norman Yardley, for one, felt that 'goodwill' came from 'good cricket' rather than diplomacy or obsequious tact. Moreover, it remained to be seen whether the selectors had chosen a squad capable of playing 'good cricket', particularly as the selection panel itself was unconvincing. It comprised the captain, Walter Hammond; two men who would act as journalists on the tour itself (raising questions about conflicts of interest); and a chairman who, after being knocked down by a London cab at the end of July, was *hors de combat*.

While Yardley thought the squad would give a good account of itself, there were those who could see significant flaws and weaknesses: a captain past his best; players physically weakened by the war; little experience of playing in Australia (only three players had toured there before); not enough specialist bowlers; and batting that looked flaky once Hutton and Compton had been dismissed. Seven years previously, in its issue of 9 September 1939, *The Cricketer* had proudly noted the 'wealth' of young batting talent in England. By the summer of 1946, however, there was a serious shortage of promising batsmen. How could it be otherwise, given the long-term absence of county cricket, the demands of wartime service and the loss of many facilities and opportunities to play the game? Of the players selected for Australia, Yardley was the only one who had not appeared against India during the summer, while three who had played in that year's Tests were left behind – Frank Smailes of Yorkshire, Bill Bowes and Alf Gover. The average age of the squad was 33. It was a sign of MCC's deep-seated determination to preserve the status quo that it was keen to ensure the selected party included at least three amateurs. In the event, there were 13 professionals augmented by the amateurs, Paul Gibb, Yardley and the ex-professional Hammond.

As well as dining with the prime minister and saying fond farewells to family – they would be away for seven long months – the players' principal concern before they left was the need to obtain spare clothing coupons. Denis Compton's wife had been deputed to shop on his behalf and label every item – the ten pairs of trousers, twelve pairs of socks, his MCC blazer, two sweaters and so on. Then, finally, at the end of August, while India were playing Middlesex at Lord's, the tour began. The MCC party travelled by train from Waterloo to Southampton and then embarked on a converted troopship, the *Stirling Castle*, which set sail on the final day of the month. Conditions on board were basic, with no variation in class of travel, and the cricketers – with one notable exception – were obliged to share rooms (Edrich billeted with Compton and the Yorkshireman Hutton with the Lancastrian Dick Pollard). The exception to the principle of shared billets was Walter Hammond, established in comfortable and splendid isolation.

Previous England tours to Australia had begun with a slow, six-week cruise punctuated by stops at Naples, Aden and Colombo. This time there was a greater sense of urgency and the *Stirling Castle*'s only port of call was Port Said. There were 900 war brides on board, en route to their Australian husbands: hence perhaps the need to complete the trip in just three and a half weeks. Evidently the plan was to get the war brides into their husbands' arms as soon as possible. England's cricketers played deck tennis and quoits and danced in the evenings, providing the novelty of strangers' arms for the travelling brides. Hammond and Joe Hardstaff played chess and, towards the end of the voyage, nets were rigged up to allow the bowlers to get some practice in.

The presence of female passengers might have stirred the cricketers' interest, but the on-board dining certainly did. The sudden abundance of food after years of wartime rationing proved to be the undoing of many a hungry English cricketer on that voyage. Denis Compton enthused about the white bread on the ship: a luxury not seen for years. At least one member of the touring party (the Yorkshire wicketkeeper Paul Gibb) had form as a big eater, even before the war. The leg-spinner Doug Wright later recalled that Gibb's appetite in South Africa was enormous, with a great fondness for oranges and peaches. His breakfasts during the Timeless Test in Durban in 1939 were judged 'unbelievable' by Wright. How much more so then after six years of privation? Spam was nowhere to be seen; instead, the availability of food – its amount and variety – was irresistible. Plates were piled high, with previously scarce and rationed items – sugar, butter and oranges – in plentiful supply. The comforting round of breakfast, lunch and dinner each day was too tempting for hungry men more used to thin, lean rations. The sustained feasting compensated, to some degree, for the fact that the ship was 'dry'.

Even an invitation to the ship captain's table brought no relaxation to the no alcohol ruling, but the special menu might have compensated, containing such treats as grapefruit, fillet of sole or chicken, 'Bombe glacé, Hammond' and 'Middlesex pastries'. Over the weeks at sea, cricketers' stomachs expanded, trouser belts were loosened and some guilty consciences stirred. The fast bowlers were weighed – on the ship's butchers' scales – and the results provoked either concern or open-mouthed scepticism. Surely Bedser couldn't be close to 18 stone? Bill Voce, 16½ stone?

After Port Said and through the Red Sea, the weather was unpleasantly hot and humid, but once out into the Indian Ocean it turned fresher, wetter and with grey skies. Until the coast of Australia appeared on the horizon there was no sight of land, or even another ship. Landfall was the port of Fremantle and the English cricketers on the motionless deck looked down at the dockside, the welcoming crowd (which included Bill Bowes), and the tanned, gritty-looking Australian stevedores and hard-boiled pressmen. The 'goodwill tour' was about to begin. As it unfolded over the following months, 'goodwill' seemed in short supply to the extent that one of the tourists could remark to the cricket writer, Clif Cary, 'We are the first ambassadors ever embroiled in war while on a goodwill mission.' Meanwhile, over four thousand miles away, the Indian tourists were returning home to a country where the concept of goodwill had long since died, and a wave of bloodshed was about to break.

25

English Winter, Australian Spring
October 1946

IT WAS the best of times to be away from England. The summer of 1946 had been unusually wet and the winter months would prove to be bitterly cold. The snow fell early – a white Christmas was scarcely compensation – and the icy conditions in early 1947 gradually worsened, proving a further trial to a weary, dispirited country. Railway points froze, water pipes burst, the newly nationalised coal industry had major problems producing sufficient fuel for the country's needs and power was in short supply. Electric fires could not be switched on between 10am and 4pm and office workers, frequently late for work because of late-running trains, were obliged to wear overcoats and mufflers in the office to preserve a glimmer of warmth. Wax candles flickered and guttered as workers strained their eyes at typewriters, trying to read office papers in the shadows. When spring arrived, it brought with it a slow thaw, snow melt leading to widespread flooding which sustained rain made much worse. It might be peacetime, but these were grim days in Britain and across war-ravaged Europe, where the Iron Curtain was cutting the continent in two. The post-war world was a dark place and the newspapers were similarly bleak, covering the barbarism associated with Indian independence, the war crimes trials in Nuremberg, the atomic bomb tests in the South Pacific and acts of terror in Palestine, among other grim trouble spots. Cricket and the prospects for Hammond's men in Australia offered some respite, a glimpse of better times.

The England players on tour were well aware of the horrors of that winter back home. Norman Yardley, for example, would write later in his account of the tour that the weather then was the worst for a hundred years. He blamed Labour's minister of power, Manny Shinwell, holding him responsible for making a bad situation substantially worse. Weather he could do little about, but producing the means by which the cold might be alleviated was surely in Shinwell's power (for want of a better word). But, in the early autumn of 1946, all this lay ahead. While the Englishmen laboured in the nets for three weeks in Perth, England was enjoying quiet autumnal weather – something which the tourists would have welcomed given the heat of Western Australia. For them the priority, however, was to acclimatise to the Australian summer, the heat and the hard, clear light, the bone-hard pitches which would prove unexpectedly slow and make Alec Bedser's feet bleed when he bowled long spells. The heat troubled tender English stomachs and the changes in diet were blamed for an outbreak of boils among the players. There was much to get used to, but there was an additional factor which had not been planned for: the fact that the Australian weather in the months ahead would prove just as quixotic as Britain's, the intensity of storms having a major bearing on the cricket to be played.

There were two months to prepare for the first Test of the Ashes series to be played at the Woolloongabba in Brisbane, time to get fit and become used to the heat. There was much for the players to learn – about the conditions and the opposition, as well as the nature of Australian life. Then, on 2 October, the real business of the tour began with a two-day warm-up game at Northam, some 60 miles east of Perth. The town had a 'Wild West' quality with its dusty main street and ramshackle buildings. The opposition was rustic too and easily folded in the face of Peter Smith's artful leg breaks – he took nine wickets in the match for only 73 runs. After the first day (Compton 61 not out, Hammond 23 not out), the players were entertained at a barbecue and barn dance held in a nearby farm – Denis Compton, for one, finding the idea of a 'barbecue' an entirely novel concept. It proved to be a straightforward evening of Aussie beers and greasy, finger-licking mutton chops coupled with dancing with partners invited in from nearby farms. Despite the evening's indulgences, the MCC XI were sprightly enough to polish off the opposition the following day, winning by an innings. All of MCC's batsmen made runs apart from Laurie Fishlock, out for 2, while Hammond scored an undefeated 131.

The party moved on to Fremantle for another gentle outing, this time against a Western Australian Colts XI, a one-day game, on 7 October which they drew. There were fifties for Gibb and Fishlock and wickets spread among all the English bowlers except Bedser. There was a more meaningful challenge four days later, against Western Australia in Perth. This match also ended in a draw, Hammond making 208, the 35th double hundred in his long career, and eight wickets falling to the two MCC spin bowlers, Peter Smith and Doug Wright. By then, the third week in October, some significant factors were beginning to emerge in the tourists' cricket: too many blunders and fumbles in the field; Norman Yardley's cool head and courage in Hammond's absence (the skipper had left himself out of the final game in Perth); and the underpowered nature of the England pace attack which consistently seemed unable to make inroads into the opposition's top order. Not one Australian in the top six had yet been dismissed by any of the English medium-pacers. That failing put considerable extra pressure on the spin bowlers.

All was not well either when it came to the captain's man-management. Hammond's relationships with the press were decidedly frosty, while there were signs of tension between him and Compton. Hammond had been unimpressed with what he saw as the Middlesex batsman's 'capering' outside of his crease when facing spin. His view was that the batsman should play the spinners from the crease, rather than using his feet. Hammond could not resist letting the free-spirited Compton know what he thought and the skipper's acid critique did not go down well with a batsman who was touched by genius and capable of finding his own way, thanks all the same.

The MCC party left Perth on the Kalgoorlie train on a Saturday night in late October, ultimately bound for Adelaide, more than a thousand miles to the east. The engine had a cow-catcher on the front, but the train itself did not run to air-conditioning and the journey across the Nullarbor desert was long, tedious and hot, the view from the window largely unchanging: sheep, a dry and empty landscape, with an occasional lonely railway depot township. For a time the track did not deviate from a ruler-straight line for 300 miles. Entertainment on board was confined to a sing-song led by the Lancashire paceman Dick Pollard at the piano in the saloon car, with Godfrey Evans offering assistance. They stopped at Port Pirie, an ugly, industrial town where the rail track ran down the main street. There they played a two-day game against a South Australia Country XI, a team whose weakness disguised the tourists' own fallibility: there were hundreds for Len Hutton (164) and Denis Compton (100), while the opposition were dismissed for 87 and 92, with both Smith and Wright taking eight wickets in the match. James Langridge, who had failed with the bat, took 4-17 in the second innings.

Nullarbor's monotony and the long journey made the players all the more appreciative of Adelaide, its overall elegance and the beauty of The Oval cricket ground. The midnight arrival at the station and chaos at the hotel check-in, which meant some of the players sleeping three to a room that night, was an unwelcome first acquaintance with the city. Pollard, Compton and Langridge, for example, were

obliged to share. The *Daily Telegraph*'s cricket correspondent
E.W. Swanton liked Adelaide but was less impressed with
the cricket to the extent that he found his eyes wandering to
the hills above the city rather than watching MCC's painful
progress against South Australia on an easy batting wicket.
Washbrook and Hutton batted assiduously for five long hours
to score 240 for the first wicket and prompted Swanton to
reflect on the origins of the tour – the Australian government
seeking the quick return of the nation's favourite sport. It had
certainly not been contemplating this kind of phlegmatic,
dour approach when it had pleaded for the English to travel
down under as soon as was possible after the war. MCC
declared at 506/5 and then laboured to bowl South Australia
out twice. This they duly did but were unable to enforce the
win, beaten by the clock. It had been stately cricket, played
at a steady three runs per eight-ball overs.

In these early days of the season, there was great
speculation as to the fitness or otherwise of the Australian
captain Don Bradman. Would he be fit enough to play in the
forthcoming Test series? To Swanton's eye, he looked frail
and somehow diminished, having lost weight and gained
years, his face looking noticeably older. He scored 76 in the
South Australian first innings, however, which seemed to
offer some promise, but he was dropped twice by the young
wicketkeeper Godfrey Evans, both off the bowling of Dick
Pollard. The medium-pacer finally succeeded in getting
the great man's wicket in the second innings for just three
runs. But the overall impression Bradman gave was of a man
struggling with fitness and touch. It was inevitable, this
damage wrought by the passing of the years. After all, he
was not alone. The same symptoms were shown by Wally
Hammond, whose once well-regarded bowling had now
become a rarity: he bowled just three overs in this game and
would not bowl again during the tour.

The travails of touring: as the Indians discovered in the
summer of 1946, no sooner had you got settled in one part of

the country than the schedule required you to move on, often to somewhere far away. On 30 October, the MCC tour party travelled to Melbourne to play Victoria at the Melbourne Cricket Ground (MCG). A rail strike and the fact that the game was due to begin the next day, meant a two-hour flight, something which Lord's had hitherto ruled out, prompted by the uncertain safety record of air travel. The English press, meanwhile, was obliged to travel the 500 miles through the night by coach, arriving jaded and sleepless. Victoria were one of the stronger state sides (the XI for that game included Lindsay Hassett and Keith Miller), but hundreds from Denis Compton and Len Hutton and ten wickets in the match for Doug Wright helped the tourists to win by 224 runs. Encouragingly, both Voce and Bedser took wickets: the Surrey man had 3-40 in the second innings while Voce took 3-48 in the first. Denis Compton broke his bat at one point and his innings was both flamboyant and carefree, characteristics which added to his growing popularity with the Australian public, but which might have been met by his captain's cold suspicion.

The win against Victoria was a welcome boost to morale, but the doubts that had surfaced earlier in the tour showed little sign of disappearing; indeed, there were other troubling signs to consider. Australian cricketers seemed tougher, fitter, and younger than their English counterparts. Then there were the early signs of umpiring issues. The Englishmen were unhappy about what they saw as a reluctance by Australian batsmen to 'walk' when clearly out, preferring to wait for the umpire's decision. In addition, there were growing doubts about the consistency and impartiality of the umpires themselves: J.D. Scott and George Borwick, the men who would officiate in the Tests and provoke controversy, made the acquaintance of the MCC players for the first time on the tour, Scott at Adelaide and Borwick at Sydney in the game against New South Wales. The weather too was oddly unreliable, sometimes hotter than India (or so was the view of those tourists who had served there in the war) and it was also occasionally very wet, with play sometimes restricted by heavy rain. The game against New South Wales, for example, was washed out – two whole days lost to the weather. Moreover, the pitches weren't what had been expected: the wicket at the MCG, for example, deteriorated rapidly after the first day – the ground staff's preparations not helped by the pounding the pitch had received from the boots of American GIs during the war. Ominously too, Australia's great batsman, Bradman, was clearly gaining in health and confidence, his hunted look becoming a thing of the past. In mid-November he scored 43 and 119 for South Australia against Victoria. England's fast bowler problem had been laid bare, highlighted by the fact that Norman Yardley was beginning to be used as a change bowler by Hammond, despite the Yorkshireman having hardly bowled during the 1946 domestic season (31 overs without taking a wicket). Then Laurie Fishlock broke a finger in the nets; Hutton and Bedser suffered bouts of stomach trouble, while Compton's knee was yet another problem. A pessimist might have wondered how many of the five Tests the tourists would manage to win – even how many first-class games, given the squad's weaknesses and the run of bad luck. Then Hammond, having won the toss six times in a row, lost it on the morning of the first Test in Brisbane.

26

D.G. Bradman, not out 28

November 1946

THE TWO Test match captains, Bradman and Hammond, somehow symbolised the weary, creaking state of the post-war world. Neither man was fully fit or in good health. The England captain looked every bit of his 43 years, his teeth stained yellow by decades of nicotine, and his back a constant source of pain. In addition to his physical decline, his domestic life was turbulent, thanks to a messy divorce and his South African wife-to-be's disquiet about her proposed new life in England. Those who cared about Hammond's wellbeing had advised him not to set out on what would be his fourth tour of Australia. Even in the best of times, he was not an easy man. That autumn, worried about cricketing form, his physical decline, his love life, and the demands of leadership, these were far from his halcyon days. He could be taciturn, prone to moods, aloof, and all too likely to produce a stinging remark if the cricket, or a team-mate, didn't meet with his approval. One of his two wicketkeepers on the tour would later comment that he didn't trust him. How corrosive must that be, to lack trust in the man in charge of the team's destiny? It didn't help that, rather than travel by train with the rest of the team, Wally and the team manager, Major Howard, drove in Hammond's newly acquired Jaguar. Rupert Howard was 57 and a former batsman with Lancashire (eight games, predominantly in the early 1920s, averaging 23.7), before becoming the county secretary. He served in both world wars, although it's doubtful whether war service figured large in his conversations with the England captain on their shared road trips across Australia. Mutterings about the skipper's distant relationship with his team-mates and his preference for Howard's company rather than theirs, did not augur well for team spirit on the resumption of Test match combat.

Don Bradman, at 38, was five years younger than the England captain, but his health at the start of the 1946 season was sufficiently poor to suggest that his involvement in the Test series was highly doubtful. As far back as 1940, his eyesight had been judged imperfect (he had been 'rundown', it was said) and, during the war, he suffered badly from fibrositis, a complaint that also plagued Wally Hammond. As a result the Don was invalided out of military service in June 1941. Five years later there were doubts about the great man putting himself through the demands of Test cricket in his present uncertain health – he was seen as a shadow of the batting colossus he had once been. The English tourists watched his struggles with mixed feelings, disturbed by his evident weakness – a fine athlete turned gaunt and thin – but knowing too that even a half-fit Bradman might well be capable of swinging the series Australia's way.

In the end, despite all the doubts, it was Bradman who led the Australians at Brisbane. There were good reasons why he wanted to do so, apart from the wish to savour the pleasure of bat striking ball in Test match conditions. He was very conscious of the inexperience of the Australian XI without him and was persuaded that by standing aside he would be denying his son the chance to see him playing Test cricket for his country. There was also the desire not to end his career on a low note. The last time the two countries had met was at The Oval some eight years earlier when the English had racked up over 900 runs (with Hutton scoring 364). This was not something that could be easily forgotten or forgiven – and the English captain that day had been Walter Hammond.

The Brisbane Test began on 29 November 1946 in weather that held little promise for the tourists. Even in the morning, the heat was unpleasant, a sticky 85°, conditions which the home side might not enjoy, but were more used to than Hammond's men. Walking out on to the field to contest the toss, the two captains – both in whites – could not have looked more different: Bradman in a familiar baggy green cap; Hammond in a rakish trilby, giving him a slightly rascally, spivish air. The Australian fiddled with the peak of his cap as if bothered by the sun, while Hammond stared morosely into the middle distance. They walked side-by-side, companionably it might have been thought, but somehow the edgy stroll out to the middle conveyed a tension between them. Then there was the physical difference: the Don was whippet-thin, while Wally was a big man, broad in the beam, his shirt straining over what was indisputably a corporation rather than a six-pack. They did not speak to each other but were evidently absorbed in their own thoughts. It was not the first time that Hammond and his opposite number had offered such a study in contrasts: when he and Pataudi – touring companions in 1932/33 – had walked out together at The Oval in August 1946, both men were photographed looking morosely at the wet grass. There the similarity ended: cigarette in hand, the England captain has the look of a physics-teaching deputy headmaster, while the pinstriped, double-breasted Pataudi might be a successful banker, or indeed an Indian prince.

Winning the toss and batting first to avoid the worst of the sun and humidity was a priority much to be desired on that Brisbane morning. But there were other worries on Hammond's mind and even more, perhaps, among his team and the English press. There were clear signs that the sides were unequal, with the Australians the stronger and more potent. With the benefit of hindsight, it can be seen that their overall career Test averages were well ahead of their English counterparts; they were younger overall, too: 29 on average as opposed to nearly 32. Dig deeper and the imbalance becomes clearer. For example, the Australian opening batsmen had greater overall flair and, in Sid Barnes, they had someone who posed a more serious, match-winning threat than either Washbrook or Hutton. There was little doubt too that the Australian fast bowlers would target Hutton because of his wartime injury.

Bradman, despite the feeling that he was not the player he had once been, remained a great threat should he ever get settled at the crease. Even Hammond – on paper the tourists' greatest batsman – was forever in Bradman's shadow. The Australian middle order was much stronger too: Keith Miller, the 'Golden Nugget', was potentially a great all-rounder; Colin McCool was a far stronger performer with bat and ball than Jack Ikin; and the Australian wicketkeeper, Don Tallon, was world-class, while there was uncertainty about whether Paul Gibb or Godfrey Evans would be the better option to play in the Test side. Finally the bowling of the home side, particularly Ray Lindwall, was quicker, younger and more dangerous than anything England could muster. Only Bradman's fitness and health; Barnes' mercurial temperament; and lingering doubts about George Tribe's left-arm wrist spin – was he actually good enough for Test cricket? – raised doubts about Australia's potential for retaining the Ashes they had held since 1934.

A cricketer of great experience and knowledge, Hammond was all too aware that any team drawn from the 16 on tour would be tested to the limit. There was much to worry him: Hutton's vulnerable, foreshortened arm; the decision to opt for Gibb behind the stumps; Bedser's inexperience and the workload he must face in the weeks ahead; Voce's age and weight; and what he saw as Doug Wright's brittleness (he had on occasion been unduly impatient with the Kent man). Then there was his own form, ill health and state of mind. The qualities that had so enthused the poet Edmund Blunden – Hammond's quickness of thought, his cricketing wisdom, his reading of the game, even his masterful batting – were all in gradual decline.

* * *

Of the 22 players, the great majority had no experience of an Ashes Test match. Only Sid Barnes, Hassett and Bradman had played against England before. Indeed, seven of the Australian XI had played only one Test: in Auckland, New Zealand, where they had won easily over two days at the end of March 1946. The home side had been dismissed for 42 and 54, the runs gathered at a funereal pace. Rather more of the English had played at least one Ashes Test: Len Hutton, Compton, Edrich, Wright and Hammond (whose Test debut stretched back to 1927 against South Africa in Johannesburg), but all of them were drawing on distant memories from the 1938 series. Interestingly, in the 1946/47 series England had no debutants at all, while Australia blooded six new players: Arthur Morris and George Tribe in the first Test, and then one in each of the subsequent games. It is as if this was a deliberate, measured strategy, far removed from England's hand-to-mouth existence.

The two teams might have within their ranks an exceptional number of players unused to Test cricket, but there were many whose life experience had included years of war service. Hutton, Washbrook, Yardley and Bradman had all, at some time or other, been physical training instructors; Bill Edrich, Keith Miller, Paul Gibb (who had been a pilot, flying Catalina and Sunderland flying boats), Ian Johnson and Colin McCool had been involved in the air war serving with either the RAF or the Royal Australian Air Force. Army service had taken a number far from home: the Middle East, India, Papua New Guinea and Italy among others. Norman Yardley was wounded in action; Hutton suffered a serious accident; Lindwall succumbed to a tropical disease; Don

Tallon, the Australian wicketkeeper, was discharged in 1943 with stomach ulcers and needed a major operation which removed part of his gut; and both captains were released from the armed forces before the war's end, each man much troubled by health issues.

Many of the players in that Brisbane Test were larger-than-life characters: John Arlott, whose natural instinct was to warm to any cricketer, thought Australia's Arthur Morris was one of the most likeable of all time, recognising his charm, philosophy of life and his easy manner. Compton and Miller were men of wit and instinct – and good friends. A number were, or had been, sportsmen in other fields: Lindwall played top-flight rugby league and George Tribe Aussie Rules football. Bill Edrich had been a footballer, a talented winger with Tottenham Hotspur before the war; Denis Compton was with Arsenal from 1936 until 1950, while Walter Hammond had been a speedy forward with Bristol Rovers, making his debut for the club against Brighton over the Christmas period in 1921 and going on to play another 19 games, scoring twice.

Lindsay Hassett and Ernie Toshack were among those whose sense of humour was greatly cherished, while Miller somehow symbolised the view that, while cricket was a joy, life itself was a delightful great adventure, bigger than the game. He anticipated that Test match cricket would be hard and competitive, but he was sure that real pressure was not playing cricket; years later he would define that as 'flying a Mosquito with a Messerschmitt up your arse'.

* * *

Before the Test's preliminaries Hammond would have been all too aware of his long run of success with the toss of the coin and worried about how long this could continue. Winning the toss in the first Test of an Ashes series would be a major bonus. Back in his first series as captain against Australia in 1938, he had won it in each of the four Tests played. After that run of success, he had gone on to win the toss three more times in South Africa, making seven consecutive successful calls. He may have pondered on the extent to which such good fortune with the pre-match coin could so easily turn to its opposite – a series of wrong calls. At all events, in Brisbane on that November day, Hammond's sequence of good luck finally broke and at the worst possible time. Bradman called correctly and with little hesitation – he thought the wicket 'splendid' – elected to bat. The Englishmen were obliged to take the field, consigned to a long day, maybe two, in the unforgiving Queensland heat.

Hammond gave the honour of the first ball delivered in the Test to the veteran pace bowler Bill Voce and he began with a maiden over, raising hopes of a disciplined, professional English performance in the field – runs hard to come by and with a steady fall of wickets. In Bedser's second over, the debutant Arthur Morris was caught at first slip, the ball ending in Hammond's big hands, the catch taken with his trademark unhurried certainty. No doubt Morris cursed his luck, disappointed but reconciled to the fact that very soon he would be listening to his music back in the dressing room: his custom was to bring his own phonograph to pass the time while others were batting. It wasn't long since the two captains had faced each other as the coin spun in the morning sun; now, the rivalry was resumed. They had never warmed to each other and, on this tour, the two men never socialised, or dined together. Bradman admired Hammond, while questioning some of his play on the leg side (notably the hook); Wally thought Bradman a great run-getter, but there were other 'greats' that he would have preferred to watch batting.

Arriving at the wicket earlier than he would have liked – only nine runs on the board – Bradman looked edgy, pale and haunted, a grim-faced shadow of his pre-war majesty, scratching for runs and clearly unhappy with his touch, timing and state of mind. Alec Bedser certainly troubled him early on and twice the ball went in the air off an ill-judged shot. So bothered was the Australian captain that he was grateful for the protection of his batting partner, Sid Barnes. Nonetheless the score mounted slowly with neither side seizing control. The game was delicately poised, but it was clear that dismissing the Australian captain at this stage would have put England on the front foot. Even more significantly, an un-Bradman-like low score might have persuaded him to call time on his playing days, with a profound impact on the rest of the series. After all, not so long ago, it had been touch-and-go whether he would appear in the series at all.

Then England struck again: Barnes losing his wicket this time – 46/2 – leaving Bradman to struggle on, in partnership with his vice-captain, Lindsay Hassett. England pressed hard, with Hammond a calm, controlling presence until, with lunch looming, the score at 74 – and Bradman on 28 – the single most dramatic moment of the series happened. Bill Voce was bowling to Bradman, the latter still edgy and brittle, struggling to recover his seemingly lost greatness, while the Nottinghamshire man was sweating hard in the sweltering mid-day heat. The critical ball was well pitched-up, virtually in the block-hole, and Bradman played an expansive drive wide of cover point, getting enough on it to send the ball flying at shoulder height to Jack Ikin at second slip, who snapped it up hungrily. It was a moment of huge relief for the English, with Hammond so certain that his opposite number and rival was out that he sat down on the grass.

Then it dawned on the England captain that Bradman had stayed put, showing every sign of intending to bat on. The fielders close to the bat were nonplussed – Norman Yardley, for example, at gully was utterly convinced that the ball had come off the top edge of Bradman's bat. Belatedly the Englishmen appealed, only for umpire George Borwick to rule 'not out!' Later the Australian captain would claim that it was a 'bump ball', hitting the ground before flying high to slip. It was troubling too that Borwick had not thought it necessary to consult with his colleague Jack Scott standing at square leg, a logical move to check whether it was indeed a bump ball. Denis Compton thought it one of the most remarkable decisions he had ever seen, a view shared by other English players and pressmen. Later, Compton described the shared sense of injustice. It was a pivotal moment, sufficiently so for those players who had never witnessed Ashes cricket before to realise for the first time that the conflict was precisely that, a war with no quarter given on either side. At the end of the over, as the fielders and umpires shifted positions, Wally Hammond gave his considered opinion to those around him, the umpires and the two batsmen above all. Accounts of the moment report Hammond as saying, 'A fine bloody way to start a series,' but, given the nature of sport, the critical nature of the moment and Hammond's fury, it is fair to say he probably used a stronger word than 'bloody'.

* * *

The incident was hard for the English to forget or forgive, while some of the Australians, including Keith Miller, thought his captain should have admitted that he was out and 'walked'. As for Bradman, he was like a man reprieved, awoken from the dead, the shackles at last removed. From that nervy 28 he went on to make 187, ominously calling for fresh gloves when he reached his century, thereby signalling his intention to bat on and on, with no thought or regret for what had happened that morning. He was perhaps driven by memories of Hammond failing to declare at The Oval eight years before when England batted for two and a half days, reaching 903/7 before declaring and then winning by an astronomical margin. Hammond hadn't even declared at 770/6 when Hutton was dismissed for 364. The Australian total of 645 at Brisbane made on 29 and 30 November 1946 was the largest in Tests on home soil to that date. The English, sent overseas as goodwill ambassadors, found themselves up to their necks in vengeful cricketing warfare.

Then, after Hutton was out cheaply, the weather took a hand, a ferocious storm hitting Brisbane accompanied by intense thunder and lightning, hail lashing the corrugated iron roof of the pavilion, winds at 80 miles per hour and lumps of ice decorating the ground. Within 30 minutes, it was possible to sail a boat across the pitch; the stumps floated away, the sightscreen was blown over and daylight turned the colour of midnight. On Brisbane's beach, surfers needed treatment for head wounds caused by shards of ice falling from the sky. It was now that the full implications of losing the toss became evident, with England obliged to bat on an evil, 'sticky dog' of a pitch – these were the days of uncovered wickets, the batting surface left open to the elements. Batting became a lottery, with the ball rearing fiercely or skidding through. Miller knocked Washbrook's cap off, then reduced his pace until Bradman insisted on him speeding up again. Hammond's painful innings of 32 was judged to be one of his greatest, so bad were the conditions. Miller took 7-60 in the England first innings; Ernie Toshack 6-82 in the second. No one scored higher than the captain in either of England's two innings. The top four were blown away twice in short order, with Denis Compton's 17 in the first innings the meagre best of them. Hutton, of whom so much was expected, scored 7 and 0. Bill Edrich, in scoring 16 in nearly two hours, was hit painfully on the body ten times, while the ball sometimes bit away the top surface of the grass. Then the sun came out and the wicket eased – before a second storm completed England's discomfiture, the game ending in an abject defeat by an innings and 332 runs.

After setting off from England with high hopes, the tourists had suddenly came face to face with reality and the inquest on the events in Brisbane was painful. There had been extenuating circumstances and considerable bad luck, with two storms (one apocalyptic); the requirement to bat second; Bradman's good fortune, or shady reprieve as some thought; and Bedser's illness that stopped him bowling for a time. That was a legacy of his war service in Italy, in itself a reminder as to why this was always going to be a difficult tour. There was much to cause concern: the poor fielding; crucial catches dropped, three of them by wicketkeeper Paul Gibb; the batting blown away twice; and the bowling attack's lack of pace and penetration.

Most worrying of all for Hammond and his men was the sense that during the sapping years of war against Germany, the English had forgotten how to wage war against Australia's unforgiving cricketers. The only glimmer of good news was that Ray Lindwall had been taken to hospital with chicken pox and would miss the next Test, due to begin in only nine days' time.

27

Ashes and Empire
1946/47

BRISBANE'S WEATHER as November turned into
December and the first Test was won and lost had been
hot, humid and sometimes tempestuous and wet. Back in
England it was dull, mild and wet, the snows of winter yet to
come. Indeed, only the Novembers of 1929 and 1940 rivalled
1946 for the amount of rainfall. News of Test cricket being
played across the other side of the world was as depressing
as the dank British weather; moreover it was perfunctory,
brief enough to be easily missed. The BBC Home Service
on 29 November, the first day at Brisbane, had just two five-
minute reports at 8.10 and 9.10 in the morning. There was no
John Arlott to ease the pain of defeat with that reassuring,
countryman's voice: he would spend that winter working
for the BBC, back at his old job as Literary Programmes
Producer, Overseas Service. He was also immersed in
writing *Indian Summer* and looking forward to the visit of
the South African tourists next year. Working late at night
at his typewriter in his house in north London, Arlott
wrote at great pace, producing 60,000 words in just ten
days, revisiting those pleasant days of touring and his fond
memories of the Indians themselves, their humour, charm,
and cricketing ability. The November rain even reminded
him of their arrival in the middle of April's cold downpours

and that dark night when their bus driver lost his way on the winding road to Worcester.

A sensitive, caring man, Arlott would have, from time to time that autumn, paused while writing about those five cricketing months, disturbed by the political chaos consuming India, its divisions and random brutality; the thousands lying dead in the streets of Calcutta (where coincidentally *Indian Summer* would be printed because of the shortages in Britain); the entrenched wrangling between Hindus and Muslims; the number of strikes and disputes; the sense that the country was spinning out of control; that independence might be gained but at what cost? While the MCC tourists were fighting to regain the Ashes in Australia (and eating for England), violence was spreading across India. As England were losing in Brisbane, the men at the head of the Indian warring parties, Jinnah and Nehru, together with Viceroy Archibald Wavell, were flying to London, the Muslim leader remaining resolutely, coldly silent in the narrow confines of the unnervingly small aeroplane. On 5 December, King George VI was obliged to sit between the two leaders, one Muslim and one Hindu, at a Buckingham Palace luncheon. The atmosphere was thoroughly unpleasant. The last attempt by the viceroy to resolve the issue of independence in a deeply divided India through a summit meeting had failed irrevocably.

By the end of the year, Wavell's days were numbered and so too was the concept of an independent All-India. It was clear too that the birth of Pakistan was now inevitable and, with it, the prospect of Tests between the two nations, with some of the All-India players transferring their allegiance. Before that, though, many of India's vast population would be killed, or lose their homes, or, in desperation, trudge east or west to find some kind of sanctuary. To outsiders it must have seemed strange that cricket, a game so rooted in British imperial history, should survive, then flourish, in both India and, eventually, in Pakistan. In the immediate aftermath of Partition, Pakistani cricketers were for some time consigned to playing for what was in effect a third-class cricketing country, unrecognised by the Imperial Cricket Conference (ICC). Meanwhile, Vijay Merchant maintained that the loss of territory deprived India of a valuable source of quick bowlers.

In a sense, cricket had been viewed by some in Britain as a branch of the country's foreign policy, a subtle form of coercion. But, conversely, there were those in India and elsewhere who viewed the game as being riddled with the toxic legacy of imperialism. Nonetheless, cricket's hold was far greater than the increasingly tenuous political links with Britain. Anti-British feeling might be intense, but this most English of games, with its rituals, subtleties and beauty would live on and flourish.

Through many decades, cricket and the empire were inextricably linked, a connection of such importance that an English cricket tour was of significant interest to those charged with British foreign policy. Hence the diplomatic furore over Bodyline. But the war had changed everything, including the concept of empire. Did it occur to anyone among the touring party that the Ashes were – as well as a symbol of a crushing Australian victory many years ago – a fitting symbol of the empire's decline? Britain's Labour government was financially hamstrung and the economic situation, if nothing else, argued for years of parsimony and the relinquishing of the country's imperial expenditure. Britain itself was grey, dismal, hungry and littered with rubble, weeds growing in the bomb sites, its citizens ashen-faced, struggling to view the future with any confidence. Its possessions overseas – how the word 'possessions' grates now – were sensing freedom, and India, at least, was increasingly aware that the road to independence was paved with blood.

Both India and Australia had been threatened from the north by the Japanese during the war: India through Burma; Australia across the Timor Sea, the prospect of

Japanese soldiers swarming ashore on the northern coast. The two countries had contributed hugely to the war effort – by the end India had two million men under arms. But with the war over, the issues facing them were very different. While India stumbled towards independence, Australia was much exercised by the sparseness of its population. There was a strongly expressed opinion that it needed to increase numbers significantly or the nation would 'perish'. Predictably, perhaps, immigration soon became a major issue; so too employment, with the trade unions wary of incomers taking jobs, while women, who had assumed men's jobs during the war, were being ruthlessly sacked and replaced by returning ex-servicemen. It was a confused picture since some politicians were looking to the homeless and destitute of war-torn Europe to fill Australia's population gap, while at the same time, non-white Asians were being deported. Moreover, those who took advantage of cheap and tempting offers to emigrate down under were obliged to take the work given them on arrival for a two-year period, a situation which was viewed by some as 'slave labour'. While the game of cricket struggled with its rebirth in the summer and autumn of 1946 – and into the winter of 1947 – each of the nations playing Tests in those years played the game against a shadowy, troubled background: thin, hungry and battle-weary Englishmen; Indian cricketers all too aware of the prospect of a consuming civil war with the loss of home, family, lives; and Australians uncertain about how it might best grow and assume a significant place in the world. (As for the South Africans, their first post-war Test wasn't until they played at Trent Bridge in June 1947, while West Indies waited until January 1948 – against England in Barbados.)

The post-war world was uncertain, damaged and dangerous. Many Australian cricket-lovers elected to ignore the world's fragility and worry instead about Bradman's continuing fitness and relish the toothless English pace attack and the tourists' limited scope for turning things around in the second Test in Sydney. Then, after the English had been whipped into submission, there was the warming prospect of India's forthcoming tour of Australia in 1947/48.

* * *

At much the same time as India's political fate was being settled, its cricket authorities had decreed that, as Partition loomed, the All-India team that had toured England in the summer should play a series of three games against the 'Rest of India' in Delhi, Bombay and Calcutta. On the same day that MCC were playing in up-country Queensland, at Gympie, and trying to forget about both Bradman's renaissance after his fortuitous 'life' at 28, and the meteorological and cricketing battering in Brisbane, the All-Indian tourists were undergoing their own brand of embarrassment, bowled out in 62 overs for a below-par 177. Only Sohoni with 76 offered much in the way of resistance, while Mushtaq Ali, Modi and Hazare were all dismissed for single figures, leaving the erstwhile tourists 45/5 at one point. Things did not improve second time round and the All-Indian XI subsided to a six-wicket defeat. They would lose again in Bombay a week or so later when England were facing Bradman's men in Sydney.

Preparation for the Sydney Test could scarcely have been more low-key: it was as if the two-day game at Gympie was designed to lull the English into a 48-hour post-prandial doze as well as underline how different Australia was from the UK. The small town was about 120 miles north of Brisbane, its climate subtropically hot, the equator not so very far away. It came into being because of the discovery of gold and the resulting mining, but by 1946 it was predominantly a farming community, growing bananas and pineapples. The town looked neat, well-ordered and picturesque, but for cricketers seeking to recover from a heavy defeat and needing to plot an alternative route to winning the Ashes after that Brisbane fiasco, it was a distraction, a chance missed. They would have been better off, perhaps, with less travelling and hard, focused practice. Getting to the town was an adventure in itself. The bus carrying the more intrepid members of the press had burst a tyre on a crumbling mountain road, leaving the passengers temporarily stranded, lathered in sweat and coated in dust. Once in Gympie, hotels were in short supply and the cricket had a picnic quality. The unreality of it all – and the cavalier waste of valuable planning and practice time – was made worse by the fact that Hammond was nearly a thousand miles away to the south. As soon as the Brisbane Test was over, he had driven to Sydney in the borrowed Jaguar, accompanied by Hutton and Washbrook. The two opening batsmen talked on and off through the Australian night as the 900 miles of country roads unwound. Hammond though was taciturn and brooding, his silence only broken when he asked one of his passengers to light him another cigarette.

Only Compton, Ikin, Yardley, Gibb and Voce from the Brisbane defeat played at Gympie. Godfrey Evans, in a move that would signal a change for the next Test match, was the preferred wicketkeeper. Laurie Fishlock, recovered from his broken finger, played and scored an encouraging 62. After two days of gentle cricket that drifted to a draw, and slightly more demanding hospitality, England's cricketers travelled down to Sydney and a reunion with Hammond and his two opening batsmen, and, soon after, another confrontation with an Australian side relishing signs of English weakness. Both sides, it can be safely assumed, were more concerned with the Ashes than the politics associated with the end of empire.

28

Facing the Storm in Sydney

December 1946

WALTER HAMMOND had fond memories of the Sydney Cricket Ground, having scored an unbeaten double hundred (231*) there back in 1936 in a Test which England won under Gubby Allen's captaincy. Allen had won the toss; England had scored 426 and then bowled out Australia for 80 in the first innings (Bradman out for 0; Bill Voce and Gubby Allen taking seven wickets between them) and 324 in the second. Hammond had even taken three wickets (for 29) when the Australians batted again. Back then, Hammond had been at the very top of his game; now he was plainly unfit and in middle-aged decline; despairing of his side's underpowered bowling attack and in the throes of a personal crisis – one which was played out in public view, thanks to the newspapers on either side of the world. After the disappointment of Brisbane, the England captain was preoccupied, both with team selection and the evident strength of the Australians – were there weaknesses as yet undiscovered that his team could exploit? Perhaps it was thinking about these two related issues which made him so withdrawn and taciturn on that long drive to Sydney in the borrowed Jaguar with Hutton and Washbrook.

When it came down to it, England made just two changes for the game beginning on 13 December: Godfrey

Evans came in for Paul Gibb (which potentially weakened the batting but improved the chances of catches being taken behind the stumps); and Peter Smith for the sadly ineffective Bill Voce, a shadow of the man of ten years before. Unlike at Brisbane, Hammond won the toss and, with little hesitation, elected to bat first: it was what you did in Sydney. Ideally, you called correctly, then batted solidly for a day and a half, thereby rendering defeat highly unlikely. Get upwards of 450, even 475, and then bowl at tired Australian batsmen as the second day draws towards its close, nipping out two or three early on. That should have been the plan.

It did not go that way: Washbrook was out within minutes of the start, his stumps in disarray. Thereafter the innings slowly subsided to a dismal 255: runs for Edrich (71) and Ikin (60), but not for Hammond, caught behind for 1. Jim Swanton was not alone in thinking the English batting 'palsied'. It was as if they were mesmerised by the unexpected turn the Australians were extracting from the wicket so early in the match. That wasn't supposed to happen in Sydney, where the ball might be expected to spin towards the end of the game; certainly not from the first day. The Englishmen had no answer to the threat, caught leaden-footed in the crease while Ian Johnson bowled an artful spell, the ball offered in slow parabolas of flight. It was a case, not for the first or last time, of Australian flair and risk against English caution and stolid defiance. Johnson took six wickets, conceding just 42 runs in his 30.1 overs. As for Hammond, his plans and hopes for a spirited recovery from the defeat at the Gabba were reduced to dust, when what he thought was the main strength of his side – the batting – had failed by early on in the second day. It was now for the bowlers to rescue the situation, something which the captain knew would be a struggle. It was a grim situation, but not an impossible one. Then the weather intervened, only nine minutes into the Australian reply.

Initially, the problem was bad light which took the players off the field. That was the overture to a torrential rainstorm, accompanied by thunder and vivid flashes of lightning. At Manchester or Headingley, it would have ended play until after the weekend, but down under, conditions were such that play could be resumed after only three hours. There were hints that the freak storm might have played to England's advantage, the pitch turning spiteful, the stuff of dreams to the English bowlers. That possibility seemed more likely when Arthur Morris was soon dismissed by Bill Edrich, the ball sufficiently hazardous to make the batsman instinctively turn his back as it reared towards him. All too aware of the risk the pitch now presented, Bradman opted to change the batting order, sending in Ian Johnson and thereby preserving his own wicket until things had eased, although there were suggestions that he was hindered by a leg injury. In the end, he batted at number 6. The Australian batsmen at the crease thereupon pressurised the umpires with five appeals against the light in quick succession and, eventually, Scott and Borwick decided that the light had deteriorated enough to pocket the bails and walk towards the pavilion. All in all, the second day ended with England still in contention: Australia were 228 behind with nine wickets standing. Looking out of the hotel window the following morning, though, Hammond might well have groaned at the sight of a bright, untroubled sun and a drying breeze. The storms, cloud and bad light of the previous day were gone and the Sunday rest day would be one of benign weather and a healing pitch.

Monday, 16 December proved a perfect day for the home side, and while Johnson, the nightwatchman, was soon dismissed (a second wicket for Edrich), the Australians increasingly batted with remorseless assurance. On the grassy slope of the Sydney Hill, the crowd baked in the sun, beer bottles close at hand, newspapers folded into sunhats, and with raucous banter aimed at the sweating English fielders growing louder by the hour. Hammond's men, fielding in temperatures of 100°, managed to keep in the game well into the day. Then, with Australia still almost 100 behind, Don Bradman walked out to bat. He and Sid Barnes stayed together in a marathon partnership, batting on and on, until nearly the close of the following day, both of them scoring 234 (it was Barnes' highest Test score). By then – the fourth day of six – there were still two days of the game left and, at 571/6, Bradman's team led by 316. The Australian captain, mindful of events at The Oval before the war, decided against a declaration and batted on until, at a massive 659/8, he eventually decided that the time was right to unleash his bowlers on the exhausted Englishmen. England were 404 runs behind with five sessions remaining: saving the game would be a major challenge. It had been a gruelling few days for them: for example, Smith and Wright, the English spinners, had taken three wickets between them, but bowled 83 overs during which they had conceded 341 runs. The sole crumb of comfort was that the wicketkeeper, Godfrey Evans, in only his second Test match, had not conceded a single bye in the innings.

There were doubts about Bradman's decision to bat on, some from within the Australian's own ranks. At lunchtime, Miller went to the English dressing room to voice his anger at Bradman's tactics. As has often been the case with England, the second innings proved a better effort than the first and the penultimate day closed with the tourists on 247/3, with Bill Edrich and Walter Hammond at the wicket and hope not quite extinguished. Earlier, the unfortunate Len Hutton had been dismissed by Miller on the last ball before lunch, hitting his wicket when he seemed to be going well. He had lost his grip on the bat when the thumb of his batting glove slipped off and the bat had then broken the stumps. Edrich went on to make a courageous 119, but wickets fell steadily, and, at the end, in a limp flurry. It was all over by the middle of the afternoon and England found themselves two down in the series, the Ashes receding into the far distance. Christmas was only six days away: the Englishmen were far from home and family; the tour still had three months to go; and the realisation was dawning that this unforgiving Australian side were stronger in every aspect of the game.

* * *

Godfrey Evans went surfing on Christmas Day. Three Yorkshiremen – the vice-captain Norman Yardley, Bill Bowes and Brian Sellers (both now working journalists) – took themselves to Palm Beach, while a fourth, Hutton, had a quiet day back in Sydney. Evans was too much of a newcomer to Test cricket to be able to analyse the overall state of play with any certainty; moreover, he was preoccupied with his novice struggles with a surfboard – that was enough to be dealing with on Christmas Day on the beach. By contrast, each of the four Yorkshiremen – the two current players and the two pressmen – could not avoid reflecting on what had gone wrong with England's cricket. Intriguingly, Sellers was a selector as well as a journalist and he knew more than a bit about captaincy, leading Yorkshire to the County Championship six times in his years at the helm (from 1933 to 1947). He was an outspoken man but a run-of-the-mill batsman, otherwise he might have been an England captain. At all events, he was less than enthusiastic about Hammond's leadership.

Len Hutton admired Hammond greatly as a batsman – the best player, he believed, on all kinds of batting surfaces. In his autobiography, *Just My Story*, he was less enthusiastic, however, about his captain's leadership qualities. Hutton's greater concern as 1946 drew to a close was that he was at the sharp end of Australia's pace attack and acutely aware of his struggle against Miller and Lindwall's bouncers, handicapped as he was by his stunted left arm. As for Bowes, he was a deep thinker about the game and his own war had been more punishing than most. He for one certainly asked himself questions about the reasons why the Australians dominated.

Was it down to the relative riches of Australian food? Were they somehow intrinsically tougher? Did the climate make a difference? Were English nerves damaged by the war and its years of air raids, tragic news, restrictions and uncertainty? Whatever the reason, England had not won an Ashes series since 1932/33. From December 1920 onwards, they had won just 15 Tests to Australia's 22. (Twelve were drawn and one, at Manchester, was abandoned without a ball being bowled.) It was 1928/29 before a series went emphatically England's way. Disconcertingly, before 1946 England had done well at both Brisbane and Sydney, never having lost at the former and with four consecutive victories at the SCG. Somehow their early and heavy defeats at grounds where they had performed well in the past suggested that the pattern of defeat might continue in Melbourne, where the third Test would begin before the Christmas decorations had been taken down.

29

Melbourne

January 1947

HAD WALTER Hammond had a choice about how he would have preferred to spend the last night of 1946, it is highly likely that he would have opted for being cosily tucked up in bed with his South African beauty queen, Sybil, looking out at the snow through the leaded windows of his rambling Cotswold mansion (Thrupp House) from beneath freshly laundered sheets. Instead, he was all too conscious of how far he was from home (enduring a hot summer's night in a Melbourne hotel, and not in a wintry Gloucestershire). Without Sybil, what was there to occupy his mind but cricket? There was much to think about, and not much of it good. Moreover, there had been only a few days in which to recover from the celebrations at Christmas and that second demoralising Test defeat in Sydney – and the Melbourne Test was due to start on the first day of 1947. Despite the need for a good night's sleep, there was much to keep Wally awake deep into the night. He, like the press and the lovers of the game back home, could not help but wonder if the English had the mental strength, let alone the cricketing ability, to claw their way back into the series.

In his dreams, Hammond would have hoped to begin by winning the toss, then bat first on a flat, benign wicket, having been able to select from a squad untroubled by injuries or poor form. The weather would have more resembled a June day in Arundel or Canterbury rather than Melbourne in the heat. Hutton and Washbrook would bat serenely through till lunch and beyond; Ray Lindwall's hamstrings would have gone and Keith Miller been warned for running on to the pitch. Even better, Bradman would succumb to a chronic stomach problem after a heavy lunch and need to lie down for hours in a darkened room. Without their captain, the Australian ship would have rapidly foundered: catches dropped and morale sinking fast. With his firm hand gone, things would fall apart for the Australians and when England bowled, the wicket would have suddenly been transformed into a pace bowler's paradise: Bedser yards quicker than Lindwall, and Bill Voce, the years stripped away, able to make the Australian batsmen tremble.

There was, though, no escaping the reality of the situation that Hammond and his men faced – and how different the two sets of players were. Physically, they even looked different: for example, there were the numbers of diminutive figures among the Australians, tanned, wiry and spare. The captain was one such; so too Lindsay Hassett and Arthur Morris; while the English looked pallid in comparison and, in the case of the medium-pace bowlers, stolid and heavy, brawny – unlike their slim, powerful Australian counterparts. Despite the weeks of sun down under, the Englishmen were unmistakeably north European, products of that continent's grey weather and long winters, the wartime years of thin rations, dark nights and fear of what might lie ahead. The England squad was older and looked it: tired cricketers, some of them clearly verging on middle age.

The differences between the two sides did not end there. For example, the absence of any significant distinction between amateur and professional in Australia reveals something of the sharp class divide in England. The English XI included a number from relatively modest backgrounds, including Hutton, Compton, Voce and Bedser. Len Hutton's father, for example, was a foreman-joiner and bricklayer; Bedser senior was also a brickie, invariably engaged in a grim struggle to find work, a preoccupation for many in the 1930s. It appears that Bedser became a Test cricketer before his family home had a bathroom. Compton's father at one time was a struggling painter and decorator before being obliged to take a job as a lorry driver, something which involved long journeys through the night. Only Norman Yardley had gone to a university (Cambridge), although he, Evans and Edrich had all been to fee-paying schools, but most of the rest were products of a school system in which many youngsters left at 14 – Butler's Education Act (which extended the leaving age to 15) had only been passed two years or so before. Some players had taken the precaution of learning work skills on which they could rely if a career in cricket failed to develop: Hutton studied technical drawing in an extra year at school; Voce was a miner; Bedser worked in a solicitor's office. Did the authorities at Lord's worry that the men representing English cricket in Australia were not all from what they might describe as the 'top drawer'? After all, Hammond had had to lose his professional status before being appointed captain of his country.

There was little evidence of such an attitude among the Australians, reflecting a different perspective on social class. Their Test side, interestingly, was mostly drawn from the south-eastern quarter of the country: Sydney and Melbourne in particular. Their backgrounds included three (Sid Barnes, Arthur Morris and Ernie Toshack) who were raised by single parents, while Lindsay Hassett was brought up in a family of nine. Their fathers' occupations ranged from sheep farmer, schoolteacher (Morris), farmer and carpenter (Bradman) and estate agent (Hassett); while their own work experience – they were all amateur cricketers – included the motor trade (Barnes, Hassett), and building (Ernie Toshack was a foreman on building sites). Bradman worked as an estate agent and stockbroker, while, incongruously, the fearsome fast bowler Ray Lindwall would later co-run a flower shop in Brisbane with his wife.

* * *

At the toss, Hammond and Bradman watched the coin spin and fall, and, despite the England captain's misleading signal to the dressing room (which had Hutton and Washbrook hurriedly, if unnecessarily, looking for their pads), it was Bradman who called correctly. England made one change from the Sydney Test (Voce coming in for Smith) and the team entered the MCG on a day reminiscent of English summer. The crowd was large and partisan – it would total 66,274 that day – and for a short while there was no sign of a cloud, either real or symbolic. It wasn't long, however, before things started to go wrong for the visitors: Arthur Morris was dropped by Godfrey Evans off Bedser. Then Bill Voce bowled a short ball to Sid Barnes whose hook shot struck Edrich, fielding close in at short leg. The blow was a brutal one on his kneecap. He collapsed like a felled tree and, soon after, limped off the field. By lunch, Australia were 71 for just one wicket, with Bradman ominously poised and Voce unable to continue, his strained groin keeping him in the treatment room and leaving England with just two front-line bowlers – against Bradman on a perfect wicket. Later, with the new ball due, there was no alternative but to give it to Norman Yardley, no more than a gutsy stock bowler. Despite everything, Australia fell away to a below-par 192/6 at one point. It would have been even better had Keith Miller not been 'caught' off a no-ball.

Thursday, 2 January was a better day for England: unexpectedly Edrich's knee responded to treatment and he was able to bowl, getting Don Tallon's wicket early on, caught behind by Godfrey Evans for 35. Colin McCool, however, continued unbeaten till the end, achieving his first Test century (104 not out). The Australian innings ended at a slightly below-par 365. The Test was broadly following the pattern of the series thus far: the Australians being able to bat right down to their last man, with England demonstrably short of bowlers, and aggressive fast bowlers in particular. It left England invariably struggling to drive home any advantage that might come their way.

When it was England's turn to bat, they soon lost Hutton (for only 2) to Lindwall whose exhilarating, ferocious aggression was of a different order to anything seen in the match thus far. For all that, the second day closed with England still in the game at 147/1. The next day, however, was one of grey cloud and darker controversy. Umpire Scott was at the centre of it, giving Edrich out leg before wicket for 89 off a ball that the Middlesex man was convinced he had edged. Up to that point he had been batting bravely, seemingly unruffled by Lindwall's pace. Once the umpire had raised his finger, Edrich walked off in a state of furious disbelief and did not keep his anger to himself, giving his opinion on the decision to anyone who would listen, including a number of newspapermen.

The incident brought echoes of the moment when Jack Ikin had 'caught' Bradman at Brisbane. No doubt, Hammond saw it as a fine way to continue the series, cursing his continuing bad luck and the umpire's fallibility. Scott later claimed that he saw clear daylight between bat and ball – the ball he believed could only have struck the pad, with no bat involved, leaving him in no doubt that Edrich was palpably lbw. Once the series was over, it would seem that Scott had had enough, retiring from the game, muttering about ill-founded reporting from the cricketing press, its English members in particular.

If the mood was soured on the pitch, any prospect of it being quickly dispelled was lost when Denis Compton was soon controversially given out to Ernie Toshack having made only 11 – another lbw and another angry batsman. Compton contended he was not out, the ball having pitched well outside leg stump. Despite such disasters, England eked out their innings, reaching a total of 351 all out, just 14 runs short of the Australian total, with Ikin, Washbrook, Edrich and Yardley all making significant contributions. By the close that lead had been extended to 47, with both openers, Barnes and Morris, still in. The crowd was even bigger on the next day, a Saturday, with 72,022 in the MCG, and now the game began to drift inexorably away from England. The tourists' meagre bowling resources were at full stretch – Voce was still off the field – and Australia flourished, despite losing Bradman just short of a fifty, caught and bowled by Yardley. Umpire Jack Scott provoked further English displeasure by turning down an appeal against Bradman for lbw, judging it 'too high'.

By that point in the game, it became a question for Hammond's men of surviving against mounting odds – why, even Ray Lindwall, batting at number 9, scored a hundred – and the England captain might have bitterly reflected on which of his own bowlers would have been capable of such a feat. England's number 9 was Voce, whose Test batting average was a little over 13. Eventually England were set 551 to win in just over seven hours, an unlikely target if ever there was one. There were short breaks for rain; insistent spells of leg spin from the Australians; another low score from Hammond (bowled by Lindwall); a hundred from Washbrook; and defiance from Yardley (undefeated for almost 90 minutes at the crease) and Bedser towards the end. So it was that England escaped with a draw, the first drawn Ashes Test in Australia since 1881/82. The result was an improvement on Brisbane and Sydney and the tourists had shown courage, particularly in a dogged bowling performance under great difficulties. There were innings to cherish from Washbrook and Edrich, while Yardley had scored 61 and 53 not out, as well as taking five wickets in the match. But there were two prevailing feelings for the English: the first was a smouldering resentment aimed at the two Australian men in white coats. Above all, though, was the wider implications of the failure to win the match. With only two Tests left and the Australians two-nil up in the series, all hope of regaining the Ashes was gone.

30

Umpires
1946–47

BORWICK AND Scott look more like ice-cream vendors than Test match umpires officiating in an Ashes series, or perhaps the resemblance is more akin to senior citizens on a budget holiday, as they walk through the pavilion gates towards the middle. There is a hint too of a music-hall duo setting off into the twilight of their vaudeville careers. Sporting broad-brimmed white hats, Australian badges on their buttoned-up jackets, white collars and funereal ties, they look imbued with confidence, late-middle-aged men possessed of certainty and stubborn, truculent determination, come what may. The two of them are in step with each other as they walk on to the playing area, presenting a unified front. Jack Scott and George Borwick are small men, both bantams – feisty and peppery. The photograph of the two, emerging from the pavilion at Sydney, is unforgiving: one of them clearly has an index finger – the digit that decides – with an arthritic, old man's gnarled look. Scott was the elder, by eight years, born in New South Wales in 1888. On New Year's Day 1947 he was approaching 60. In his time, he had been an aggressive quick bowler for South Australia, good enough to be the first man to dismiss Don Bradman in first-class cricket, and possessing a fiery temperament, a man not averse to querying an umpire's judgement. It was perhaps a case of poacher turned gamekeeper. Both men look older than their age, a distant generation from the young men over whom they presided.

Borwick and Scott had stood in each of the Tests a decade before in the 1936/37 tour, without provoking much in the way of controversy. That particular 'Goodwill Tour', after the trauma of Bodyline, was always likely to be a less heated affair and so it proved. But now Scott and Borwick were ten years older, inevitably rustier – short of recent matchday experience after years without umpiring – and less able perhaps to cope with pressure, their older eyes struggling with Australian light, their faculties challenged by the game's sudden twists and turns, and moments of unexpected doubt. They were, however, judged to be the best umpires that Australia could muster. On 11 November, over a fortnight before the first Test, Norman Yardley had observed 'a shadow no bigger than a man's hand' when Denis Compton was surprisingly given out stumped in a game against an Australian XI at Melbourne. So taken aback was the Middlesex man that he was smiling at the absurdity of the appeal before it reached its crescendo. He hadn't even bothered to look behind him to check whether his back foot was behind the line, so sure was he of his position.

Yardley was also unnerved by the custom the Australian batsmen had of staying put, choosing not to 'walk' but rather to wait for an appeal to the umpire, even when they were clearly out. It was this difference between the two sides that provided the context in which Bradman survived the notorious Ikin 'catch' at Brisbane. The Australian captain simply stared at the ground throughout the incident, the belated appeal and the contentious decision, then resumed his guard, waiting for the next ball. It became a matter of cricketing legend; moreover, there were some, both English and Australian, who were greatly troubled by what had happened and by the fitness of the umpires for their job. The former Australian batsman Jack Fingleton was disturbed both by the fact that umpire Scott was perhaps unduly close to the cricket establishment and that he could remember all too clearly an occasion when the young Scott – when he was still playing the game, rather than standing in judgement on it – jumped into the midst of the crowd in Sydney to take matters up with a group of barrackers, thereby provoking a lively fracas, and a subsequent lengthy ban.

Despite his concerns about the quality of the umpiring in Brisbane and Sydney, and to his great credit, Hammond did not ask for their replacement and Borwick and Scott had duly officiated at Melbourne in the New Year Test. They would preside at Adelaide, too, in the fourth Test that began on 31 January. Concern about the umpiring did not go away in Adelaide, a new cause for doubt arising over the discrepancy between the number of 'no-balls' called by the umpires: twice as many as committed by the English bowlers, mainly Bedser and Doug Wright, whose confidence suffered through the slow drip-drip of the umpires' decisions. The issue was sufficiently disturbing for the England captain to ask Yardley to field at mid-on, instructing him to watch for overstepping and to check on the legitimacy of the umpires' calls. Over the series as a whole, the Australian bowlers were 'called' just 13 times; the English 34, a ratio not entirely explained by the greater amount of bowling the English were obliged to do. After Melbourne, Hammond wrote to the Australian Board expressing his dissatisfaction with the standard of umpiring, deeming that both Borwick and Scott were 'incompetent'. It cut no ice with the board, although they did seek evidence. Hammond was unwilling to provide examples and the outcome was that the umpires were left unchanged for the series.

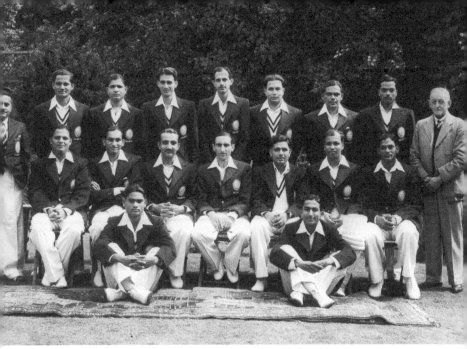

The All-India tourists in 1946. The captain, the Nawab of Pataudi, is in the centre; the manager, Pankaj Gupta, is on the far left.

Photographed at Lord's in late summer 1946, the MCC tourists before sailing for their Ashes assignation down under.

Pataudi, Amarnath and Banerjee arrive at Bournemouth courtesy of BOAC and via New Delhi, Karachi and Cairo: 'on the aerodrome tarmac in the rain.'

With Pataudi ill, Vijay Merchant assumed the captaincy at Lord's against MCC on 25 May 1946. The stand-in skipper scored 148.

Wally Hammond, captain of Gloucestershire and England, on 1 May 1946: 'Feeling pretty good. See you for pre-season. We want to win the Championship.'

Hedley Verity of Yorkshire and England photographed in 1932. That year he was named one of the Wisden Cricketers of the Year.

England's Paul Gibb and the Indian keeper Hindlekar. Gibb made 60 but John Arlott thought it 'perhaps the least impressive match-winning innings ever played'.

All smiles from the Ashes captains, Bradman and Hammond, at a reception in Adelaide. The mood would change as the series unfolded.

Refugees after India's Partition: millions displaced and fleeing for their lives.

John Arlott on his last day of commentary, 2 September 1980: '…after Trevor Bailey, it'll be Christopher Martin-Jenkins.'

The new Viceroy Lord Mountbatten meets Nehru, Liaquat Ali Khan and Field Marshal Claude Auchinleck, March 1947. George Abell, civil servant and cricketer, is doing the introductions.

Walter Hammond drives Keith Miller in the third Victory Test, July 1945 at a packed Lord's.

Joe Hardstaff (England) nudges the ball between Australian fielders Ray Lindwall and Colin McCool in the drawn fourth Test, Adelaide (1947).

'Three chilly days in spring': Worcestershire v All-India, 4 May 1946.

The Lord's Test, England v India, June 1946: cricket and a beer, rediscovering the joys of peacetime.

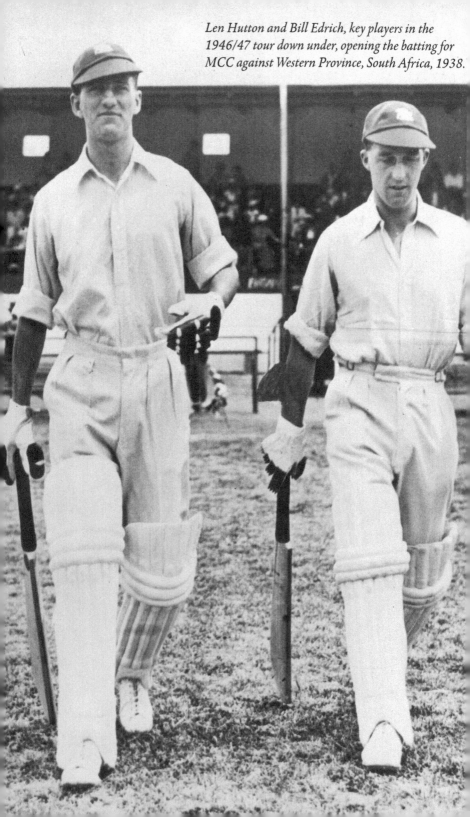

Len Hutton and Bill Edrich, key players in the 1946/47 tour down under, opening the batting for MCC against Western Province, South Africa, 1938.

31

A Tour Too Far?

January 1947

THERE WERE still two months of England's tour remaining and the strain was beginning to tell, not least on the captain. Hammond was struggling both physically and mentally and it showed all too clearly in his batting form and in the way that he conducted himself as captain. His fibrositis never really went away and, at its worst, caused him crippling back pain. It was said that he would take a dozen aspirins before batting, a desperate ritual watched by his team-mates with a mixture of concern and disbelief. He felt jaded, too tired and listless to raise his game. His form in the Tests thus far had been disappointing – he was not alone in that respect – but for a man with his pedigree, his feeble total of 128 runs in the three Tests to date (at an average of just 21.3) was deeply worrying. Had he been a young hopeful, his form would have seen him left out of the side. He was very aware that his dearth of runs rendered the England middle order uncomfortably fragile. His bleak form also compared badly with that of his opposite number – there was a man who had been thought, at one time, too unfit and unwell to play at all in the series. In the event Don Bradman had defied predictions of his imminent retirement, scoring 549 runs to that point in the series at an average of 137.3. Significantly, perhaps, Hammond, once known around the cricketing world for his grace and footwork against spinners, had lost his wicket five times in the three Tests to leg-break bowlers. At Melbourne it was the speed of Ray Lindwall which had shattered his stumps in the second innings.

Hammond was low enough, without taking into account what he and others regarded as the deeply flawed umpiring decisions that had characterised the series. Their contentious nature was made worse by the fact that some of the officials' errors happened at the most critical of moments, just when England could see a breakthrough or a chance to seize the initiative. There was that 'life' at Brisbane given to Bradman when he had been all at sea, scratchy and uncertain, and Ikin's 'catch' had been judged no such thing. He had gone on to score 159 more runs. Then there was the lbw judgement against Bill Edrich at Melbourne as he was closing in on his century, the blow made worse by Denis Compton being given out soon after in what were similarly controversial circumstances. Those two dubious decisions had reduced England from a healthy 167/2 to 176/4 in a matter of minutes. All this contributed to the pressures mounting on the England captain. As well as the unrelenting disappointments of the tour, there was the ongoing public drama of his divorce, together with the loneliness back in England of his wife-to-be. By the time his thoughts turned to the next Test match, to be played in Adelaide, his mood matched his batting form – sinking lower by the day. The signs of considerable stress were very evident and, later, he would say that he had been close to a breakdown. Cricket is a team game but one which also places the individual into situations of the highest pressure when a player is conclusively alone and highly vulnerable. By January 1947, Hammond felt isolated and fragile, understandably contemplating walking away from the things that had brought him so low.

So, walking away is what he did, albeit temporarily. From Melbourne the team was scheduled to travel to Tasmania to play two matches, but Hammond elected to opt out, handing over the captaincy to Yardley. At a press conference the team manager, Major Rupert Howard, who had grown accustomed to sitting beside his taciturn captain in the leathered luxury of the borrowed Jaguar as they bowled along dusty Australian tarmacadam, sought to reassure reporters that Hammond simply needed a holiday, having played in nine of the last ten matches, including all three Tests. It was a somewhat disingenuous argument since a number of other players had pushed themselves equally hard in the previous weeks. Alec Bedser, for example, had bowled some 233 eight-ball overs during the same period, while both Hutton and Washbrook had also missed only the one game. Howard preferred to plead the case of a tired man needing a break, rather than admitting that his captain was suffering from the acute strain of being in charge of an underpowered and outplayed XI, as well as the pain of facing the end of his long and illustrious career. The Australian press took a dim view of Hammond's stepping aside.

The team was on the island for nine days, playing two three-day games, both of which ended in draws. It was significantly cooler there, more reminiscent of an English summer, and in Hobart the game was played on a ground set between the blue of the city's harbour and the looming shadow of Mount Wellington. Yardley won the toss and presided over the familiar Hammond experience of watching the batting collapse early on. This particular batting crisis – 53/4 – was inflicted by a Tasmanian travel agent who could bowl uncomfortably and inhospitably fast. A solid second innings, with runs being shared throughout the team, managed to save the game. It was noticeable that Denis Compton, freed of Hammond's baleful shadow, struck form at last, scoring 124.

Six relatively tranquil days of cricket were played on the island and the rest of the time was spent enjoying a Tasman holiday. Yardley went fishing and yachting, for example. On one day, the players were bussed up into the mountains for a sightseeing trip, although the coach lacked the horsepower to manage the full sweep of hairpin bends to the summit – or perhaps it was the burden of too many overweight cricketers. The interlude of peace couldn't last, of course: instead, the cricketers took a ship back across the Bass Straits, then spent a Sunday in Melbourne, before taking the night train to Adelaide and a few days off. On Friday, 24 January, they began a game against South Australia. Any semblance of holiday was gone by then, however: the weather was stiflingly hot (over 100°), making rooms oven-like and wrecking any prospect of a good night's sleep. If that wasn't enough, Bradman would be playing and Hammond would be obliged to face him once again after his nine days of freedom.

It seemed that the short break had worked for Hammond: he scored 188, batting for nearly seven hours, while James Langridge also scored a hundred. The Sussex man, however, further aggravated his groin injury and would not play again in the tour. MCC's mammoth 577 provoked a similarly weighty riposte from South Australia (443), but with Bradman falling to Doug Wright for only 5. The inevitable draw ensued and thoughts turned towards the next Test in Adelaide beginning in three days' time.

* * *

An Australian series down under has always been the ultimate test of an English cricket captain. Over the period 1900 to 1946, only four had won in Australia: Pelham Warner (in 1903/04), J.W.H.T. Douglas (1911/12), Percy Chapman (1928/29) and Douglas Jardine (1932/33) – all of them from southern teams (Middlesex, Essex, Kent and Surrey). Four more have won there since 1946: Len Hutton (1954/55), Raymond Illingworth (1970/71), Mike Brearley (1978/79), Mike Gatting (1986/87) and Andrew Strauss (2010/11) – two Yorkshiremen, two from Middlesex and one born in Johannesburg. Only Strauss, who played for Middlesex, achieved the feat in the first two decades of the 21st century.

Walter Hammond played under three different captains during his pre-war tours of Australia. Like him, all three of them struggled for runs in the Tests: Percy Chapman in 1928 scored just 165 runs at an average of 23.57; four years later Douglas Jardine made 199 at 22.11 on the Bodyline tour; and Gubby Allen, in 1936, scored 150 at 18.75, as well as taking 17 wickets at 30.94. There was nothing Wally could learn from them as batsmen but taken together they offered interesting models of captaincy: Chapman and Allen worked hard to forge a positive atmosphere – a 'splendid harmony' was a feature of Chapman's regime and Hammond later reflected on his 'sanguine' attitude and his ability to form strong friendships. Hammond regarded Allen as a good captain. In the last pre-war Ashes tour, Allen had been keen to foster team spirit, although privately he held a more acerbic perspective on his men. Writing to his 'Darling Dad' in September 1936, from the Royal Mail ship *Orion*, he reported that so far no one had yet 'got tight'. At a fancy-dress party on board – where the wicketkeeper Les Ames appeared as Hitler – he reluctantly stayed up late to ensure that there would be no unfortunate incidents. It seems that Bill Voce removed his shoes and socks and helped the deckhands wash the decks, but overall, everyone had behaved, even one of the fast bowlers who, contrary to expectations, stayed quiet and held back on his drinking. What caused Allen most bother once the tour had begun wasn't the behaviour or performances of his players, but the constant, tedious treadmill of speech-making. He regarded that as the principal reason why captains of touring teams in Australia were destined to fail. An added burden was that he felt obliged to play in every game himself since MCC did not want to see a professional leading the side. Team spirit might have been crucial to Allen, but it didn't stem private disdain – player X was not very bright; player Y was unduly stubborn; and Z was far too fat.

Percy Chapman was also a gifted tactician and a captain who inspired the team with his excellent fielding, usually close in at gully or silly mid-off. Douglas Jardine, for his part, was tough and uncompromising, although off the field he was a genial figure with a sense of humour. He inspired fierce loyalty, ran a tight, disciplined ship and took great pains to look after his players, for example, allegedly quenching the thirst of his star fast bowler Harold Larwood with champagne on at least one occasion. Moreover, he was a thoughtful and adroit tactician on the field. Significantly, though, all three were younger than Hammond when captaining in Australia. Percy Chapman was 28, Jardine 32 and Allen 34.

There was evidently bad blood between the two captains in the 1946/47 Ashes series; perhaps there was always going to be ill feeling between them – jealousy and resentment – from the moment when Bradman's greatness outshone Hammond's unparalleled stardom early in the previous decade. The bump ball/catch by Jack Ikin at Brisbane guaranteed that the first post-war series would not be the celebration of brotherhood between the two countries, the grand tour of ambassadorial goodwill that Attlee had signalled before the tour began. Hammond had played under some good captains, not only with England; Gloucestershire's Bev Lyon, for example, was a strong influence too – not just his sartorial style (the off-field trilby and suit; the on-field nonchalantly placed handkerchief) – but where Bradman had received praise from many quarters for his leadership, Hammond was seen as plodding and defensive. The Australian captain would long remember the perverse decision by his opposite number to bat on for one ball after lunch in the Adelaide Test before declaring, a ploy that wasted valuable time. A later captain of England, Mike Brearley, would write about the key characteristics of cricket captaincy, emphasising, for example, the importance of lateral thinking, empathy, the avoidance of 'drift', leading by example, the ability to motivate, the need to consult and the skill of 'making something happen'.

The manager, Rupert Howard, had also been on Gubby Allen's tour before the war, working in the same capacity.

He would have found it hard to resist making comparisons between Bradman and Hammond and could not have been blind to the latter's problems: his domestic situation; his physical decline; his tendency to be over-cautious as captain; his reluctance to seize an advantage when it had been all too apparent; his questionable field placements, particularly for Doug Wright; and his equally dubious man-management. Morose and moody, he took too long to make decisions, allowing his opposite number to seize the initiative and dictate the game's tempo. Moreover he could not, it seemed, in these twilight days of his illustrious career, even secure a fair share of luck.

But perhaps things would change in the fourth Test in Adelaide, beginning on 31 January. After all, Walter had enjoyed a rest and had then scored a big hundred only a few days before. It would, however, prove to be his last Test in Australia, with only a curtain-call appearance in the solitary Test in New Zealand in the tour's final days.

32

The Ageing British Umpire

1942–47

WHILE MESSRS Borwick and Scott were gearing up for the beginning of the New Year and the opening overs of the Melbourne Test, the Indian players from the summer tour to England were discovering the kind of batting solidity that would have served them well earlier in the year. Playing against a Rest of India XI in Calcutta, they had finished the first day's play at an eye-watering 449/2, with Modi 156 not out and Amarnath unbeaten on 243. Back in England, winter was closing in, while in Australia Hammond's men were facing up to the realisation that they were simply not good enough, choosing to attribute that inferiority to the war, the weather, bad luck and two flawed Australian umpires. India, by contrast, was on the very edge of civil war. Cricket might be continuing but the country was increasingly divided, fragile and volatile, its peace threatened by the potent mix of religious difference and the rising anger of those seeking freedom from the British. During the war years India had been shaken by things beyond its control: the 'Quit India' movement had gathered momentum; there had been a massive cyclone in Bengal in October 1942, followed by three tidal waves; the Japanese had long threatened an invasion, its troops infiltrating from across the border with Burma and attacking India's northern territories; and Bengal had suffered famine the impact of which was of biblical proportions.

In March 1943, a cricket match was played between a Bijapur Famine XI and a Bengal Cyclone XI at the Brabourne Stadium, Bombay, to raise funds for those affected by the two disasters. The game included a number of players who, three years later, would be part of the Indian tour to England: Mushtaq Ali, Hazare (he scored a double century), Gul Mohammad and Nayudu, for Bengal; Sohoni, Sarwate, Amarnath and Merchant for Bijapur. The famine situation deteriorated rapidly, however, and by August that year some 2,000 people were dying of hunger and disease on the streets of Calcutta every week. At the best of times, the state of Bengal was difficult to administer – it was heavily overpopulated and desperately poor, conditions far beyond the creaking machinery of government administered by the British, a situation which worsened as the war ground on. By 1946 many British troops and officials were keen to leave a land where murder and arson were becoming commonplace. Britain was essentially bankrupt, its government preoccupied with how best to revitalise the country without spiralling even further into debt. Dispensing with the financial drain of empire seemed both wise and inevitable, as well as being in tune with the gathering demands for independence. On the playing fields of empire, the ageing British Umpire had settled for a quiet life, hands resolutely in his pockets, just letting the game flow, keen for the final innings to end.

Britain's pride in its 'jewel in the crown' had long stood on the shakiest of foundations. It could boast of its infrastructure improvements in India, its canal building and its railway system, but the latter, in truth, was more to do with facilitating the rapid deployment around the country of British soldiers. The canals boosted the fertility of the Punjab, but there was no escaping the fact that, by 1944, in a land where half the population of India was under the age of 20, life expectancy was shamefully low. The insensitive paternalism of the Raj was nowhere more evident than in the way India had been brought into the war: its governor-general and viceroy, Lord Linlithgow, had seen fit to declare that India was at war with Germany on 3 September 1939, the same day as the 'mother country'. Other than the Muslim scholar charged with translating the announcement into Urdu, not one Indian was consulted. The leader of the Indian Congress, Jawaharlal Nehru, was understandably furious. Throughout the war, Nehru, the Muslim leader, Muhammad Ali Jinnah, and Mahatma Gandhi, the erstwhile lawyer and non-violent exponent of Indian independence, were all variously engaged in resistance to British rule and, in the case of Jinnah and Nehru, to each other. The British government was much exercised by the damage that could be done to the war effort in India by those imprisoned for supporting 'an illegal mass movement' – as a draft Cabinet Office note described it in May 1943. Gandhi's refusal to abandon his movement's policies and practices guaranteed his continuing captivity. This was a man who when asked in 1933 for his view of Western civilisation replied that he thought it would be a good idea.

On 15 August 1945, the day when war with Japan ended, it was announced in King George VI's speech that the new Labour government would seek an 'early realisation of self-government in India'. The viceroy, Archibald Wavell, had already opened discussions in Simla with the Indian political leaders who had been imprisoned for years. Gandhi himself had been released earlier, in 1944, as a result of concerns that his hunger strikes might end his life. He had been imprisoned in Poona in a former palace of the Aga Khan, while Nehru had been kept in the fort at Ahmednagar, 160 miles east of Bombay, his confinement lasting almost three years. Wavell knew India well – he had spent 13 years of his life there – and he was a considerable improvement on his predecessor as viceroy. Nonetheless, he had not enjoyed Churchill's full trust, nor did he get on well with the incoming prime minister,

Clement Attlee. Moreover, Labour's new foreign secretary, Ernest Bevin, was keen to replace Wavell with someone who could disentangle his country's destiny from that of India's. The objective was for Britain to leave the subcontinent with, as Bevin put it, the empire's 'dignity' upheld. At the same time, there was also the question of India's strategic importance in the post-war world, particularly its north-west frontier and the proximity to it of both China and Russia. A further factor in the determination of British policy was that Jawaharlal Nehru was on friendly terms with both of those communist countries.

Those with power, both British and Indian, were at odds and pulling in very different directions in the latter part of 1945 and on into the following year. Indeed, the months when the Indian cricketers were progressing from Bradford through Manchester to Lord's and Scarborough – July until September 1946 – were the critical ones for hopes of any peaceful resolution to the question of Indian independence. As the clock ticked, hope faded and diplomatic words proved woefully inadequate. On 15 August 1946, Nehru wrote to Jinnah suggesting that they meet for talks in Bombay. After an hour and 20 minutes, the meeting, held at Jinnah's mansion, broke up with no agreement reached. In Calcutta, the capital of Bengal, tensions were now very high. Jinnah had declared that 16 August should be a day of 'Direct Action' and Bengal's chief minister, H.S. Suhrawardy, raised the stakes by designating it an official holiday. Predictably, street demonstrations soon turned into violent riots and the Calcutta police were rapidly overwhelmed. Gangs of killers roamed the streets hunting down victims. It more resembled a pogrom than a riot, with thousands of dead – perhaps 5,000 – both Hindu and Muslim. The scattered bodies reminded American photographer Margaret Bourke-White, then working for *Life* magazine, of the Nazi death camps at Auschwitz and Buchenwald. The butchery was at its worst in the south of Calcutta, but the city as a whole was affected, disfigured, bloody corpses scattered far and wide. Moreover, the killing spread throughout northern India: in Bihar, for example, 8,000 Muslims were massacred in October by Hindu gangs. There were many instances of enforced religious conversions, of grotesque atrocities, of homes and shops razed to the ground.

At the same time the political manoeuvring grew ever more shrill and embittered. At the end of August 1946, Wavell met Gandhi and Nehru in an attempt to find a constructive way forward, a forlorn aspiration whose hopelessness was best summed up by Gandhi's despairing comment, 'If India wants her bloodbath, she shall have it!' Gandhi's philosophy somehow seemed out of step with the present situation: after the 'Great Calcutta Killing' he begged Hindus to resist retaliation and, instead, to 'die fearlessly', and he exhorted women to commit suicide rather than be raped. By September, he was actively advocating Wavell's removal from the viceroyalty.

This was the country to which India's cricketers returned from their long tour in England; it was deeply troubled, with every indication that things would get worse, such was the level of venom and uncertainty. For those in the squad with homes or family connections in the Punjab or Bengal – Pataudi, Lala Amarnath, Gul Mohammad, Shute Banerjee and Abdul Hafeez – the situation would have been highly disturbing. Each day of cricket coincided with more evidence of political turmoil on the road to civil war. On 2 September, when the disenchanted Viceroy swore in Nehru's interim administration, India's cricketers were thrashing Middlesex at Lord's, Shute Banerjee taking four wickets as the county subsided to 82 all out and an innings defeat.

The 1946 tourists had been called 'All-India' but geographically the team was largely drawn from Bombay and the northern half of India. Religiously they were mixed, although predominantly Hindu and Muslim, though not quite in the broadly equal ratio that was the case in the populations of Bengal and the Punjab. Once back in India, and given the volatile mood in the country, it was inevitable that the Muslims among the squad would be contemplating the prospect of playing for Pakistan sooner rather than later. Certainly, the birth of that country seemed ever more likely as 1946 drew to a close and the bitter intensity of religious opposition grew.

In October 1946 Nehru decided to visit the tribal areas along the Indian border with Afghanistan. It was an unsettling experience: he was faced with considerable hostility and feared for his life. It brought home to him the desperate state the country was in – thousands of refugees traversing the land in desperate and forlorn attempts to find safety, often obliged to leave most of their possessions behind, and private militias growing now that the regulations governing their existence had been lifted. The same month Jinnah appointed two new deputy commanders to the Muslim League National Guard, whose numbers increased rapidly, reaching 60,000 by the end of the year.

The December meeting in London, to which Wavell, Nehru and Jinnah travelled together in virtual silence, achieved nothing but bitterness and frustration, not helped by events outside the meeting room: Wavell's impending removal in favour of Viscount Louis Mountbatten (later Earl Mountbatten of Burma) who had been offered the viceroyalty on 18 December 1946; the backing that the leader of the opposition, Winston Churchill, gave to the Muslim cause and the establishment of the Pakistan state; and the shaky economic foundations of Britain, with its government's attendant anxieties and fears about foreign policy – Burma and Palestine as well as India. So far as the latter was concerned, if the British stood back and let India descend into civil war, would Russia take it upon itself to intervene?

The situation for the British in India was the classic umpire's dilemma: if in doubt, avoid making a decision, keep the declaratory finger in the white jacket pocket and rely on an impassive, stern face. Or ignore any scintilla of doubt, look firm and unflinching, and make a brave, irrevocable decision. The British Umpire, presiding over this shadowy game between India's past and future, as well as the chaotic, blood-stained end of empire, felt there was little option but to stand back and let the two sides make up their own rules. The problem was that the divisions in India seemed ever wider, with both sides preferring to shun the other. So it was, for example, that in February 1947, the Ranji Trophy semi-final between Northern India and Holkar fell victim to the widening bloodshed and violence. The game, due to begin on 8 February, was awarded to Holkar without a ball being bowled. Two days earlier, the fourth Ashes Test in Adelaide had ended.

33

Hammond's End

February–March 1947

THOSE IN the know feared for Len Hutton, recognising that the injury he had sustained in that York gymnasium during the war might eventually even end his career. Shortly before the Adelaide Test, a former England Test cricketer – was it Bill Bowes? – suggested to Hutton that the Australian quick bowlers were intent on trying to put him in hospital. The mix of hard wickets, high-quality pacemen and a key English batsman with a visible weakness was too tempting a target. After all, Hutton's injury had been career-threatening, so restricting that he had been unable to hold his first-born son in his arms – Richard had been born in September 1942, 18 months after his father's accident. (Hutton Junior would go on to make his Test debut at Lord's against Pakistan in 1971.)

The fourth Test in Adelaide was played in terrible heat and high humidity, with the temperature most days over the 100° mark and reaching 105° on occasions. England's dismal sequence of bad luck, however, seemed to have receded. After Hammond had won the toss, and Hutton and Washbrook had put on 137 for the first wicket, England batted themselves into a strong position, with Denis Compton scoring a fine hundred (147) without giving a chance. The total of 460 was England's highest of the series. The *Daily Telegraph*'s

E.W. Swanton dined with the Bradmans on the evening of the second day but missed the concluding over in which the stalwart, persistent Bedser bowled Australia's captain for a duck. Bradman thought the delivery from the Surrey man – a fast leg break – was the finest he ever faced. The day ended with Australia on 24/2 – a position of some comfort, unlike the England team's hotel which had no air-conditioning on a night when the heat was unrelenting. Bedser was among those who suffered from it, unsurprisingly since he had bowled 22 eight-ball overs during the day. On the field, Bedser's legs in his heavy woollen cricket flannels were slick with sweat and, after his bowling stint was over, he had been violently sick in the shower.

Australia ended the second day a daunting 436 behind, with Harvey and Bradman both out. That was the high point of the Test for the English since only Bedser tested the opposition when the Australia innings resumed; the rest of the bowling – Edrich, Wright, Yardley, Ikin and Compton – was simply not good enough, only one of them a front-line bowler. Keith Miller and Arthur Morris both scored hundreds and the first innings ended with England behind by 27. The heat got worse as the Test unfolded and a sharp storm on the fourth day made the likelihood of a draw more certain. Hammond was faced with a dilemma: when should he declare? What target would give his men a chance of snatching victory, tempt the Australians, but guarantee that they did not take an unlikely win? In great pain, the skipper failed once again with the bat, scoring just 22, and England were grateful to Compton for another century. Hammond's final stroke in Australia proved to be a cavalier swish to the leg side off Ernie Toshack, worth four runs, but instead plucked from the air brilliantly by Ray Lindwall, fielding just 20 yards from the bat.

Whether it was the heat, or frustration with the Adelaide pitch – a bowlers' graveyard – the energy levels had flagged and tempers had risen. Bradman was irritated by Compton's adroit manipulation of the strike when batting with Godfrey Evans, managing to face most of the bowling himself. The Australian captain sourly told him that 'it wasn't cricket'. Compton's response was sharp, suggesting that the Don might bring his men in from where they had been patrolling on the boundary edge. Bradman did so – and then fumed as Compton split the field with a cleanly hit four. Later Bradman protested again, this time about the Middlesex man's spikes roughing up the pitch as he ran between the wickets, pointing out that his team would have to bat last on it. 'I am *terribly* sorry,' Compton said, 'but I'm playing for our side.' Then, perversely, it seemed to Bradman, Hammond delayed the English declaration until after the first ball of the afternoon session – thus losing from what was left of the game the time allowed for the change between innings. It was no surprise when the Australians made no attempt to get the 314 runs they needed to win in the three and a quarter hours that remained and so the game meandered to a draw, with Australia 215/1 at the close.

* * *

So, the England squad returned to Sydney for the final Test after six long months of touring. It was the end of February and the final Test of the series was about to begin. The opportunity to regain the Ashes had been lost long ago and now Hammond's end had come. For 27 consecutive matches he had played for his country, 19 of them as captain, the run stretching back to July 1936. He had not scored a hundred for England since August 1939 (against West Indies a matter of days before their touring party had sailed for home and the war had begun). Wally was one final Test away from the end of it all, but it would not be against Australia. A further bout of fibrositis kept him out of the side for the fifth Test.

For now, with that final New Zealand Test to come at Christchurch in March, the captaincy passed to Norman Yardley. It was anticipated, in view of the amount of rain in

Sydney, that the pitch would favour the ball and England played the extra bowler they should have deployed at Adelaide: Laurie Fishlock and Peter Smith came in for Hammond and Joe Hardstaff. Don Bradman spun a Victorian four-shilling piece at the toss and Yardley duly won it, electing to bat. Since the Adelaide Test, Hutton, as some had feared, had been hospitalised by an Australian quick bowler, Ginty Lush of New South Wales, but he had recovered and was declared fit to open with Cyril Washbrook. The latter departed early and Edrich came in to replace him; thereafter progress was slow, with the wicket already taking some spin. The batting on that first day was patchy at best, and England subsided from a healthy 151/2 to 237/6 at the close. Hutton was undefeated with 122, but the Australian pacemen had battered all the English batsmen: a rearing bouncer from Lindwall removed Bill Edrich, who made 60, and Denis Compton fell for 17, treading on his wicket trying to avoid yet another bouncer.

With Hutton still at the wicket, England might have hoped perhaps to reach 350, but overnight he was struck down with tonsillitis, suffering a temperature of 103° and leaving him unable to speak. He was taken to hospital and played no further part in the game. The England innings without Hutton fell away to a disappointing 280. When it came to the Australian first innings, Doug Wright and Alec Bedser bowled well, but it was not enough: England's frail batting had determined the result. Compton thought the cricket in this Test was the best of the series, but, Yardley's promising captaincy apart, little went right: selection had been limited by injuries (Hammond, Hardstaff and Langridge all unfit); the weather was unhelpful, so wet that mushrooms were seen growing in the outfield on the Sunday; the umpires – the fireproof Borwick and Scott still standing – refused justifiable appeals against the light; the temperature again topped 100°; Laurie Fishlock, deputising for Hutton as a makeshift opener in the second innings, was out first ball; and Edrich dropped Bradman in the second innings.

Hammond had long presided over events from first slip, but he was gone and the former captain's safe pair of hands was greatly missed. On 5 March 1947, England lost the final Test of the series by five wickets. The series was won 3-0 by Australia, with two matches drawn.

* * *

The day the Sydney Test ended, Lahore in India's Punjab was in flames. Two days before, on 3 March, the premier of the Punjab had resigned and, the following day, Muslim gangs in Lahore had attacked both Sikhs and Hindus. On 7 March, in Amritsar, law and order had broken down. Through the previous month, India had burned: in the United Provinces instances of robbery had risen by 56% and murder by nearly a half. The Wavells were preparing to leave Delhi, the viceroy less than enamoured of his treatment by the British government – 'dismissed like a cook' he wrote to Field Marshal Auchinleck, Commander-in-Chief, British India.

Wavell's replacement, 'Dickie' Mountbatten, would arrive in India on 22 March, the second day of England's one-off Test in New Zealand. It was a time when cricket was far from the minds of politicians, administrators and those caught up in the struggle for Indian independence. It is, though, an interesting quirk of history that the man who served both Wavell and Mountbatten as private secretary, and advised on matters relating to the Punjab, was a former county cricketer. George Abell, who had an important role in the plan for the Partition of India, also played for Worcestershire, among others. He began his county career in August 1923 – aged 19 – and played against Gloucestershire that month in a game where the 20-year-old Walter Hammond scored ducks in both innings. For his part, Abell made 50 in the Worcestershire second innings. Overall he played some 75 first-class games, averaging nearly 25 with the bat. Making his debut for Northern India against the Army in December 1934 in Lahore, he scored 210; he also kept wicket and had six victims in the match. Over his career he played with or against a number of the cricketers in this book, including Vijay Merchant, Dattaram Hindlekar, Mushtaq Ali, Harold Gimblett, Douglas Jardine, Alf Gover, Tom Goddard, Charlie Barnett, Maurice Turnbull and the captain of the 1936 Indian tourists, the Maharajkumar of Vizianagaram – the much maligned 'Vizzy'. He also played *for* India against Ceylon in Lahore in December 1932.

Sir George Abell – knighted shortly after Indian independence – was also instrumental in the shaping of an organised cricket structure in what would become Pakistan after 1947. Of much greater significance than his cricketing pedigree, however, was his detailed, day-to-day policy work on Indian independence, working with Wavell, Mountbatten and others, including Sir Cyril Radcliffe, the Inner Temple lawyer charged with drawing the new border between India and Pakistan – and someone who had never been to India (and who, after the arbitrary line across the Punjab had been drawn, never went back to the country). Perhaps amid the intrigue, bloodshed and mayhem, George Abell turned a weary eye to the cricket score from New Zealand and imagined for a moment a world where the threat to life and limb was confined to a short rising ball from a genuine quick bowler on a fiery pitch.

34

What Went Wrong, Mr Hammond?
March 1947

LYING WIDE awake beside a sleeping Sybil on their wedding night, Walter Hammond juggled thoughts of a new life thankfully empty of cricketing responsibility and living in some sprawling, ivy-covered mansion, in Stroud, perhaps, or Dursley – the heart of Gloucestershire, anyway – with all-too-vivid recollections of the six months in Australia. At some point, he knew, he would have to report back on what had gone well (not much) and explain away the disappointments (legion). No longer captain, indeed no more a cricketer, there would still be demands upon him – from an MCC concerned that this powerful Australian team would be touring England in the summer of 1948 and wondering what needed to change (other than the captain). Then there was the press, both sportswriters and scandalmongers, keen to point the finger of blame. Hammond's defence to questions about overall defeat and the manner of each disappointment boiled down to one simple fact, namely that, man for man, the Australians were clearly superior. Stronger, younger, fitter. Hammond remembered sitting in a deckchair on the sun-deck of the *Stirling Castle* and looking with a jaundiced eye at his men, disconcertingly pale, war-weary, uncomfortably bloated after a large ship's breakfast on stomachs used to thin porridge, and many of them nudging an age when they would have preferred a quiet time pruning the roses.

Hammond turned over, looked across at the slim tanned back on the other side of the bed, and reran the grim sequence of bad luck that had plagued his final series as captain: the injuries, the idiosyncratic umpiring, the dropped catches, and the weather that impacted negatively on practice in the nets. But, as a thinking cricketer, he recognised some uncomfortable truths about his own leadership. Not only was his batting now much inferior to the Australian captain's, so too was his captaincy. It was less ruthless, more passive, less incisive. Bradman's field setting was more considered; inventive too. Was there value in pointing out to MCC that the Australians tended to choose their eleven players first and then nominate a captain from those selected? England usually did it the other way round and perhaps that should change? Wally knew too that his preference for his own company – was it shyness, anxiety, mean-spiritedness, or something deeper? – set him apart from the team. Uncomfortably, he recalled the long drive to Sydney, with Hutton and Washbrook chatting amicably while he stared beyond the Jaguar's windscreen wishing he was done with Australia.

He knew that not everything was his fault. The selectors should take some of the blame and, in truth, the hand they had been dealt was flawed. There was no Hedley Verity nor Ken Farnes, and there was no escaping the absence of bowlers offering anything resembling genuine pace. But the selection overall was clearly weak in certain areas. Included in the party were players who were simply not good enough, while they had chosen all-rounders who fell short of Test standard as both batsmen and bowlers.

Hammond nestled against Sybil's back, out of fondness, but also for warmth – this was England in early April, remember – and he found himself thinking of the baleful weather down under, particularly the gruelling heat and the cataclysmic rainstorms, and the influence of both on the flaky cricket England had played. He knew too that his frame of mind and health were damaged. Perversely, Bradman had approached the series uncertain whether he had the necessary level of fitness: he had looked wan and weak, and yet, as games came and went, so his strength returned, as well as his unparalleled batting. Hammond by contrast was a martyr to his back and his worries. On top of that came the endless travelling with the added burden of nights sleeping on trains, the long sequence of anonymous hotel rooms, the social pressures of captaincy – the speeches, the queries from the press, the cycle of receptions and dinners, and the worries about his own batting which included an unexpected, sudden weakness against spin. It had all served to put him into a downward spiral.

It was little comfort that there was a precedent for the debacle. In the series played in the aftermath of the Great War, in 1920/21, England had also failed to win a Test. Hammond's back ached – when did it not? – and he got out of bed, went to the window and looked out over the lights of London, remembering the days of blackout. Behind him he heard Sybil sigh and turn away from the light. He was glad to be home, cricket done with, but there was the little matter of what would become of them both. How would he cope without the sun on his back, a bat in his hand and runs on the board? And how would Sybil cope with exile from South African sun?

* * *

By the time the opening overs of the Test in New Zealand were bowled, the start of the 1947 English cricket season was barely a month away. The weather in Christchurch over the four days of the Test provided a sharp reminder of England in April – indeed, the three-day game was extended to a fourth day to compensate for a washout on the third. Then that day was abandoned too. There was insufficient time for more than one innings per side and it was telling that New

Zealand made 345 (Walter Hadlee 116), whereas against Australia 12 months before, they had been dismissed for 42 and 54. In his final Test match, Hammond top-scored with 79 in an England total of 265/7 declared.

The tour ended on 25 March and then there was just the slow return home, not by boat (except for the heavy bags and three team members – Gibb, Hardstaff and Langridge – who sailed on the *Largs Castle*), but by air. That meant the languid luxury of a BOAC flying boat, a flight of a week or so with a precise ritual that would all too soon be a thing of the past: the weigh-in (to check whether each passenger was below the maximum safe weight); the distinctive smell on board of coffee, oil, the sea and polish; the reassuring words of *Hints for your Comfort* to read as waves of harbour water swept past the windows and the aircraft reached for the sky. The pace of the experience was as slow as the opening overs of a Roses match, but there were comforts you didn't get at Leeds or Old Trafford: a steward provided cocoa, aspirin, Bovril, bridge cards – what you will – plus a mouth-watering menu and the elegant rhythms of silver service. There were 12 stops on the return flight, the players crossing Partitioned India, landing briefly at Calcutta and Karachi – the latter now in Pakistan – as well as Singapore and Cairo.

The week-long flight gave ample time – too much perhaps – for each man to reflect on six months of cricket and exile, its highs and lows, inescapable thoughts in the slow air-tour from the ceiling of 10,000 feet. Alec Bedser sat back and contemplated his improvement, an education in cricket, courtesy of Bradman, Barnes and Arthur Morris. Denis Compton had struck convincing form in the second half of the tour; Bill Edrich had scored more runs than anyone; while Doug Wright and Cyril Washbrook had both impressed, if only at times.

In any squad of 16 tourists there will be times when injuries prompt concerns about whether the reserves are sufficient or good enough. There will be other occasions when everyone is fit and five will not be selected and cannot play. Inevitably then there were some members of the England tour party who had been on the periphery of the trip and whose memories of those long months criss-crossing Australia will have been tinged with regret and disappointment. Dick Pollard, for example, had played in four of the five 'Victory Tests' in 1945: 'Sergeant R. Pollard' was then the leading wicket-taker on either side, with 25. The following year he was still waiting to be discharged from the armed forces and he played only 12 games for Lancashire, taking 55 wickets. He and Bill Voce were given special leave from the army to make the Australian tour, but neither bowler was quick enough to trouble Test-class batsmen in the conditions down under. Pollard took 28 wickets, averaging 36, but didn't appear in any of the Ashes Tests, although he played in Christchurch against New Zealand and took three wickets. In the main part of the tour, his weight, rabbit-like batting and ponderous fielding all counted against him.

James Langridge would celebrate his 41st birthday halfway through the 1947 season. Even in those days of mature, battle-hardened cricketers determined to squeeze the last moments out of their cricketing lives, Langridge could see the end of his career looming. It had been a bitterly disappointing tour for him, the regret heightened by the way the war years had confined his Test career to just eight games. There had been eyebrows raised when he was selected for the tour, some hard-nosed critics arguing that he was always destined to be a passenger, not enough of a specialist as a batsman or a bowler to force his way into Hammond's team. His selection stemmed from a strong season with the ball in the summer of 1946, although when picked for the final, rain-soaked Test against India at The Oval, he bowled 29 wicketless overs and didn't get a chance to bat. That proved to be his final Test match, although he played on for Sussex until 1953. Australian pitches and its climate combined to defeat him. He was chosen for the Melbourne Test only to suffer a groin injury in the preparation for the game and, if he had been fit enough, he might have been selected for the last two Tests. In the event he played just four games during the whole tour. The 1947 season couldn't come quickly enough – ah, the prospect of Sussex versus Hampshire at Portsmouth in the middle of May!

For his part Joe Hardstaff would go on to play four more Tests, but his contribution to the Ashes series was limited to Adelaide in January where he scored 67. He had been a regular member of the England XI before the war but played only eight games on the tour. Like Langridge, he would be left out of matches against the state sides to allow batting practice for those earmarked to play in the Tests. Poignantly, his cricketing father, Joe Hardstaff Senior, died on 2 April as his son was travelling home.

It was 9 April before the returning tourists landed in Poole harbour with the County Championship due to begin in a month's time. The following day, Walter Hammond married his South African beauty queen, Sybil Ness-Harvey, in Kingston Registry Office in south-west London. Major Rupert Howard and his wife were two of the four guests in the quintessential 'quiet wedding'. The opening match for the South African tourists would be played at Worcester, beginning on 30 April, while Gloucestershire's first game – against Oxford University – was on 3 May. Hammond was not in the side, having retired from cricket. At some point he had informed Gloucestershire that he intended to resign from the captaincy and leave the first-class game.

* * *

No doubt Hammond would have worried about how best to explain the disappointing performance of England down under. He knew that there were important lessons to be learned for the future of English cricket, if not for his own career. It was, after all, only a year before the Australians toured over here and it was essential that the mistakes

WHAT WENT WRONG, MR HAMMOND?

and weaknesses evident down under should be addressed. Hammond knew too that he was likely to be both questioned and blamed for the limp resistance the English had displayed in the Tests. At the same time he was preoccupied with his own future, both domestic – the imminent wedding – and professional, given that retirement was equally close.

What follows is not Walter Hammond's work but an attempt to capture what he knew in his heart of hearts. It is, of course, fiction, but based on the reality of that difficult tour down under.

A Report on MCC's Tour of Australia and New Zealand, 1946/47

1. **Fitness of the squad**: Despite my best efforts, both on board our outward-bound ship and in the nets, we were not fit enough to combat the much sharper, battle-hardened Australians. We had injuries that hit us hard, while the opposition was significantly more fortunate in that regard. Indeed, the man we expected to withdraw from the series, Don Bradman, simply recovered his health and strength throughout the series. His runs took hope away from us.

2. **Age**: We were overburdened with older cricketers, myself included, I have to say! The average age was 33, while Evans was the youngest at 26. The war can be blamed for the failure to identify young cricketing prospects, but the fact remains that three of our party were over 40 years old.

3. **The bowling**. We lacked firepower, possessing none with the venom and energy of Lindwall and Miller. Bedser and Wright, although always willing, were overworked. The spinners were a mixed bag: Wright was good on his day, but his 23 Test wickets were too expensive (at over 43 each). Smith was simply not up to the task.

4. **The batting**. Quite simply, we were unable to score enough runs. In the game where we posted our highest total (460 in the fourth Test at Adelaide) we were able to secure a comfortable draw. But overall we averaged only 287 per innings, while Australia's equivalent was 422 (including two incomplete innings of 215/1 and 214/5). Key batsmen took time to run into form. The combination of the Bodyline legacy and Hutton's wartime injury seemed to provoke a bouncer war from the Australians. Hard to show goodwill in such circumstances! All too often the batting collapsed like a pack of cards (Sydney for example) and none of our left-handers came good.

5. **The fielding**. Overall ours compared unfavourably with Australia's.

6. **The Australian umpires**: Both Borwick and Scott who officiated throughout were barely competent; worse, their errors seemed to affect us significantly more than they did the Australians.

7. **Weather**: If the umpires' decisions largely went against us, so did the weather, both in terms of storms (which always seemed to work in the Australians' favour) and the intensity of the heat and light.

8. **Other considerations**. Two spring to mind: first the pitches frequently surprised by their characteristics – excessive turn on the first day in a Test match, for example. The itinerary too was over-demanding, given the distances involved and the fragility of our thin squad.

We turn now to the players:

- **Len Hutton**: Unquestionably a fine batsman and a potential captain at some future date (if one can ignore his professional status). However, his wartime injury seemed to spur the Australian pacemen on: hence the barrage of bouncers he endured. Nonetheless, with a top score of 122 not out, he was our most successful batsman, averaging 52.12 in the Tests. His average overall was nearly 20 runs higher, however.

- **Cyril Washbrook**: At his best a capable performer with the bat and a top-class fielder in the covers. Less free in his strokeplay than in England, but solid and dependable. His Test average of 36.3 slightly disappointed, however, and his top score of 112 disguises a run of low scores: 6 and 13 at Brisbane; 1 and 0 (Sydney).

- **Denis Compton**: Second in the batting averages in the Tests (459 runs at 51). He struggled for runs, however, in the first three Tests, scoring 17, 15, 5, 54, 11 and 14.

Popular with the crowd and better when attacking. Not the easiest man to advise.

- **Joe Hardstaff**: Deserted by his touch for much of the tour and played in just one Test (at Adelaide where he scored 67 and 9).

- **James Langridge**: One of three men over 40 in the touring party. He certainly tried hard, but his bowling was marred by his erratic length and a reluctance to give the ball air – and when he did he was punished for it. There were considerable issues over his fitness and he only played in four matches.

- **Bill Edrich**: He was a key member of the touring party, performing well in the Tests with both bat and ball: (he averaged 46.2 as a batsman, often in particularly difficult circumstances; and also took nine wickets, albeit expensively).

- **Laurie Fishlock**: Another 'senior' cricketer. . He proved injury-prone (a badly strained muscle in his leg, as well as a finger injury). I do, however, stand by his original selection: his form in the summer certainly justified it. Having said that, his previous tour down under, in 1936/37 was equally underwhelming: after a sound start (91 against a Western Australia Combined XI at Perth in October 1936), his batting deteriorated to the extent that he had eight single-figure scores in his ten games. Thus he made only 318 runs throughout that tour at a disappointing average of just over 21. That wasn't enough to earn Test selection in Gubby Allen's XI and his pre-war memories of Australia would have been more bitter than sweet. Ten years later, things hadn't changed much: Fishlock played only ten matches altogether on this tour, averaging a fraction over 20. His one Test was disappointing: at Sydney where he scored 14 and 0.

- **Jack Ikin**: He is a fine fieldsman, but not good enough as a bowler of spin at Test level. Batted soundly and with courage, often at key moments.

- **Norman Yardley**: Surprised with his ability to assume the role of stock bowler. Staunch support and responsible. A fighter. Excellent in the field.

- **Godfrey Evans**: Perhaps our most improved player and, with hindsight, should have played at Brisbane. It was telling that he conceded no byes when he was brought in to replace Gibb for the Test at Sydney.

- **Paul Gibb**: Began the tour as first-choice wicketkeeper and was behind the stumps in the first Test, although I had been exercised as to whether he or Evans should have the gloves at Brisbane. Frankly, he struggled, often seeming unable to read Doug Wright's spin. He dropped several crucial catches, while his form with the bat was no better than mediocre. After Brisbane he played only three more games, with Evans keeping his Test place and benefiting from playing in the state games.

- **Peter Smith**: Tended to bowl too slowly and was reluctant to toss the ball up. Flimsy batting disappointed since there had been high hopes he would contribute with the bat. There were occasions when he did well, but not on the highest stage. His finger injury on his bowling hand and his appendix-related hospital stay at one point were both handicaps. In his two Tests he failed to trouble the Australian batsmen, taking just two wickets at 109 runs each – scarcely figures that win Test matches.

- **Doug Wright**: Weaknesses elsewhere in the squad meant he had too much bowling to do. His ability to spin the ball both ways was a boon and he was our leading wicket-taker with 23, but they were expensive, at over 43 each.

- **Alec Bedser**: Found things harder than in the summer against the Indians. At times he reminded me of Maurice

Tate: that late swing and his ability to hit both the pitch and the bat hard. Eager and strong.

- **Bill Voce**: Remained a trier and in the Brisbane Test showed his old aggression, but it was a tour too far for him (he was not alone!) His weight was a problem and basically he lacked pace. He, more than most, succumbed to the gastronomic delights of life in unrationed Australia and put on too much weight. His classic bowling action was unimpaired by the passing of time and the polishing off of substantial breakfasts and dinners, but the venom and zip of his prime had faded. He had lost the very thing that batsmen facing pace most feared – the ability to make you duck and weave. After appearing in the Melbourne Test, he only played three more games on the tour.

- **Dick Pollard**: Too heavy and was an unwise selection lacking the skills and pace to compensate for the absence of English conditions. Food and the conditions were his undoing.

So, in summary, there are some key points of learning for future tours: the squad's average age must come down; all-rounders must be good enough to make an impact with both bat and ball; and we need to develop quick bowlers if we are to challenge the Australians in 1948.

Respectfully presented
Signed for Hammond in his absence, Richard Knott.

Pankaj Gupta's report on the Indian tour was submitted only to the ocean, while Hammond's report – not this piece of informed fiction – was duly submitted and consigned to the archives.

35

'And That's Over'

1947 and after

THE ENGLISH tourists returned to a halcyon summer, one that would forever be associated with a benign sun beating down, Compton and Edrich batting as if in a blue-skied paradise, and with crowds basking in peacetime torpor. The South African tourists came and went, beaten 3-0 in the series and England's stout performance offered hope for the visit of the Australians in 1948. India's cricketers – without those who had opted to give their allegiance to Pakistan – would not return to play a series in England until 1952; Pakistan came two years later, seven years after Partition. Oddly, India played Tests against Pakistan before the latter came to play a series in England.

But what of India, its politics and cricketers, its blood-stained transformation into two separate countries at midnight on 15 August, the day before England began the final Test against South Africa at The Oval? The All-India tourists had returned home as their country toyed with civil war and the Labour government in London, notably the foreign secretary, Ernest Bevin, wanted the viceroy, Field Marshal Wavell, summarily removed and India left to its own political devices. The important proviso was that Britain's prestige must be undamaged, its empire upheld. Bevin was in sympathy with Winston Churchill who, in 1942, had remarked that he had not 'become the King's first minister to preside over the liquidation of the British Empire'. Bevin even considered the possibility of sending the British Army to India, its numbers made up of recently demobbed soldiers. The whole crisis was being played out at a time when Britain was burdened by debt and struggling with problems in other parts of the empire. There were troubles in Palestine, Malaya and Burma, for example, and the world seemed a dangerous place with a third world war threatening. In truth, the workings of the British Raj in India were disintegrating and violence was rapidly escalating. The country was in turmoil, beset with private armies, desperate refugees trudging to somewhere – anywhere – else, indiscriminate killings spreading westwards, forced religious conversions and burnings.

On 18 December 1946, the viceroyalty of India was offered to Mountbatten – among the notes of congratulation he received was one from Hampshire County Cricket Club – and three weeks later he formally asked the prime minister to set a precise date for the ending of the British Raj. A further three weeks passed before Attlee informed Wavell in a letter that it was time for him to leave India, an act which infuriated the departing viceroy. As for the Mountbattens, soon to leave London for Delhi, the playwright Noël Coward wondered if the couple would return alive. When the new viceroy and his wife flew over the Punjab on his journey to assume his duties, he could see far below the tell-tale swirls of smoke across the land.

* * *

Eventually an agreement was reached for Indian independence to begin on 1 June 1948, albeit with a few weeks' flexibility built in. In the end, in a move which seemed to smack of British exhaustion, a weariness of the imperial spirit, rather than a wish to free India from its chains, the date was brought forward to 15 August 1947. At midnight. It is extremely doubtful whether, if it had been held back to the original date ten months later, that the fury and bloodshed of post-Partition would have been avoided. There were, for example, desperate riots involving Hindus and Muslims in the Sindh province in the newly created Pakistan. By the time the turmoil of Partition had reached some sort of resolution, estimates suggest that some 20 million would become refugees, while perhaps three million would be slaughtered. More immediately some 100,000 refugees were relocated to military camps near Bombay. Those Indian cricketers with roots in or near the city – Shinde, Merchant, Hindlekar, Modi and Mankad – would have witnessed the consequences on a daily basis.

Some of the All-India tourists of 1946 remained in England or returned later. A number played Lancashire League cricket: for example, Mankad (for Haslingden); Hazare (Rawtenstall); Sohoni (Rishton and Lowerhouse); and Gul Mohammad (Ramsbottom). Both Pataudi and Hafeez played for counties (Worcestershire and Warwickshire respectively). Abdul Hafeez stayed in England to read philosophy at Oxford where he won a Blue for cricket. His friendship with the Nawab of Pataudi had helped secure him a place. Hafeez would change his name to Abdul Kardar, marry an Englishwoman and play cricket for Pakistan. The Nawab of Pataudi never played Test cricket again – indeed his last first-class game was against Middlesex at Lord's at the end of August 1946. The two wicketkeepers, Nimbalkar and Hindlekar, also retired from Test cricket. Five of the squad were named Indian Cricketers of the Year in 1946/47: Pataudi, Amarnath, Hazare, Mankad and Merchant. Gul Mohammad played for India against Pakistan at Lucknow in October 1952 and then for Pakistan against Australia four years later. Mushtaq Ali was offered Pakistani citizenship on two occasions but remained firm that his home was in India.

Just three months after Partition, India – no longer 'All-India' – travelled to Australia to play a series of five Test matches. Preparation for the tour was problematic in the extreme, not least because the selectors had chosen the Indian squad on the basis that independence day would have been in June 1948 as originally planned. A number of players withdrew, including both the captain, Vijay Merchant, and Mushtaq Ali, his vice-captain. Lala Amarnath assumed the captaincy. The pre-tour training camp in Poona was eventually abandoned, washed out by monsoon rains. The quick bowler Fazal Mahmood was in the squad, having been left out of the tour to England in 1946, and to reach the camp he had to travel from Lahore via Karachi and Bombay to Poona, travelling against the flow of the mass migration of Muslims heading for Pakistan. With the camp abandoned, he was obliged to return home prior to leaving for Australia. On the Poona to Bombay train he would have been murdered by a Hindu mob were it not for the intervention of the great Indian cricketer C.K. Nayudu wielding his bat.

Before the series began the Australian Cricket Board and Don Bradman had tried to get the Indian tourists to agree to covered pitches for the Tests at the end of play and in the event of rain. The request was turned down. From the moment they were dismissed for 58 in their first innings on a sticky Brisbane wicket, India struggled – Ernie Toshack took 11 wickets for 31 in the match – and they were defeated in the series 4-0, three of them by an innings. The emphatic victory underlined the extent of the gap between Australia and England, as well as showing the relative weakness of the Indian tourists. Like England, the Indians had discovered that playing a Test series in Australia meant coming up against the combined weight of its fine cricketers, its challenging conditions and its crowds. There were some who would question its umpiring too. The Indians had found the 1946 tour less harrowing than the four crushing Australian victories. Lala Amarnath had been confronted more than most by the troubled politics in India. Obliged to flee his home in Lahore because of a Muslim mob, Partition was very disruptive for him, both financially and mentally. The house in Lahore was his ancestral home and he would never return there – like much of the old Hindu quarter of the city, it was burned to the ground. Moreover, Amarnath lost most of his silver and gold trophies, and many other things of value, including, for example, the Gunn & Moore bat with which he had scored a hundred on his Test debut in Bombay. Soon after Partition, Amarnath took the train from Patiala to Delhi in order to attend a meeting about the forthcoming Australian tour. Normally the journey would have taken some four hours, but in the febrile atmosphere of an independent India, the train stopped without explanation every mile or so. Train travel at this time was notoriously dangerous: in August 1947, 'death trains' would arrive in Lahore, for example, with blood dripping from the carriages on to the track.

At one point, Amarnath witnessed a bloodbath in his train compartment, the work of a frenzied mob. Then when the train drew to a halt in Ambala, the newly appointed captain of India stepped down from his carriage before registering the disconcertingly threatening presence of a gang of thugs on the platform. The fact that he was wearing a Sikh bangle on his wrist saved his life. 'We were planning to kill you,' he was told. The overcrowded train continued to be delayed and eventually Amarnath transferred to a goods train before abandoning the railway altogether, opting instead for travelling by road in a series of buses, lorries and a bullock cart. In comparison, the tour of Australia, with its sequence of Tests – Brisbane (Bradman 185); Sydney; Melbourne (Bradman 132 and 127*); Adelaide (Bradman 201, Hassett 198*) and Melbourne again (Neil Harvey, in his second Test for Australia, 153) – was painful, unforgiving and hard work, but not blood-stained, intractable or murderous.

The relentless passing of time both in cricket and in life is inescapable. For those gallant Indian tourists of 1946, the years between when they first walked out on the green arena of Lord's, and then later stepping away from the game forever, were all too short – the length of the war years, or even less. A number of them retired from Test cricket in the early 1950s: Merchant, Sohoni and Sarwate in 1951; Amarnath, Mushtaq, Shinde and Hazare soon afterwards. Mankad ploughed on until February 1959 by which time he was 42. Against West Indies in Delhi, he remained fit enough to bowl a marathon 55 overs in the only innings, failing to take a single wicket and conceding 167 runs. Shute Banerjee, who had missed out on a first Test appearance on the 1946 tour, finally – at the age of 38 – entered the world of international cricket three years later, in 1949, taking four West Indian wickets in the first innings. Having waited 15 years to make his Test debut, he never played another.

The overall love of the wider game went beyond the honour of Test match appearances and so it was the norm for players to keep on playing until middle age: Lala Amarnath turned out for Northern Punjab at the age of 49; Nayudu for Madya Pradesh when he was 47; and Sarwate for Vidarbha in the Ranji Trophy aged 48. Vijay Hazare, despite a discomfort against the bouncer acquired in his later years, played cricket in the Ranji Trophy until October 1960 when he was 45. The same reluctance to leave the stage was true for English cricketers, too. County players, stoically, each passing April, contemplated beginning all over again, each year a little bit stiffer and more prone to injury. What was it about the game that players in those days did not want to leave? There are some prosaic reasons, including the less arduous physical demands of cricket in the immediate post-war era – the absence of frenetic one-day cricket, the tolerance of plodding fielders, the forgiving nature of fitness training where the balance between beer consumption and press-ups was heavily tipped in favour of sociability. Above all perhaps, the years lost to the war needed to be both exorcised and compensated for – there was a longing to make up for time that had been taken away.

Inevitably there were mixed fortunes for those disappointed English cricketers who had returned without the Ashes in 1947. The Lancashire quick bowler Dick Pollard, whose Test aspirations were scuppered by his two stone weight-gain, was not selected for the 1947 home series against South Africa. By then he was 35, but that glorious summer he bowled impressively for his county, taking 131 wickets. He had to wait another year for his next international chance. Two heavy defeats inflicted by the Australians led to his recall and he played in the Old Trafford Test, alongside two Gloucestershire men – Jack Crapp and George Emmett – making their debuts. Pollard did well in combination with Alec Bedser and England's supremacy in the game was only thwarted by Manchester's rain. His three wickets (in 32 overs) were valuable; so too the ferocious pull shot against the off-spinner, Ian Johnson, which poleaxed Sid Barnes, fielding close in at short leg on the fringe of the batting strip. The blow badly damaged Barnes's ribs and he was taken off on a stretcher, eventually having to retire hurt and then spending ten days in hospital, missing the next Test. Another feather in Pollard's England cap was that one of his wickets was Don Bradman, lbw for 7.

A draw where England had held a significant advantage encouraged the selectors to stick with the same fast-medium combination at Headingley. Although Pollard took the wicket of Bradman again, as well as Lindsay Hassett, Australia made 404/3 on the final day to win the match. For the remaining Test at The Oval, Pollard was dropped to accommodate an extra spin bowler and that ended his short-lived Test match career. Fifty-four years later the ball with which he took Bradman's wicket at Leeds was sold at auction for £1,700. At the end of the 1950 season, Dick Pollard – fondly remembered by Old Trafford devotees as the 'Owd Chain Horse' because, in his pomp, he could bowl all day – retired from the county game and moved into Lancashire League cricket.

Other English tourists from the 1946/47 squad followed a similar path – that reluctant decline into retirement – although James Langridge, at the age of nearly 44, was appointed captain of Sussex in 1950, a role he occupied until 1952. The last man dismissed before war broke out in 1939, he was only the third professional player that century to be appointed the regular captain of a county club. After retirement, he served as county coach at Sussex until 1959.

Another cricketer for whom Australia in 1946/47 was a disappointment, Nottinghamshire's Joe Hardstaff, toured the West Indies with England in 1947/48 under the captaincy this time of Gubby Allen. Hardstaff and Allen fell out to such an extent that when the tour was over, Allen assured Hardstaff that he would never appear again in a Test for his country. Not to be outdone in terms of grand gestures, Hardstaff asked Allen to name his odds on the possibility of his recall. Allen put the chances at 100–1 against; Hardstaff duly took the bet, proffering a five-pound note and had the triple satisfaction of winning the bet, receiving a cheque for £500 from a chagrined Allen and then tearing it up, before posting the scraps of paper back to his former captain. The bad feeling went back 12 years to the 1936 Australian tour when Allen considered it his duty as captain to insist on bedtimes for players, just one among many curtailments. In the post-war West Indies tour, the straight-talking Hardstaff left the captain in no doubt about his opinion: 'Listen, I didn't come through six years of war to be treated like a schoolboy.' His run-scoring continued well into the 1950s but Allen's baleful influence ensured that his Test appearances were strictly limited.

Life after cricket? For many retirees from the game, the preferred option was to continue to be involved in the game in some form or other: perhaps as county coach (Bill Voce); school cricket coach (Laurie Fishlock and Doug Wright); umpire (Paul Gibb – who later become a bus driver in Guildford, Surrey); Minor Counties cricketer (Bill Edrich) and so on. There were exceptions: Gloucestershire's Tom Goddard, for example, ran a furniture shop in Gloucester. Of the 16 members of the England squad that toured in

1947, only Hutton, Ikin and Pollard retired before they were 40, while the average age of retirement among them was 43.

Of the other cricketers whose careers are touched in this book, Harold Gimblett became a coach at Millfield School in Somerset and died of an overdose of prescription drugs in 1978. Bill Bowes became a respected journalist and writer and died in 1987. Alec Bedser became chairman of the England selectors and was knighted in 1997. He died in 2010, four years after his brother, Eric: the twins finally separated. Sir Leonard Hutton also served as a selector as well as working as a journalist. He died in 1990. Douglas Jardine died in 1958 in Switzerland where he had gone for cancer treatment. He was only 57. Denis Compton played in 78 Tests, averaging over 50, and died of septicaemia on the first day of the 1997 cricket season. Norman Yardley captained Yorkshire; became a Test selector; then president of Yorkshire before resigning. He died in 1989. Don Bradman's last Test match was at The Oval: he was dismissed by Eric Hollies for 0 and denied the chance to bat in the second innings by England's abject batting (they were all out for 52 and 188) with the 'Invincible' Australians winning by an innings. He died in Adelaide in 2001, aged 92.

Of the Indians, several died relatively young: the captain, Pataudi, suffered a heart attack playing polo in Delhi on 6 January 1952 (it was his son's 11th birthday); Shinde died of typhoid in 1955, aged 35; Nimbalkar died at 49, never having played in a Test match; Hindlekar was 40 when he died, leaving a wife and seven children. His continuing poverty resulted in vital treatment being received too late to save him. Others continued to contribute to the game: Hazare and Sarwate became selectors, the latter helping to pick the team that won the World Cup in 1983; Gul Mohammad became a cricket administrator, while Vijay Merchant went back to the family's textile business as well as involving himself in charity work (for the rights of the disabled). Lala Amarnath was employed to encourage the development of cricket in Patiala and could be heard on All-India radio; later, in 1978, he would be invited by Pakistan television to commentate on the Test match with India in Lahore. He was given a warm and emotional welcome by the home crowd for a game in which both his sons – Surinder and Mohinder – were playing for India. Like the English Test cricketers of the time, many Indians who had toured England in 1946 played on for many years: Amarnath and Mushtaq Ali both played their last games in 1963; Modi and Nayudu in 1961; Abdul Kardar in 1966; Hazare in 1967 and Sarwate in December 1968.

Abdul Hafeez Kardar, whose tour of England as a young cricketer in 1946 had been decidedly underwhelming, emerged as a future captain of his country and eventually became chairman of selectors. It was five years after Partition, however, before Kardar returned to Pakistan, his time away including gaining his degree at University College Oxford, followed by two seasons playing for Warwickshire in the County Championship. He was by then a cricketer with an interest in politics and a passionate belief in the new country that had emerged from Partition. In October 1952, when India played Pakistan for the first time, the opposing captains were Lala Amarnath and Kardar, two comrades from that last All-India tour of England. Kardar's political career benefited from having travelled during the war with Zulfiqar Ali Bhutto, who was to become the country's prime minister, serving in that capacity for four years in the mid-1970s, and founding the Pakistan People's Party (PPP) which Kardar duly joined. The two men had first met during the war years when Kardar took the train from Lahore to Bombay. Bhutto loved the game and was a capable player in his own right, having been coached by both Mushtaq Ali and Vinoo Mankad. He would be executed in the Central Jail in Rawalpindi under the orders of the military junta that seized power in Pakistan in March 1979. As for Kardar, he was in many ways the father of Pakistani cricket, although in later life his involvement in the game faded. He died, aged 71, in 1996, 50 years after the last All-India tour of England.

* * *

In time the weeds on Britain's bomb sites withered and died; rationing faded away to nothing; the Labour government was toppled; Churchill returned as the nation's prime minister and the war's shadow faded. English cricket produced some fast bowlers at last and something closer to parity was achieved in the games against Australia, until, in 1953, the Ashes were finally regained, under a professional captain for the first time. That in itself was proof that cricket's administrators presided over a game that evolved with painful slowness. For years a pre-war mindset persisted, one which was deeply suspicious of change and took the view that playing the great game in peacetime again was enough. The great England fast bowler, John Snow, talking of the 1960s, commented that those who ran the game in those days held on for too long to the view that 'after fighting for five years, having a game of cricket was heaven' and so nothing needed to be changed in a hurry – or at all.

As for All-India, its division after Partition into two separate countries – bitter rivals soured by religion and politics – saw the game's development held back, only for it to flourish mightily as the years passed. The volatility of its politics rumbled on: Mahatma Gandhi, for example, was assassinated in 1948 and riot and bloodshed was never far away. India's cricketers had to wait until 1952 before beating England (at Madras) and until August 1971 in England at The Oval; Pakistan had first beaten the English (also at The Oval) in 1954. It wasn't until 1952 that Pakistan played its first Test. Significantly perhaps, the great Indian slow bowler, Bishan Bedi, born in the first year after the war and a key member of Indian Test sides in the 1960s and 1970s, observed that it was 'Tiger' Pataudi, the son of the 1946 captain, who 'was the first Indian captain who gave us a feeling of Indianness'.

Religion and politics and its impact on sport, however, did not go away. In Pakistan, where so much was new and fragile, cricket suffered in both the short and medium term. There was, for example, only one first-class game played in the country during 1947/48: the new nation was starved of first-class cricket. Moreover, Pakistan was stranded outside the ICC, its very name – the Imperial Cricket Conference – revealing much about the old world of British imperialism. These were difficult times far beyond the game of cricket: the city of Karachi, for example, was a giant refugee camp, while almost all the Pakistani cricketers were caught up in the carnage of 1947. The cricketing enterprise was essentially on a shoestring, to the extent that Pakistan had no official scorer, a gap filled by the players themselves. It would take many years for Pakistan to become fully fledged: only four Tests were played against Australia in the 25 years after Partition, while, between the 1950s and 1974/75, no Tests took place between West Indies and Pakistan. Between 1960/61 and 1978/79 there were no Tests between India and Pakistan; there were, however, two wars, in 1965 and 1971. The impact of race, religion and politics was all too evident: only one cricketer from East Pakistan, Niaz Ahmed, ever played for Pakistan, while it was not until 1984 that the first Hindu (Anil Dalpat) played for that country. Significantly, the Pakistani batsman, Javed Miandad, was one of those who took the view that cricket was less a game than it was warfare.

While few Hindu cricketers have played for Pakistan, the World Cup of 1987 was jointly organised by India and Pakistan. The close relationship between cricket and politics was exemplified by the establishment of the Nehru Cup in 1989: Indian cricket firmly linked to the name of the nation's first prime minister. But the violence didn't end: the desperate riots of 1992 testifying to the continuing, virulent hatred. In 2008 a terror attack in Mumbai (formerly Bombay) led to the banning of Pakistani cricketers from the Indian Premier League. Moreover, 60 years after Partition, Pakistan was obliged to play their home Tests out of the country (in the United Arab Emirates) more than a decade after the terrorist attacks on the United States of America in September 2001. A different kind of war was casting a shadow over the game of cricket and cricketers' lives were at the mercy once again of failed diplomats and military men.

* * *

At a dinner held at the Royal Hotel in Bristol, with Gloucestershire CCC's president, the Duke of Beaufort in the chair, and a menu that included turbot, chicken, 'Pommes Delmonico' and 'abricot glacé Aurore', Wally Hammond was presented with a portrait of himself painted by Edward Halliday. At the end the diners sang 'For He's a Jolly Good Fellow'. No doubt someone remarked that the county's erstwhile captain had been given a 'damn good send-off'. Soon after, Hammond emigrated to South Africa, taking up an appointment at Natal University as a sports administrator. He died in 1965, aged only 62.

* * *

And the Ashes rivalry – what of that after Bradman had finally left the stage? It took England until 1953 to win a series. The rival captains that year, Hutton and Hassett, were veterans of previous Ashes series and the margin of victory was narrow; four draws and a win in the final Test at The Oval. The Ashes remained England's through the series played between 1954 and 1956, courtesy of the fast bowling that had been missing in 1946/47 – Brian Statham and Frank 'Typhoon' Tyson – and the spin of Jim Laker, who took 19 wickets in the match at Old Trafford in 1956. By then only two Australians – Keith Miller and Ray Lindwall – had survived from the series of a decade before, and two Englishmen, Godfrey Evans and Cyril Washbrook, who by then was 41. The fact that the Lancashire batsman had been recalled at that age after a six-year gap from Test cricket was thought highly unusual that season. Unlike ten years before, cricketers tended no longer to eke out careers to compensate for the time that had been lost.

It was 1954 before John Arlott went to Australia for the first and only time. He was there to watch England defend the Ashes which they had won in the previous year, playing under the country's first professional captain, Len Hutton. Arlott flew there via Karachi, Hong Kong, Tokyo and Korea, aiming to arrive in time for MCC's game against Queensland, followed by the first Test at Brisbane. He was excited by the prospect, recognising that the true 'cricket critic' must have made at least one tour down under and seen cricket 'in the game's second home.' Like others before him, he worried about the selection of the touring party, particularly the absence of the young fast bowler, Fred Trueman of Yorkshire. The party did, however, include two genuine quick bowlers in Brian Statham and Frank Tyson. Arlott was disconcerted by the Brisbane crowd which he thought truculent; Adelaide's heat was unbearable; Hutton batted like 'a weary man' – it all had an echo of previous tours, but the outcome, with England retaining the Ashes by winning in Adelaide, was very different. In Tom Graveney of Gloucestershire, the batsman who topped the Test averages that series, Arlott saw a worthy successor to the great Wally Hammond. He had regarded the now exiled Hammond as a cricketer for whom the label 'great' was entirely right – he put him in the very top bracket alongside W.G. Grace and Jack Hobbs. He recognised too that Hammond was undoubtedly remote with a profound shyness but would never forget his kindness to the novice broadcaster, taking 'JA' as Arlott called himself in his autobiography, out for dinner and revealing some of the secrets of the great game, from the lofty perspective of a giant of the sport.

Arlott himself was commentating on cricket on the BBC until 1980, signing off in a Test against Australia at Lord's in characteristically avuncular fashion, the low-key delivery pitched on a perfect length: '… It's 69 for two, nine runs off the over, 28 Boycott, 15 Gower, 69 for 2, and after Trevor Bailey, it'll be Christopher Martin-Jenkins …' He died in 1991 on the island of Alderney.

* * *

A year or so after Mr Gupta and Mr Arlott had met in the foyer of the Berners Hotel in Westminster, the Indian tour manager was in Australia performing the same function for the 1947/48 Indian tourists. One wonders if the two men were on first-name terms when they met on that April day in 1946 – 'Good to see you Pankaj!' 'The pleasure's mine, John.' As for the Australian captain, Don Bradman, he found 'Peter' Gupta and India's captain, Lala Amarnath 'charming'. Pankaj Gupta was a man of many talents and highly regarded in Indian sporting history. He had been to the 1932 Olympics in Los Angeles as non-playing captain and to Berlin for the Games four years later. In his official capacity at the Berlin Olympics, he shook hands with Joseph Goebbels, one of those moments when sport found itself cheek-by-jowl with raw, unsavoury politics. It seems that Mr Gupta shook hands with the Nazi minister for propaganda, and intimated his disapproval of Great Britain, an antipathy that he presumed the German shared. Ten years later, John Arlott would clasp Gupta's hand, thinking only of cricket, the weather, the first game at Worcester in May and the long summers of peace that lay ahead.

All-India tour results

Worcestershire	Worcester 191 and 284; India 192 and 267	**Lost**
	Shinde 5-50; Modi 84	
Oxford Uni.	Oxford 256 and 245/3; India 248	**Drawn**
	Mankad 4-58; Hazare 64	
Surrey	India 454 and 20/1; Surrey 135 and 338	**Won**
	Sarwate 124*; Sarwate 5-54	
Cambridge U.	Univ. 178 and 138; India 335/6 dec.	**Won**
	Sarwate 5-58; Nawab of Pataudi 121	
Leicestershire	India 198/7 dec and 107/6 dec	
	Leicester 144 and 24/1	**Drawn**
	Merchant 111*; Amarnath 4-14	
Scotland	India 247; Scotland 101 and 90;	**Won**
	Hazare 101; Sarwate 7-42	
MCC	India 438; MCC 139 and 105	**Won**
	Merchant 148; Mankad 7-37	
Indian Gymkhana	Indian Gymkhana 97; India 149/8	**Won**
	Modi 51	
Hampshire	Hampshire 197 and 142; India 130 and	
	212/4	**Won**
	Hazare 4-18; Modi 41	
Glamorgan	India 376/6 dec; Glamorgan 149 and 73/7	**Drawn**
	Amarnath 104*; Sarwate 5-30	
Combined Services	Combined Services 241/4 dec. and 135	**Drawn**
	India 159 and 116/5	
	Hazare 7-66; Hazare 62*	

Nottinghamshire	India 345/5 dec.; Nottinghamshire 24/1	Drawn
	Nawab of Pataudi 101*	
England	India 200 and 275; England 428 and 48/0	**Lost**
	Mankad 63; Amarnath 5-118	
Northants	India 328 and 171/1; Northants 362	**Drawn**
	Merchant 110; Mankad 5-99	
Lancashire	Lancashire 140 and 185; India 126 and 200/2	
	Banerjee 4-32; Merchant 93*	**Won**
Yorkshire	India 138 and 124; Yorkshire 344/9 dec.	**Lost**
	Hazare 29, Nayudu 29; Nayudu 5/27	
Lancashire	Lancashire 406 and 172; India 456/8 dec.	**Drawn**
	Mankad 5-62; Merchant 242*	
Derbyshire	India 380/9 dec. and 313/8 dec.	**Won**
	Derbyshire 366 and 209	
	Nawab of Pataudi 113; Mankad 4-69	
Yorkshire	Yorkshire 300/6 dec. and 64/0;	**Drawn**
	India 490/5 dec.	
	Mankad 3-56; Hazare 244*	
Durham	India 149/5 dec.; Durham 109/5	**Drawn**
	Merchant 64	
England	England 294 and 153/5 dec.	**Drawn**
	India 170 and 152/9	
	Amarnath 5-96; Merchant 78	
Club Cricket Conf.	India 281/5 dec.; CCC 223/4	**Drawn**
	Merchant 141	
Sussex	India 533/3 dec. and 148/1	**Won**
	Sussex 253 and 427	
	Merchant 205; Mankad 5-140	
Somerset	India 64 and 431; Somerset 506/6 dec.	**Lost**
	Merchant 87	
Glamorgan	Glamorgan 238 and 237/8 dec.	**Won**
	India 203 and 274/5	
	Mankad 4-81; Mushtaq Ali 93	

Warwickshire	Warwickshire 375/9 dec. India 197 and 21/1	
	*Hazare 4-47; Merchant 86**	**Drawn**
Gloucestershire	Gloucestershire 132/3 dec. and 187	**Drawn**
	India 135/8 dec. and 177/9	
	Mankad 5-72; Nawab of Pataudi 71	
England	India 331; England 95/3	**Drawn**
	Merchant 128; Mankad 2-28	
Essex	Essex 303 and 201/3 dec.	**Won**
	India 138 and 370/9	
	Shinde 4-69; Merchant 181	
Kent	Kent 248/3	**Drawn**
Middlesex	India 469/5 dec.; Middlesex 124 and 82	**Won**
	Hazare 193; Mankad 5-48*	
South of England	India 241 and 253/3 dec.; South of England 219/9 dec. and 266	**Won**
	Merchant 82; Amarnath 4-57	
Leveson-Gower's XI	India 139 and 194/8; Leveson-Gower's XI 345	**Drawn**
	Mankad 4-127; Gul Mohammad 57	

MCC in Australia and New Zealand 1946/47 tour results

Northam & Country	Northam 123 and 71; MCC 409/6 dec.	**Won**
	Smith 5-55; Hammond 131 retired	
Western Australian Colts	MCC 197/4 dec.; WA Colts 138/6	**Drawn**
	Gibb 51; Langridge 2-21	
Western Australia	WA 366 and 48/1; MCC 477	**Drawn**
	Wright 4-55; Hammond 208	
WA Country XI	WA Country XI 462; MCC 302	**Drawn**
	Ikin 4-172; Compton 98	
South Australia Country	MCC 487/6 dec.; SA Country 87 and 92	**Won**
	Hutton 164; Smith 5-16	
South Australia	MCC 506/5 dec.; S. Australia 266 and 276/8	**Drawn**
	Hutton 136; Smith 5-93	
Victoria	MCC 358 and 279/7 dec.; Victoria 189 and 204	**Won**
	Hutton 151; Wright 6-48*	
Australian XI	Australian XI 327/5; MCC 314	**Drawn**
	Hutton 71; Smith 3-111	
New South Wales	NSW 165/4 dec.; MCC 156/2.	**Drawn**
	Hutton 97; Bedser 2-48	
Queensland	Queensland 400 and 230/6 dec.; MCC 310 and 238/6	**Drawn**
	Washbrook 124; Yardley 3-19	

Australia	Australia 645; England 141 and 172 *Wright 5-167; Hammond 32, Ikin 32*	**Lost**
Queensland Country	Queensland Country 208 and 311/9; MCC 282 *Smith 5-80; Hardstaff 64*	**Drawn**
Australia	England 255 and 371; Australia 659/8 dec. *Edrich 119 and 3-79*	**Lost**
Northern NSW	MCC 395 and 146/6; Northern NSW 202 *Hammond 142; Voce 4-45*	**Drawn**
Southern NSW	MCC 465; Southern NSW 11/4 *Hutton 133; Pollard 4-2*	**Drawn**
Victoria Country	Victoria C. 156; MCC 200/4 *Smith 6-43; Edrich 62*	**Won**
Australia	Australia 365 and 536; England 351 and 310/7 *Edrich 3-50; Washbrook 112*	**Drawn**
Tasmanian Country XI	MCC 278 and 353/9; Tasmania Country XI 374 and 145/2 *Compton 124; Edrich 2-40*	**Drawn**
Tasmania	MCC 467/5 dec.; Tasmania 103 and 129/6 *Compton 163; Edrich 4-26*	**Drawn**
South Australia	MCC 577 and 152/2; S. Australia 443 *Hammond 188; Voce 4-125*	**Drawn**
Australia	England 460 and 340/8; Australia 487 and 215/1 *Compton 147; Bedser 3-97*	**Drawn**
Victoria Country	Victoria Country 268 and 70/5; MCC 288 *Voce 3-28; Evans 82*	**Drawn**
Victoria	MCC 355 and 118; Victoria 327 *Compton 93; Wright 4/108*	**Drawn**
New South Wales	NSW 342 and 262/6 dec.; MCC 266 and 205/3 *Smith 9-121; Compton 75*	**Drawn**

Australia	England 280 and 186; Australia 253 and 214/5 *Hutton 122*; Wright 7–105*	**Lost**
Wellington	MCC 176 and 271/6 dec.; Wellington 160 and 73 *Voce 6–38; Washbrook 133*	**Won**
Otago	Otago 340 and 262/7 dec.; MCC 385/6 dec. and 216/9 *Pollard 4–92; Yardley 126*	**Drawn**
New Zealand	New Zealand 345/9 dec. England 265/7 dec. *Hammond 79; Bedser 4–95*	**Drawn**
Auckland	MCC 240; Auckland 85 and 90 *Compton 97* and 7–36*	**Won**

Acknowledgements

FOR THE past four years our postman has regularly been obliged to deliver a steady supply of book-sized packages through the letterbox. Appropriately, perhaps, he is of Indian origin (from Kerala in the south of the country) and I am grateful to him for the weight of books he has had to carry – the volumes of cricketers' memoirs that have contributed to this account of two cricketing tours more than seven decades ago. I admire cricketers – as John Arlott did – and the literature of the game has been invaluable in the writing of this book.

In addition, I should like to acknowledge the following sources which have been of particular value: *Wisden Cricketers' Almanack* (the editions of 1946 and 1947 in particular), Cricket Archive, the British Library, the National Archives and Bristol Archives. In addition I am grateful to:

> *rajumukerjioncricket.blogspot.com*
> *The Cricketer*
> *ESPN.com*
> *The London Gazette* (12 September 1941)
> *Wisden Cricket Monthly,* and
> *The Wisdener.*

A long shelf in my office at home holds the books I have drawn on in writing *All-India and Down Under.* They are listed in the bibliography that follows. In particular, I should like to note the work of the following that have been inspirational and invaluable: John Arlott, Bill Bowes, Clif Cary, David Foot, Peter Oborne, E.W. Swanton and Marina Wheeler. Finally I should like to thank my wife, Vanessa, who read the book at a critical stage and whose help and encouragement I value beyond any other. Her father, Arthur Spencer, whose sporting memories of Southampton FC and Hampshire CCC go back to the 1920s, is also owed a fond debt of gratitude.

Bibliography

Alvi, Moniza, *At the Time of Partition* (Tarset, Northumberland: Bloodaxe, 2013)

Amarnath, Rajender, *Lala Amarnath: The Making of a Legend* (Cheltenham: Sportsbooks Ltd., 2007)

Andrews, Bill, *The Hand that Bowled Bradman* (Newton Abbot, Devon: Sportsman's Book Club, 1974)

Arlott, John & Brearley, Mike, *Arlott in Conversation with Mike Brearley* (London: Hodder & Stoughton, 1986)

Arlott, John, *Basingstoke Boy* (London: Willow Books, 1990)

Arlott, John, *Indian Summer* (London: Longmans, Green, 1947)

Arlott, Timothy, *John Arlott, a Memoir* (London: Andre Deutsch, 1994)

Astill, James, *The Great Tamasha* (London: Bloomsbury, 2013)

Bailey, Thorn & Wynne-Thomas, *Who's Who of Cricketers* (Feltham, Middlesex: Newnes, 1984)

Bandyopadhyay, Kausik, *Mahatma on the Pitch* (New Delhi: Rupa, 2017)

Bannister, Jack, *The History of Warwickshire County Cricket Club* (London: Helm, 1990)

Bedser, Alec, *Twin Ambitions* (London: Stanley Paul, 1986)

Blunden, Edmund, *Cricket Country* (London: Collins, 1944)

Bose, Mihir, *A History of Indian Cricket* (London: Andre Deutsch, 1990)

Bose, Mihir, *A Maidan View* (London: Allen & Unwin, 1986)

Bowes, Bill, *Express Deliveries* (London: Stanley Paul, 1949)

Bradman, Don, *Farewell to Cricket* (Sydney: Hodder & Stoughton, 1950)

Brearley, Mike, *The Art of Captaincy* (Sydney: Hodder & Stoughton, 1985)

Cardus, Neville, *The Roses Matches 1919-1939* (London: Souvenir Press, 1982)

Cary, Clif, *Cricket Controversy* (London: Werner Laurie, 1948)

Chalke, Stephen, *The Way It Was* (Bath, Somerset: Fairfield, 2008)

Compton, Denis, *End of an Innings* (London: Oldbourne, 1958)

Compton, Denis, *'Testing Time' for England* (London: Stanley Paul, 1948)

Douglas, Christopher, *Douglas Jardine, Spartan Cricketer* (London: Allen & Unwin, 1984)

Farnes, Kenneth, *Tours and Tests* (London: Lutterworth, 1940)

Fay, Stephen & Kynaston, David, *Arlott, Swanton and the Soul of English Cricket* (London: Bloomsbury, 2018)

Ferguson, W.H., *Mr Cricket* (London: Kaye, 1957)

Ferris, P. (ed.), *The Collected Letters of Dylan Thomas, vol. 2* (London: Weidenfeld & Nicolson, 2007)

Foot, David, *Walter Hammond – the Reasons Why* (London: Robson Books, 1996)

Foot, David, *Harold Gimblett – Tormented Genius of Cricket* (London: W.H. Allen, 1984)

Foot, David, *Sunshine, Sixes and Cider* (Newton Abbot, Devon: David & Charles, 1986)

Frindall, Bill, *The Wisden Book of Test Cricket* (London: Macdonald & Jane's, 1978)

Gover, Alfred, *The Long Run* (London: Pelham Books, 1991)

Green, Benny (ed.), *The Wisden Book of Obituaries* (London: Queen Anne Press, 1986)

Guha, Ramachandra, *A Corner of a Foreign Field* (London: Picador, 2002)

Hammond, Walter, *Cricket My World* (London: Stanley Paul, 1949)

Harris, Bruce, *With England in Australia* (London: Hutchinson's, 1947)

Hayhurst, Keith, *The Pictorial History of Lancashire County Cricket Club* (Leicester: Polar, 2000)

Hazare, Vijay, *Cricket Replayed* (Calcutta: Rupa, 1974)

Heald, Tim, *Denis Compton* (London: Pavilion Books, 1994)

Hill, Alan, *The Bedsers: Twinning Triumphs* (Edinburgh: Mainstream, 2001)

Hill, Alan, *Bill Edrich – A Biography* (London: Andre Deutsch, 1994)

Hill, Alan, *Hedley Verity – Portrait of a Cricketer* (Edinburgh: Mainstream, 2000)

Hodgson, D., *The Official History of Yorkshire County Cricket Club*, (Marlborough, Wiltshire: The Crowood Press, 1989)

Howat, Gerald, *Walter Hammond* (London: Allen & Unwin, 1984)

Howat, Gerald, *Len Hutton – The Biography* (London: Heinemann Kingswood, 1988)

Hughes, Simon, *Cricket's Greatest Rivalry* (London: Cassell, 2013)

Hutton, Len, *Fifty Years in Cricket* (London: Stanley Paul, 1984)

Hutton, Len, *Just My Story* (London: Hutchinson, 1956)

Khan, Yasmin, *The Raj at War* (London: Vintage, 2015)

Khan, Yasmin, *The Great Partition* (New Haven and London: Yale, 2017)

Knightley, Phillip, *Australia: A Biography of a Nation* (London: Vintage, 2001)

Kynaston, David, *Austerity Britain* (London: Bloomsbury, 2007)

Lazenby, John, *Edging Towards Darkness* (London: Bloomsbury, 2017)

Lee, Christopher, *From the Sea End* (London: Partridge Press, 1989)

Lemmon, David, *The History of Surrey County Cricket Club* (London: Helm, 1989)

Lemmon, David & Marshall, Mike, *Essex County Cricket Club – The Official History* (London: Kingswood, 1987)

Lemmon, David, *A History of Middlesex CCC* (London: Helm, 1988)

Lemmon, David, *Changing Seasons* (London: Andre Deutsch, 1997)

Lindwall, Ray, *Flying Stumps* (London: Stanley Paul, 1954)

McCrery, Nigel, *The Coming Storm* (Barnsley, South Yorkshire: Pen & Sword, 2017)

Marshall, Michael, *Gentlemen and Players* (London: Grafton, 1987)

249

Midwinter, Eric, *The Lost Seasons 1939-1945* (London: Methuen, 1987)

Mukherjee, Sujit, *Between Indian Wickets* (New Delhi: Orient, 1976)

Oborne, Peter, *Wounded Tiger* (London: Simon & Schuster, 2014)

Parker, Graham, *Gloucestershire Road* (London: Pelham, 1983)

Paynter, Eddie, *Cricket All the Way* (London and Leeds: Richardson, 1962)

Peel, Mark, *Ambassadors of Goodwill* (Worthing, Sussex: Pitch Publishing, 2018)

Perry, Roland, *The Don – a Biography* (Sydney: Macmillan, 1995)

Ricquier, Bill, *The Indian Masters* (Stroud, Gloucestershire: Tempus, 2005)

Rowe, Mark, *The Victory Tests* (Cheltenham, Gloucestershire: Sportsbooks, 2010)

Sandford, Christopher, *Godfrey Evans: a Biography* (London: Simon & Schuster, 1990)

Schofield, Victoria, *Wavell: Soldier and Statesman* (London: John Murray, 2006)

Swanton, E.W., *Cricketers of My Time* (London: Andre Deutsch, 1999)

Swanton, E.W., *Swanton in Australia* (Glasgow: Collins, 1975)

Swanton, E.W., *Gubby Allen – Man of Cricket* (London: Hutchinson, 1985)

Thurlow, David, *Ken Farnes – Diary of an Essex Master* (Manchester: The Pars Wood Press, 2000)

Tunzelmann, Alex von, *Indian Summer* (London: Simon & Schuster, 2007)

Turbervill, Huw, *The Toughest Tour* (London: Aurum, 2010)

Wheeler, Marina, *The Lost Homestead* (London: Hodder & Stoughton, 2020)

White-Spunner, Barney, *Partition* (London: Simon & Schuster, 2017)

Whitington, R. S., *Keith Miller – The Golden Nugget* (Adelaide: Rigby, 1981)

Wilde, Simon, *England: the Biography* (London: Simon & Schuster, 2018)

Williams, Charles, *Bradman* (London: Little Brown, 1996)

Wooller, Wilfred, *Glamorgan* (London: Arthur Barker, 1971)

Yardley, Norman, *Cricket Campaigns* (London: Stanley Paul)

Presenting Indian Cricket (Calcutta: Sporting Publications (India), 1946)

Wisden Cricketers' Almanack – for 1946, 1947 and 1948

Yorkshire CCC Handbooks – for 1939 and 1947

Pamphlets and Articles
Dutta, Anindya, *A Dinner in 1946* (ESPN.com, June 2018)

Edwards, Paul, *When Play Resumes* (The Cricketer, July 2020)

Guha, Ramachandra, *The Other Side of Merchant* (ESPN.com, November 2011)

Williamson, Martin, *A Right Royal Indian Mess* (ESPN.com, July 2007)

Williamson, Martin, *The Tour That Never Was* (ESPN.com, October 2011)

Index

251